CHELSEA HOUSE PUBLISHERS
Modern Critical Views

HENRY ADAMS
EDWARD ALBEE
A. R. AMMONS
MATTHEW ARNOLD
JOHN ASHBERY
W. H. AUDEN
JANE AUSTEN
JAMES BALDWIN
CHARLES BAUDELAIRE
SAMUEL BECKETT
SAUL BELLOW
THE BIBLE
ELIZABETH BISHOP
WILLIAM BLAKE
JORGE LUIS BORGES
ELIZABETH BOWEN
BERTOLT BRECHT
THE BRONTËS
ROBERT BROWNING
ANTHONY BURGESS
GEORGE GORDON, LORD BYRON
THOMAS CARLYLE
LEWIS CARROLL
WILLA CATHER
CERVANTES
GEOFFREY CHAUCER
KATE CHOPIN
SAMUEL TAYLOR COLERIDGE
JOSEPH CONRAD
CONTEMPORARY POETS
HART CRANE
STEPHEN CRANE
DANTE
CHARLES DICKENS
EMILY DICKINSON
JOHN DONNE & THE
   17th-CENTURY POETS
ELIZABETHAN DRAMATISTS
THEODORE DREISER
JOHN DRYDEN
GEORGE ELIOT
T. S. ELIOT
RALPH ELLISON
RALPH WALDO EMERSON
WILLIAM FAULKNER
HENRY FIELDING
F. SCOTT FITZGERALD
GUSTAVE FLAUBERT
E. M. FORSTER
SIGMUND FREUD
ROBERT FROST

ROBERT GRAVES
GRAHAM GREENE
THOMAS HARDY
NATHANIEL HAWTHORNE
WILLIAM HAZLITT
SEAMUS HEANEY
ERNEST HEMINGWAY
GEOFFREY HILL
FRIEDRICH HÖLDERLIN
HOMER
GERARD MANLEY HOPKINS
WILLIAM DEAN HOWELLS
ZORA NEALE HURSTON
HENRY JAMES
SAMUEL JOHNSON
BEN JONSON
JAMES JOYCE
FRANZ KAFKA
JOHN KEATS
RUDYARD KIPLING
D. H. LAWRENCE
JOHN LE CARRÉ
URSULA K. LE GUIN
DORIS LESSING
SINCLAIR LEWIS
ROBERT LOWELL
NORMAN MAILER
BERNARD MALAMUD
THOMAS MANN
CHRISTOPHER MARLOWE
CARSON MCCULLERS
HERMAN MELVILLE
JAMES MERRILL
ARTHUR MILLER
JOHN MILTON
EUGENIO MONTALE
MARIANNE MOORE
IRIS MURDOCH
VLADIMIR NABOKOV
JOYCE CAROL OATES
SEAN O'CASEY
FLANNERY O'CONNOR
EUGENE O'NEILL
GEORGE ORWELL
CYNTHIA OZICK
WALTER PATER
WALKER PERCY
HAROLD PINTER
PLATO
EDGAR ALLAN POE

POETS OF SENSIBILITY &
   THE SUBLIME
ALEXANDER POPE
KATHERINE ANNE PORTER
EZRA POUND
PRE-RAPHAELITE POETS
MARCEL PROUST
THOMAS PYNCHON
ARTHUR RIMBAUD
THEODORE ROETHKE
PHILIP ROTH
JOHN RUSKIN
J. D. SALINGER
GERSHOM SCHOLEM
WILLIAM SHAKESPEARE (3 vols.)
   HISTORIES & POEMS
   COMEDIES
   TRAGEDIES
GEORGE BERNARD SHAW
MARY WOLLSTONECRAFT SHELLEY
PERCY BYSSHE SHELLEY
EDMUND SPENSER
GERTRUDE STEIN
JOHN STEINBECK
LAURENCE STERNE
WALLACE STEVENS
TOM STOPPARD
JONATHAN SWIFT
ALFRED LORD TENNYSON
WILLIAM MAKEPEACE THACKERAY
HENRY DAVID THOREAU
LEO TOLSTOI
ANTHONY TROLLOPE
MARK TWAIN
JOHN UPDIKE
GORE VIDAL
VIRGIL
ROBERT PENN WARREN
EVELYN WAUGH
EUDORA WELTY
NATHANAEL WEST
EDITH WHARTON
WALT WHITMAN
OSCAR WILDE
TENNESSEE WILLIAMS
WILLIAM CARLOS WILLIAMS
THOMAS WOLFE
VIRGINIA WOOLF
WILLIAM WORDSWORTH
RICHARD WRIGHT
WILLIAM BUTLER YEATS

Further titles in preparation.

Modern Critical Views

HERMAN MELVILLE

Modern Critical Views

HERMAN MELVILLE

Edited with an introduction by

Harold Bloom

Sterling Professor of the Humanities
Yale University

1986
CHELSEA HOUSE PUBLISHERS
New York
New Haven   Philadelphia

PROJECT EDITORS: Emily Bestler, James Uebbing
ASSOCIATE EDITOR: Maria Behan
EDITORIAL COORDINATOR: Karyn Gullen Browne
EDITORIAL STAFF: Laura Ludwig, Perry King
DESIGN: Susan Lusk

Cover illustration by Richard Martin

Library of Congress Cataloging in Publication Data

Herman Melville.
     (Modern critical views)
     Bibliography: p.
     Includes index.
     Summary: A collection of critical essays on Melville
and his works. Also includes a chronology of events in
the author's life.
     1. Melville, Herman, 1819–1891—Criticism and
interpretation—Addresses, essays, lectures.
[1. Melville, Herman, 1819–1891—Criticism and interpretation—Addresses, essays, lectures.   2. American
literature—History and criticism]   I. Bloom, Harold.
II. Series.
PS2387.H4   1986   813'.3   85–26892
ISBN 0–87754–670–3

Chelsea House Publishers
Harold Steinberg, Chairman and Publisher
Susan Lusk, Vice President
A Division of Chelsea House Educational Communications, Inc.
133 Christopher Street, New York, NY 10014

Contents

Editor's Note

This book gathers together a representative selection of the best criticism devoted to the works of Herman Melville during the last forty years, arranged in the chronological order of its publication. The editor wishes to thank Ms. Ingrid Holmberg, whose erudition brought several of these articles to his attention. The volume begins with the editor's "Introduction," which speculates upon a demiurgical self-identification in Melville's imagination, particularly as it is represented in the story, "The Bell-Tower," from *The Piazza Tales*, and in certain crucial episodes in *Moby-Dick*. The suggestion is made that Melville's emergent religion, *as a writer*, was an overt Gnosticism, though the precise extent of Melville's knowledge of ancient religious heresies remains to be determined by future scholarly research.

Charles Olson, Melvillean poet and spiritual father of modern Melville criticism, begins the chronological sequence with his remarkable meditative reverie on *Moby-Dick*, "Call Me Ishmael." The discussion of four early novels—*Typee, Omoo, Redburn, White-Jacket*—by Newton Arvin, is the proper start for modern scholarly criticism of Melville, nearly all of which has benefited from Arvin's overview.

Melville after *Moby-Dick* is the focus of Hershel Parker's commentary upon *The Confidence Man*, Guy Cardwell's study of symbolism in "Benito Cereno," and of the tales in general by R. W. B. Lewis. With Paul Brodtkorb, Jr.'s classic phenomenological reading of Ishmael's natural despair, we return to *Moby-Dick*, necessarily the center of Melville's achievement. Robert Penn Warren, a strong poet and novelist who is Melville's true heir, deepens our sense of how central Melville's poetry is to that achievement.

In her consideration of Melville's comic sense, Elaine Barry usefully outlines the increasing abstraction that develops into an almost Kafkan version of the absurd. Richard H. Brodhead's masterly reading of *Mardi* also illuminates *Pierre*, the most problematic of all Melville's works, which receives a detailed consideration as the interpretive problem it most certainly represents in Edgar Dryden's essay.

The nearly as problematic long poem (immensely long) *Clarel* is illuminated by Bryan C. Short's superb study, with its acute sense of Melville's revisionary relationship to precursor authors and texts. Michael Paul Rogin brings a Marxist historical perspective to *Billy Budd,* in order to place Melville's lyrical, late short novel in a more societal context than it is usually afforded. Finally, P. Adams Sitney returns us to *Moby-Dick* with a previously unpublished, and radically advanced reading of the poignant chapter 132, "The Symphony," in which the hero asks the crucial and unanswerable question: "Is Ahab, Ahab?"

Introduction

I

Melville's *The Piazza Tales* was published in 1856, five years after *Moby-Dick*. Two of the six tales—"Bartleby, The Scrivener" and "Benito Cereno"—are commonly and rightly accepted among Melville's strongest works, together with *Moby-Dick* and (rather more tenuously) *The Confidence-Man* and *Billy Budd, Sailor*. Two others—"The Encantadas, or Enchanted Isles" and "The Bell-Tower"—seem to me even better, being equal to the best moments in *Moby-Dick*. Two of the *The Piazza Tales* are relative trifles: "The Piazza" and "The Lightning-Rod Man." A volume of novellas with four near-masterpieces is an extraordinary achievement, but particularly poignant if, like Melville, you had lost your reading public after the early success of *Typee* and *Omoo*, the more equivocal reception of *Mardi*, and the return to a wider audience with *Redburn* and even more with *White-Jacket*. *Moby-Dick* today is, together with *Leaves of Grass* and *Huckleberry Finn*, one of the three candidates for our national epic, but like *Leaves of Grass* it found at first only the one great reader (Hawthorne for Melville, Emerson for Whitman) and almost no popular response. What was left of Melville's early audience was killed off by the dreadful *Pierre*, a year after *Moby-Dick*, and despite various modern salvage attempts *Pierre* certainly is unreadable, in the old-fashioned sense of that now critically-abused word. You just cannot get through it, unless you badly want and need to do so.

The best of *The Piazza Tales* show the post-*Pierre* Melville writing for himself, possibly Hawthorne, and a few strangers. Himself the sole support of wife, four children, mother and several sisters, Melville was generally in debt from at least 1855 on, and Hawthorne and Richard Henry Dana, though they tried, could not get the author of *Pierre* appointed to a consulate. In the late 1850's, the tormented and shy Melville attempted the lecture circuit, but as he was neither a pulpit-pounder like Henry Ward Beecher, nor a preternaturally eloquent sage like Ralph Waldo Emerson, he failed rather badly. Unhappily married, mother-ridden, an apparent literary failure; the author of *The Piazza Tales* writes out of the depths. Steeped, as were Carlyle and Ruskin, in the King James Bible, Melville no more believed in the Bible than did Carlyle and Ruskin. But even as *Moby-Dick* found its legitimate and overwhelming precursors in the Bible, Spenser, Shakespeare and Milton, so do *The Piazza Tales*. Melville's rejection of Biblical theology, his almost Gnostic distrust of nature and history alike, finds powerful expression in *The Piazza Tales*, as it did throughout all his later fictional prose and his verse.

II

"The Bell-Tower" is a tale of only fifteen pages but it has such resonance and strength that each rereading gives me the sense that I have experienced a superb short novel. Bannadonna, "the great mechanician, the unblest foundling," seeking to conquer a larger liberty, like Prometheus, instead extended the empire of necessity. His great Bell-Tower, intended to be the noblest in Italy, survives only as "a stone pine," a "black massed stump." It is the new tower of Babel:

> Like Babel's, its base was laid in a high hour of renovated earth, following the second deluge, when the waters of the Dark Ages had dried up, and once more the green appeared. No wonder that, after so long and deep submersion, the jubilant expectation of the race should, as with Noah's sons, soar into Shinar aspiration.
>
> In firm resolve, no man in Europe at that period went beyond Bannadonna. Enriched through commerce with the Levant, the state in which he lived voted to have the noblest Bell-Tower in Italy. His repute assigned him to be architect.
>
> Stone by Stone, month by month, the tower rose. Higher, higher; snail-like in pace, but torch or rocket in its pride.
>
> After the masons would depart, the builder, standing alone upon its ever-ascending summit, at close of every day saw that he overtopped still higher walls and trees. He would tarry till a late hour there, wrapped in schemes of other and still loftier piles. Those who of saints' days thronged the spot—hanging to the rude poles of scaffolding, like sailors on yards, or bees on boughs, unmindful of lime and dust, and falling chips of stone—their homage not the less inspirited him to self-esteem.
>
> At length the holiday of the Tower came. To the sound of viols, the climax-stone slowly rose in air, and, amid that firing of ordnance, was laid by Bannadonna's hands upon the final course. Then mounting it, he stood erect, alone, with folded arms; gazing upon the white summits of blue inland Alps, and whiter crests of bluer Alps off-shore—sights invisible from the plain. Invisible, too, from thence was that eye he turned below, when, like the cannon booms, came up to him the people's combustion of applause.

> That which stirred them so was, seeing with what serenity the builder stood three hundred feet in air, upon an unrailed perch. This none but he durst do. But his periodic standing upon the pile, in each stage of its growth—such discipline had its last result.

We recognize Captain Ahab in Bannadonna, though Ahab has his humanities, and the great mechanician lacks all pathos. Ahab plays out an avenger's tragedy, but Bannadonna's purpose lacks any motivation except pride. His pride presumably is related to the novelist's, and the black stump that is the sole remnant of the Bell-Tower might as well be *Pierre*, little as Melville would have welcomed such an identification. The sexual mortification of the image is palpable, yet adds little to the comprehensiveness of what will become Bannadonna's doom, since that necessarily is enacted as a ritual of castration anyway. Melville's Prometheans, Ahab and Bannadonna, have an overtly Gnostic quarrel with the heavens. Melville's narratives, at their strongest, know implicitly what Kafka asserted with rare explicitness in his great parable:

> The crows maintain that a single crow could destroy the heavens. Doubtless that is so, but it proves nothing against the heavens for the heavens signify simply: the impossibility of crows.

In Melville, the heavens signify simply: the impossibility of Ahab and of Bannadonna. Ahab is a hunter and not a builder, but to destroy Moby-Dick or to build the Bell-Tower would be to pile up the Tower of Babel and get away with it:

> If it had been possible to build the Tower of Babel without ascending it, the work would have been permitted.

Kafka's aphorism would be an apt title for Melville's story, with Bannadonna who has built his tower partly in order to ascend it and to stand "three hundred feet in air, upon an unrailed perch." Kafka could have told Bannadonna that a labyrinth underground would have been better, though of course that too would not have been permitted, since the heavens would have regarded it as the pit of Babel:

> What are you building? — I want to dig a subterranean passage. Some progress must be made. My station up there is much too high.
> We are digging the pit of Babel.

Bannadonna is closest to the most extraordinary of the Kafkan parables concerning the Tower, in which a scholar maintains that the Great Wall of China "alone would provide for the first time in the history of mankind a secure foundation for the new Tower of Babel. First the wall, therefore, and then the tower." The final sentence of "The Great Wall and the Tower of Babel" could have impressed Melville as the best possible commentary upon Bannadonna-Melville, both in his project and his fate:

> There were many wild ideas in people's heads at that time—this scholar's book is only one example—perhaps simply because so many were trying to join forces as far as they could for the achievement of a single aim. Human nature, essentially changeable, unstable as the dust, can endure no restraint; if it binds itself it soon begins to tear madly at its bonds, until it rends everything asunder, the wall, the bonds and its very self.

The fall of Bannadonna commences with the casting of the great bell:

> The unleashed metals bayed like hounds. The workmen shrunk. Through their fright, fatal harm to the bell was dreaded. Fearless as Shadrach, Bannadonna, rushing through the glow, smote the chief culprit with his ponderous ladle. From the smitten part, a splinter was dashed into the seething mass, and at once was melted in.

That single blemish is evidently Melville's personal allegory for whatever sense of guilt, in his own pained judgment, flawed his own achievement, even in *Moby-Dick*. More interesting is Bannadonna's creation of a kind of *golem* or Frankensteinean monster, charmingly called Haman, doubtless in tribute to the villain of the Book of Esther. Haman, intended to be the bell-ringer, is meant also: "as a partial type of an ulterior creature," a titanic helot who would be called Talus, like the rather sinister iron man who wields an iron flail against the rebellious Irish in the savage Book V of Spenser's *The Faerie Queene*. But Talus is never created; Haman is quite enough to immolate the ambitious artist, Bannadonna:

> And so, for the interval, he was oblivious of his creature; which, not oblivious of him, and true to its creation, and true to its heedful winding up, left its post precisely at the given moment; along its well-oiled route, slid noiselessly towards its mark; and aiming at the hand of Una, to ring one clangorous note, dully smote the intervening brain of Bannadonna, turned backwards to it; the manacled arms then instantly upspringing to their hovering poise. The falling body clogged the thing's return; so there it stood, still impending over Bannadonna, as if whispering some post-mortem terror. The chisel lay dropped from the hand, but beside the hand; the oil-flask spilled across the iron track.

Which of his own works destroyed Melville? Juxtapose the story's deliberately Addisonian or Johnsonian conclusion with the remarkable stanza in Hart Crane's "The Broken Tower" that it helped inspire, and perhaps a hint emerges, since Crane was a superb interpreter of Melville:

So the blind slave obeyed its blinder lord; but, in obedience, slew him. So the creator was killed by the creature. So the bell was too heavy for the tower. So that bell's main weakness was where man's blood had flawed it. And so pride went before the fall.

> The bells, I say, the bells break down their tower;
> And swing I know not where. Their tongues engrave
> Membrane through marrow, my long-scattered score
> Of broken intervals . . . And I, their sexton slave!

Crane is both Bannadonna and Haman, a complex fate darker even than Melville's, who certainly had represented himself as Bannadonna. The Bell-Tower of Bannadonna perhaps was *Pierre* but more likely *Moby-Dick* itself, Melville's "long-scattered score / of broken intervals" even as *The Bridge* was Hart Crane's. This is hardly to suggest that Haman is Captain Ahab. Yet Melville's "wicked book," as he called *Moby-Dick* in a famous letter to Hawthorne, indeed may have slain something vital in its author, if only in his retrospective consciousness.

III

"Canst thou draw out Leviathan with a hook?," God's taunting question to Job, can be said to be answered, by Captain Ahab, with a "Yes!" in thunder. Job's God wins, Ahab loses, and the great white Leviathan swims away, harpooned yet towing Ahab with him. But Ahab's extraordinary last speech denies that Moby-Dick is the conquerer:

> I turn my body from the sun. What ho, Tashtego! let me hear thy hammer. Oh! ye three unsurrendered spires of mine; thou uncracked keel; and only god-bullied hull; thou firm deck, and haughty helm, and Pole-pointed prow,—death-glorious ship! must ye then perish, and without me? Am I cut off from the last fond pride of meanest shipwrecked captains? Oh, lonely death on lonely life! Oh, now I feel my topmost greatness lies in my topmost grief. Ho, ho! from all your furthest bounds, pour ye now in, ye bold billows of my whole foregone life, and top this one piled comber of my death! Towards thee I roll, thou all-destroying but unconquering whale; to the last I grapple with thee; from hell's heart I stab at thee; for hate's sake I spit my last breath at thee. Sink all coffins and all hearses to one common pool! and since neither can be mine, let me then tow to pieces, while still chasing thee, though tied to thee, thou damned whale! *Thus*, I give up the spear!

Beyond the allusions — Shakespearean, Miltonic, Byronic — what rings out here is Melville's own grand self-echoing, which is of Father Mapple's sermon as it concludes:

He drooped and fell away from himself for a moment; then lifting his face to them again, showed a deep joy in his eyes, as he cried out with a heavenly enthusiasm,—"But oh! shipmates! on the starboard hand of every woe, there is a sure delight; and higher the top of that delight, than the bottom of the woe is deep. Is not the main-truck higher than the kelson is low? Delight is to him—a far, far upward, and inward delight—who against the proud gods and commodores of this earth, ever stands forth his own inexorable self. Delight is to him whose strong arms yet support him, when the ship of this base treacherous world has gone down beneath him. Delight is to him, who gives no quarter in the truth, and kills, burns, and destroys all sin though he pluck it out from under the robes of Senators and Judges. Delight,—top-gallant delight is to him, who acknowledges no law or lord, but the Lord his God, and is only a patriot to heaven. Delight is to him, whom all the waves of the billows of the seas of the boisterous mob can never shake from this sure Keel of the Ages. And eternal delight and deliciousness will be his, who coming to lay him down, can say with his final breath—O Father!—chiefly known to me by Thy rod—mortal or immortal here I die. I have striven to be Thine, more than to be this world's, or mine own. Yet this is nothing; I leave eternity to Thee; for what is man that he should live out the lifetime of his God?"

Father Mapple's intensity moves from "a sure delight, and higher the top of that delight" through "a far, far upward, and inward delight" on to "Delight,—top-gallant delight is to him," heaven's patriot. Ahab's equal but antithetical intensity proceeds from "unsurrendered spires of mine" through "my topmost greatness lies in my topmost grief" to end in "top this one piled comber of my death." After which the Pequod goes down with Tashtego hammering a hawk to the mainmast, an emblem not of being "only a patriot to heaven" but rather of a Satanic dragging of "a living part of heaven along with her." Admirable as Father Mapple is, Ahab is certainly the hero, more Promethean than Satanic, and we need not conclude (as so many critics do) that Melville chooses Mapple's stance over Ahab's. William Faulkner, in 1927, asserted that the book he most wished he had written was Moby-Dick, and called Ahab's fate "a sort of Golgotha of the heart become immutable as bronze in the sonority of its plunging ruin," characteristically adding: "There's a death for a man, now."

As Faulkner implied, there is a dark sense in which Ahab intends his Golgotha, like Christ's, to be a vicarious atonement for all of staggering Adam's woes. When Melville famously wrote to Hawthorne: "I have written a wicked book," he was probably quite serious. The common reader does not come to love Ahab, and yet there is a serious disproportion between that reader's awe of, and admiration for, Ahab, and the moral dismissal of the monomaniacal hero by many scholarly critics. Ahab seems to provoke academic critics rather more even than Milton's Satan does. Ishmael, presumably speaking for Melville, consistently emphasizes Ahab's greatness. And so does Ahab himself, as when he confronts the corposants or St. Elmo's fire, in the superb Chapter 119, "The Candles":

> Oh! thou clear spirit of clear fire, whom on these seas I as Persian once did worship, till in the sacramental act so burned by thee, that to this hour I bear the scar; I now know thee, thou clear spirit, and I know that thy right worship is defiance. To neither love nor reverence wilt thou be kind; and e'en for hate thou canst but kill; and all are killed. No fearless fool now fronts thee. I own thy speechless, placeless power; but to the last gasp of my earthquake life will dispute its unconditional, unintegral mastery in me. In the midst of the personified impersonal, a personality stands here. Though but a point at best; whensoe'er I came; wheresoe'er I go; yet while I earthly live, the queenly personality lives in me, and feels her royal rights. But war is pain, and hate is woe. Come in thy lowest form of love, and I will kneel and kiss thee; but at thy highest, come as mere supernal power; and though thou launchest navies of full-freighted worlds, there's that in here that still remains indifferent. Oh, thou clear spirit, of thy fire thou madest me, and like a true child of fire, I breathe it back to thee.

If Ahab has a religion, it is Persian or rather Parsee, and so Zoroastrian. But Melville has not written a Zoroastrian hymn to the benign light for Ahab to chant. Ahab's invocation is clearly Gnostic in spirit and in substance, since the light is hailed as being both ambiguous and ambivalent. Ahab himself knows that the clear spirit of clear fire is not from the Alien God but from the Demiurge, and he seems to divide the Demiurge into both the "lowest form of love" and the "highest . . . mere supernal power." Against this dialectical or even self-contradictory spirit, Ahab sets himself as personality rather than as moral character: "In the midst of the personified impersonal, a personality stands here." As a personality, Ahab confronts "the personified impersonal," which he astonishingly names as his father, and defies, as knowing less than he, Ahab, knows:

> I own thy speechless, placeless power; said I not so? Nor was it wrung from me; nor do I now drop these links. Thou canst blind; but I can then grope. Thou canst consume; but I can then be ashes. Take the homage of these poor eyes, and shutter-hands. I would not take it. The lightning flashes through my skull; mine eye-balls ache and ache; my whole beaten brain seems as beheaded, and rolling on some stunning ground. Oh, oh! Yet blindfold, yet will I talk to thee. Light though thou be, thou leapest out of darkness; but I am darkness leaping out of light, leaping out of

thee! The javelins cease; open eyes; see, or not? There burn the flames! Oh, thou magnanimous! now I do glory in my genealogy. But thou art but my fiery father; my sweet mother, I know not. Oh, cruel! what hast thou done with her? There lies my puzzle; but thine is greater. Thou knowest not how came ye, hence callest thyself unbegun. I know that of me, which thou knowest not of thyself, oh, thou omnipotent. There is some unsuffusing thing beyond thee, thou clear spirit, to whom all thy eternity is but time, all thy creativeness mechanical. Through thee, thy flaming self, my scorched eyes do dimly see it. Oh, thou foundling fire, thou hermit immemorial, thou too hast thy incommunicable riddle, thy unparticipated grief. Here again with haughty agony, I read my sire. Leap! leap up, and lick the sky! I leap with thee; I burn with thee; would fain be welded with thee; defyingly I worship thee!

The Gnosticism here is explicit and unmistakeable, since "some unsuffusing thing beyond thee, thou clear spirit, to whom all thy eternity is but time, all thy creativeness mechanical" is certainly what the Gnostics called the true or alien God, but off from our cosmos. But who is Ahab's "sweet mother"? Ahab scarcely recognizes a benign aspect of our cosmos, so that his mother, in Gnostic terms, must be the original abyss, preceding the Demiurge's false creation. But, as Melville knew, that motherly abyss, in Gnosticism, is also the forefather or Alien God. Echoing the Gnostics' savage reading of the opening of Genesis, Ahab insinuates that his father, the Demiurge, begat him upon the true God, or abyss, his mother. Rebelling (though equivocally) against his father, Ahab proudly asserts his mother's knowledge of origins against his father's ignorance. When Ahab cries out that he wishes to be welded with his father, we rightly should flinch, because that is the book's true wickedness. Ahab, like Bannadonna, like Melville himself, desires to be one with the Demiurge.

IV

The visionary center of *Moby-Dick,* and so of all Melville, as critics always have recognized, is Chapter 42, "The Whiteness of the Whale." It is Ishmael's meditation, and not Ahab's, and yet how far is it from Ahab? Ishmael is himself half a Gnostic:

Though in many of its aspects this visible world seems formed in love, the invisible spheres were formed in fright.

Closer to Carlyle than to Emerson, this extraordinary sentence is the prelude to the final paragraph of Ishmael's reverie:

But not yet have we solved the incantation of this whiteness, and learned why it appeals with such power to the soul; and more strange and far more portentous—why, as we have seen, it is at once the most meaning symbol of spiritual things, nay, the very veil of the Christian's Deity; and yet should be as it is, the intensifying agent in things the most appalling to mankind.

Is it that by its indefiniteness it shadows forth the heartless voids and immensities of the universe, and thus stabs us from behind with the thought of annihilation, when beholding the white depths of the milky way? Or is it, that as in essence whiteness is not so much a color as the visible absence of color, and at the same time the concrete of all colors; is it for these reasons that there is such a dumb blankness, full of meaning, in a wide landscape of snows—a colorless, all-color of atheism from which we shrink? And when we consider that other theory of the natural philosophers, that all other earthly hues—every stately or lovely emblazoning—the worst tinges of sunset skies and woods; yea, and the gilded velvets of butterflies, and the butterfly cheeks of young girls; all these are but subtle deceits, not actually inherent in substances, but only laid on from without; so that all deified Nature absolutely paints like the harlot, whose allurements cover nothing but the charnel-house within; and when we proceed further, and consider that the mystical cosmetic which produces every one of her hues, the great principle of light, for ever remains white or colorless in itself, and if operating without medium upon matter, would touch all objects, even tulips and roses, with its own blank tinge—pondering all this, the palsied universe lies before us a leper; and like wilful travellers in Lapland, who refuse to wear colored and coloring glasses upon their eyes, so the wretched infidel gazes himself blind at the monumental white shroud that wraps all the prospect around him. And of all these things the Albino whale was the symbol. Wonder ye then at the fiery hunt?

Ishmael's "visible absence of color" becomes the trope of whiteness, "a dumb blankness," similar to its descendant in the beach-scene of Wallace Stevens's "The Auroras of Autumn":

> Here, being visible is being white,
> Is being of the solid of white, the accomplishment
> Of an extremist in an exercise . . .
>
> The season changes. A cold wind chills the beach.
> The long lines of it grow longer, emptier,
> A darkness gathers though it does not fall.
>
> And the whiteness grows less vivid on the wall.
> The man who is walking turns blankly on the sand.

Melville and Stevens alike shrink from "a colorless, all-color of atheism," not because they are theists, but precisely because they both believe in and fear the Demiurge. When Ishmael cries out: "Wonder ye then at the fiery hunt?", he refutes all those critics, moral and psychoanalytic, who condemn Ahab as being immoral or insane. It was Melville, after all, who wrote two memorable quatrains, in the mode of Blake, which he entitled "Fragments of a Lost Gnostic Poem of the 12th Century":

> Found a family, build a state,
> The pledged event is still the same:
> Matter in end will never abate
> His ancient brutal claim.
>
> Indolence is heaven's ally here,
> And energy the child of hell:
> The Good Man pouring from his pitcher clear,
> But brims the poisoned well.

There the Gnosticism is overt, and we are left a little cold, since even an heretical doctrine strikes us as tendentious, as having too clear a design upon us. Perhaps "The Bell-Tower" is a touch tendentious also. *Moby-Dick*, despite its uneven rhetoric, despite its excessive debt to Shakespeare, Milton and Byron, is anything but tendentious. It remains the darker half of our national epic, complementing *Leaves of Grass* and *Huckleberry Finn*, works of more balance certainly, but they do not surpass or eclipse Melville's version of darkness visible.

CHARLES OLSON

Call Me Ishmael

I take SPACE to be the central fact to man born in America, from Folsom cave to now. I spell it large because it comes large here. Large, and without mercy.

It is geography at bottom, a hell of wide land from the beginning. That made the first American story (Parkman's): exploration.

Something else than a stretch of earth—seas on both sides, no barriers to contain as restless a thing as Western man was becoming in Columbus' day. That made Melville's story (part of it).

PLUS a harshness we still perpetuate, a sun like a tomahawk, small earthquakes but big tornadoes and hurrikans, a river north and south in the middle of the land running out the blood.

The fulcrum of America is the Plains, half sea half land, a high sun as metal and obdurate as the iron horizon, and a man's job to square the circle.

Some men ride on such space, others have to fasten themselves like a tent stake to survive. As I see it Poe dug in and Melville mounted. They are the alternatives.

Americans still fancy themselves such democrats. But their triumphs are of the machine. It is the only master of space the average person ever knows, oxwheel to piston, muscle to jet. It gives trajectory.

To Melville it was not the will to be free but the will to overwhelm nature that lies at the bottom of us as individuals and a people. Ahab is no democrat. Moby-Dick, antagonist, is only king of natural force, resource.

I am interested in a Melville who decided sometime in 1850 to write a book about the whaling industry and what happened to a man in command of one of the most successful machines Americans had perfected up to that time—the whaleship.

This captain, Ahab by name, knew space. He rode it across seven seas. He was an able skipper, what the fishing people I was raised with call a highliner. Big catches: he brought back holds barrel full of the oil of the sperm, the light of American and European communities up to the middle of the 19th century.

This Ahab had gone wild. The object of his attention was something unconscionably big and white. He had become a specialist: he had all space concentrated into the form of a whale called Moby-Dick. And he assailed it as Columbus an ocean, LaSalle a continent, the Donner Party their winter Pass.

I am interested in a Melville who was long-eyed enough to understand the Pacific as part of our geography, another West, prefigured in the Plains, antithetical.

The beginning of man was salt sea, and the perpetual reverberation of that great ancient fact, constantly renewed in the unfolding of life in every human individual, is the important single fact about Melville. Pelagic.

He had the tradition in him, deep, in his brain, his words, the salt beat of his blood. He had the sea of himself in a vigorous, stricken way, as Poe the street. It enabled him to draw up from Shakespeare. It made Noah, and Moses, contemporary to him. History was ritual and repetition when Melville's imagination was at its own proper beat.

It was an older sense than the European man's, more to do with magic than culture. Magic which, in contrast to worship, is all black. For magic has one purpose: compel men or non-human forces to do one's will. Like Ahab, American, one aim: lordship over nature.

I am willing to ride Melville's image of man, whale and ocean to find in him prophecies, lessons he himself would not have spelled out. A hundred years gives us an advantage. For Melville was as much larger than himself as Ahab's hate. He was a plunger. He knew how to take a chance.

The man made a mess of things. He got all balled up with Christ. He made a white marriage. He had one son die of tuberculosis, the other shoot himself. He only rode his own space once—Moby-Dick. He had to be wild or he was nothing in particular. He had to go fast, like an American, or he was all torpor. Half horse half alligator.

Melville took an awful licking. He was bound to. He was an original, aboriginal. A beginner. It happens that way to the dreaming men it takes to discover America: Columbus and LaSalle won, and then lost her to the competent. Daniel Boone loved her earth. Harrod tells the story of coming upon Boone one day far to the west in Kentucky of where Harrod thought any white man had ever been. He heard sound he couldn't place, crept forward to a boulder and there in a blue grass clearing was Boone alone singing to himself. Boone died west of the Mississippi, in his own country criminal—"wanted," a bankrupt of spirit and land.

Beginner—and interested in beginnings. Melville had a way of reaching back through time until he got history pushed back so far he turned time into space. He was like a migrant backtrailing to Asia, some Inca trying to find a lost home.

We are the last "first" people. We forget that. We act big, misuse our land, ourselves. We lose our own primary.

Melville went back, to discover us, to come forward. He got as far as *Moby-Dick.*

Ortega y Gasset puts it that the man of antiquity, before he did anything, took a step like the bullfighter who leaps back in order to deliver the mortal thrust.

Whitman appears, because of his notation of the features of American life and his conscious identification of himself with the people, to be more the poet. But Melville had the will. He was homeless in his land, his society, his self.

Logic and classification had led civilization toward man, away from space. Melville went to space to probe and find man. Early men did the same: poetry, language and the care of myth, as Fenollosa says, grew up together. Among the Egyptians Horus was the god of writing and the god of the moon, one figure for both, a WHITE MONKEY.

In place of Zeus, Odysseus, Olympus we have had Caesar, Faust, the City. The shift was from man as a group to individual man. Now, in spite of the corruption of myth by fascism, the swing is out and back. Melville is one who began it.

He had a pull to the origin of things, the first day, the first man, the unknown sea, Betelgeuse, the buried continent. From passive places his imagination sprang a harpoon.

He sought prime. He had the coldness we have, but he warmed himself by first fires after Flood. It gave him the power to find the lost past of America, the unfound present, and make a myth, *Moby-Dick,* for a people of Ishmaels.

The thing got away from him. It does, from us. We made AHAB, the WHITE WHALE, and lose them. We let John Henry go, Negro, worker, hammering man:

> He lied down his hammer an' he died.

Whitman we have called our greatest voice because he gave us hope. Melville is the truer man. He lived intensely his people's wrong, their guilt. But he remembered the first dream. The *White Whale* is more accurate than *Leaves of Grass.* Because it is America, all of her space, the malice, the root.

WHAT LIES UNDER

Melville prepared the way for *Moby-Dick* by ridiculing, in 1850, the idea that the literary genius in America would be, like Shakespeare, "a writer of dramas." This was his proposition:

> great geniuses are parts of the times, they themselves are the times, and possess a corresponding colouring.

Melville raised his times up when he got them into *Moby-Dick* and they held firm in his schema:

> e.g. his *crew*, a "people," Clootz and Tom Paine's people, all races and colors functioning together, a forecastle reality of Americans not yet a dream accomplished by the society;
>
> e.g. his *job on the whaling industry*, a problem in the resolution of forces solved with all forces taken account of: (1) OWNERS Bildad and Peleg (Aunt Charity interested party); (2) Ahab, hard MASTER; (3) the MEN, and TECHNOLOGY, killer boat, tryworks and underdeck storage of yield permitting four-year voyage.

We forget the part the chase of the whale played in American economy. It started from a shortage of fats and oils. The Indian had no cattle, the colonist not enough. It was the same with pigs and goats. Red and white alike had to use substitutes. It accounts for the heavy slaughter of the passenger pigeon and the curlew, plentiful birds; and the slaughter of the buffalo.

The Indians appear to have taken shore whales from an early time. The Makahs around Cape Flattery knew tricks only the present day Norwegian whalers have applied. They blew up seal skins to slow the run of a wounded whale like a sea anchor and to float the dead whale when heavier than water.

The American Indian continued to be a skilled part of the industry down to its end, a miserably paid tool. Melville had reason to name his ship *Pequod* and to make the Gayhead Tashteego one of his three harpooneers.

COMBUSTION. All whales yield oil. Most of the oil is a true fat, a glyceride of the fatty acids. Unlike the Indians the settlers did not find it edible. They boiled the blubber down for tallow. In addition to this fat, commonly called whale oil, the sperm whale and the bottlenose yield a solid wax called spermaceti and a liquid wax called sperm oil. The spermaceti wax is contained in the cavity of the head (vide chp. CISTERN AND BUCKETS, *Moby-Dick*), and in the bones.

Economic historians, lubbers, fail to heft the industry in American economic life up to the Civil War. (In 1859 petroleum was discovered in Pennsylvania. Kerosene, petroleum, and paraffin began rapidly to replace whale oil, sperm oil, and spermaceti wax as illuminating oil, lubricants, and raw materials for candles.)

Whaling expanded at a time when agriculture not industry was the base of labor and when foreign not domestic commerce was the base of trade. A few facts:

by 1833, 70,000 persons and $70,000,000 were tied up in whaling and such associated crafts as shipbuilding, sail-lofts, smiths to make toggle irons, the thieving outfitters, their agents and the whores of ports like New Bedford;

by 1844 (peak years roughly 1840-1860) the figure is up to $120,000,000, whaling competes successfully in attracting capital to itself with such opening industries as textiles and shoes, and the export of whale products—one-forth of the catch—is third to meat products and lumber.

A NECESSARY DISSOCIATION: the notion that the China trade and clipper ships made and made up the maritime America which went down as did agrarian America before land and finance speculation, hard metal industry.

The China trade was, economically, distribution, appeared after England closed the West Indies to our rum merchants following the Revolution. It was the way the smugglers, themselves the answer to England's pre-Revolutionary restrictions, went straight.

Whaling was production, as old as the colonies and, in capital and function, forerunner to a later America, with more relation to Socony than to clippers and the China trade.

As early as 1688 there is a record at Boston of a New York brig petitioning Governor Andross for permission to set out "upon a fishing design about the Bohames Islands, And Cap florida, for sperma Coeti whales and Racks."

This was new to whaling, BRAND NEW, American. A FIRST. All the way back to French and Spanish Basques of the Middle Ages it had been cold water whales, the black, right or Greenland whales of northern waters, which had been hunted. But the Yankees had discovered that the Sperm whale had the finest oil and brought the biggest price.

They went after it. And it led them into all the oceans. And gave whaling its leading role in making the Pacific the American lake the navy now, after a lapse of 100 years, has been about the business of certifying.

A FACT: whale logbooks are today furnishing sea lawyers first claims to islands—the flag & all that;

for whaler as pioneer, cf. chp. THE ADVOCATE, *Moby-Dick*.

You will also discover in that chapter Melville's figures on the value of the industry. Compare to mine above. Thus:

we whalemen of America now outnumber all the rest of the banded whalemen in the world; sail a navy of upward of seven hundred vessels; manned by eighteen thousand men; yearly consuming 4,000,000 dollars; the ships worth, at the time of sailing, $20,000,000; and every year reporting into our harbours a well-reaped harvest of $7,000,000.

About this outnumbering: of 900 whaling vessels of all nations in 1846, 735 were American.

All this is by way of CORRECTION. I don't intend to dish up cold pork. There are histories of whaling if you are interested. BUT no study weighs the industry in the scale of the total society. What you get is this: many of the earliest industrial fortunes were built on the "blessing" of the whale fishery!

TWO INTERPOLATIONS. Melville did not know Number 1. Maybe somewhere he does point out Number 2. For he was wide. Add to his knowledge of whaling:

merchant marine	(read *Redburn*)
the Navy	(ditto *White-Jacket*)
assorted carriers of the Pacific	(*Omoo, Mardi,* etc.)
and the Spanish	(by all means read "Benito Cereno" and "The Encantadas," the finest things outside *Moby-Dick*)

Interpolation 1
1762: the colonies still very English, so much so they have little to do with one another, face and act toward London.
Rhode Island: makers of spermaceti candles meet and make covenant to raise the price of wax candles—and keep it raised, it goes without saying. The first American TRUST.
Name: The United Company of Spermaceti Chandlers.

Importance: "shows how colonial boundaries were being eliminated in the minds of the moneyed groups as contrasted with the as yet extremely provincial outlook and provincial patriotism of the smaller people of town and country."

I'm putting a stress Melville didn't on whaling as *industry.* Cutting out the glory: a book *Moby-Dick* turns out to be its glory. We still are soft about our industries, wonder-eyed. What's important is the energy they are a clue to, the drive in the people. The things made are OK, too, some of them. But the captains of industry ain't worth the powder etc. Take the Revolution so long as we're on the subject: whose revolution was it but the "moneyed groups' ''; Breed's Hill two weeks after Lexington and it was all over the for the "smaller people" until Jefferson gave them another chance.

Don't think whaling was any different from any other American industry. The first men in it, the leaders, explorers, were WORKERS. The money and the glory came later, on top with the exploiters. And the force went down, stayed where it always does, at the underpaid bottom. Where the worker is after the leader is gone.

Whaling started, like so many American industries, as a collective, communal affair. See any history of Sag Harbor or Nantucket. And as late as 1850 there were still skippers to remember the days when they knew the fathers of every man in their crew. But it was already a sweated industry by the time Melville was a hand on a lay (1841–43).

THE TRICK—then as now:

reduce labor costs lower than worker's efficiency—during the 1840's and '50's it cost the owners 15¢ to 30¢ a day to feed each crew member

combine inefficient workers and such costs by maintaining lowest wages and miserable working conditions—vide TYPEE, early chps., and *Omoo,* same.

THE RESULT: by the 1840's the crews were the bottom dogs of all nations and all races. Of the 18,000 men (Melville above) *one-half* ranked as green hands and more than *two-thirds* deserted every voyage.

There were so many Pacific natives like Queequeg, the second colored harpooneer, that a section of Nantucket came to be known as New Guinea.

There were so many Portuguese from the Islands that a section of New Bedford was called Fayal.

The third of Melville's harpooneers was the imperial African Negro Ahasuerus Daggoo.

For bottom dogs made pretty SEE the balletic chapter called MIDNIGHT, FORECASTLE, in *Moby-Dick*.

I insert here a document of our history left out of the published works of Herman Melville. It was written at the same time as *Moby-Dick* and is headed:

What became of the ship's company of the whaleship 'Acushnet,' according to Hubbard who came home in her (more than a four years' voyage) and who visited me at Pittsfield in 1850.

Captain Pease—retired & lives ashore at the Vineyard
Raymond, 1st Mate—had a fight with the Captain & went ashore at Payta
Hall, 2nd Mate—came home & went to California
3rd Mate—Portuguese, went ashore at Payta
Boatsteerer Brown—Portuguese, either ran away or killed at Ropo one of the Marquesas
Smith—went ashore at Santa coast of Peru, afterwards committed suicide at Mobile
Barney, boatsteerer—came home
Carpenter—went ashore at Mowee half dead with disreputable disease

The Crew:
Tom Johnson—black, went ashore at Mowee half dead (ditto) & died at the hospital
Reed—mulatto—came home
Blacksmith—ran away at St. Francisco
Backus—little black—Do
Bill Green—after various attempts at running away, came home in the end
The Irishman—ran away at Salango, coast of Columbia
Wright—went ashore half dead at the Marquesas
John Adams & Jo Portuguese—came home
The old cook—came home
Haynes—ran away aboard of a Sidney ship
Little Jack—came home
Grant—young fellow—went ashore half dead, spitting blood, at Oahu
Murray—went ashore, shunning fight, at Rio Janeiro
The Cooper—came home

Melville himself is a case in point. He deserted the *Acushnet*, his first whaleship, at the Marquesas. He was one of eleven mutineers aboard his second, a Sidney ship the *Lucy Ann*, at Tahiti. Nothing is known of his conduct on the third, except that he turned up after it, ashore, at Honolulu.

So if you want to know why Melville nailed us in *Moby-Dick*, consider whaling. Consider whaling as FRONTIER, and INDUSTRY. A product wanted, men got it: big business. The Pacific as sweatshop, Man, led, against the biggest damndest creature nature uncorks. The whaleship as factory, the whaleboat the precision instrument. The 1840's: the New West in the saddle and Melville No. 20 of a rough and bastard crew. Are they the essentials?

BIG? Melville may never have seen the biggest of whales, the blue, the principal kill of the present day. He reaches his full size, 100 feet, at 11 years, lives 20 to 25 years, and weighs 150 tons—or four times the estimated weight of the biggest prehistoric monster and equal to the weight of 37 elephants or 150 fat oxen.

There are two classes of whale: the baleen and the toothed whale. The blue is a baleen. Melville was satisfied with the biggest of the toothed whales, the sperm.

Whales have lungs. To breathe they come to the surface about every half hour. It is this fact that makes them vulnerable to attack by the only important enemy they have—the whaleman.

Melville didn't put it all on the surface of *Moby-Dick*. You'll find the frontier all right, and Andrew Jackson regarded as heavyweight champion (READ end of first KNIGHTS AND SQUIRES chapter for finest rhetoric of democracy). And the technic of an industry analyzed, scrupulously described. But no economics. Jefferson and John Adams observed that in their young days very few men had thought about "government," there were very few writers on "government." Yes, the year *Moby-Dick* was being finished Marx was writing letters to the N.Y. *Daily Tribune*. But Melville . . . . . .

SOME NECESSARY ECOLOGY. With his baleen the blue whale strains out of the water and eats KRILL. Krill is a shrimplike fish which itself feeds on floating green diatoms. These algae develop in summer in the neighborhood of drift ice.

> color: krill spawn at the border of arctic and antarctic ice. The offspring drift with the currents toward the equator. They are in such abundance they turn the waters pink.

The sperm whale feeds on cuttlefish, particularly on the GIANT SQUID which grows to a 33-foot spread of tentacles and an arm length of 21 feet. Compare *Moby-Dick*, LIX, SQUID. The squid lives on big prawn and small fish, and to catch him the whale dives into depths of several hundred fathom. The struggle leaves sores and marks of the armed suckers on the whale's skin around the mouth.

. . . . . . what counts, Melville had, the *experience*, what lies under. And his own force to resolve the forces.

Interpolation No. 2
Quote. The American whaling era—in contrast to the
            Basque, French, Dutch and English—
            developed independently
            concentrated on different species of whale
            covered all seas including the Arctic
            yielded on a larger scale than in any other coun-
            try or group of countries before.

                                                    Unquote. . . .

SHAKESPEARE, OR THE DISCOVERY OF "MOBY-DICK"

Which is the best of Shakespeare's plays? I mean in what mood and with
what accompaniment do you like the sea best?"
                            Keats, Letter to Jane Reynolds Sept. 14, 1817

Moby-Dick was two books written between February, 1850 and August,
1851.
        The first book did not contain Ahab.
        It may not, except incidentally, have contained Moby-Dick.
        On the 7th of August, 1850, the editor Evert Duyckinck reported
to his brother:

> Melville has a new book mostly done, a romantic, fanciful & most literal
> & most enjoyable presentment of the Whale Fishery—something quite
> new.

It is not surprising that Melville turned to whaling in February,
1850, on his return from a trip to England to sell his previous book, *White-
Jacket*. It was the last of the materials his sea experience offered him.
        He had used his adventures among the South Sea islands in *Typee*
(1846) and *Omoo* (1947). He had gone further in the vast archipelago of
Mardi, written in 1847 and 1848, to map the outlines of his vision of life.
The books of 1849, *Redburn* and *White-Jacket*, he had based on his experiences aboard a merchant ship and a man-of-war. The whaling voyage in
the *Acushnet* was left.
        There is no evidence that Melville had decided on the subject before
he started to write in February. On the contrary. Melville's reading is a
gauge of him, at all points of his life. He was a skald, and knew how to
appropriate the work of others. He read to write. Highborn stealth, Edward
Dahlberg calls originality, the act of a cutpurse Autolycus who makes his
thefts as invisible as possible. Melville's books batten on other men's books.
Yet he bought no books on whaling among the many volumes purchased

in England on his trip and soon after his return Putnam's, the publishers, were picking up in London for him such things as Thomas Beale's *The Natural History of the Sperm Whale.*

He went at it as he had his last two books, "two jobs," as he called *Redburn* and *White-Jacket* in a letter to his father-in-law, "which I have done for money—being forced to it, as other men are to sawing wood." He had a family to support.

By May it was half done. So he told Richard Henry Dana in a letter on the 1st, the only other information of the first Moby-Dick which as survived. The book was giving Melville trouble. Referring to it as "the 'whaling voyage,' " he writes:

> It will be a strange sort of a book, I fear; blubber is blubber you know; tho you may get oil out of it, the poetry runs as hard as sap from a frozen maple tree;—& to cook the thing up, one must needs throw in a little fancy, which from the nature of the thing, must be ungainly as the gambols of the whales themselves. Yet I mean to give the truth of the thing, spite of this.

That's the record of Moby-Dick No. 1, as it stands. There is nothing on why, in the summer of 1850, Melville changed his conception of the work and, on something "mostly done" on August 7th, spent another full year until, in August, 1851, he had created what we know as *Moby-Dick or, The Whale.*

"Dollars damn me." Melville had the bitter thing of men of originality, the struggle between money and me. It was on him, hard, in the spring of 1850. He says as much in the Dana letter: "I write these books of mine almost entirely for 'lucre'—by the job, as a wood-sawyer saws wood," repeating on Moby-Dick what he had said about *Redburn* and *White-Jacket.*

He knew the cost if he let his imagination loose. He had taken his head once, with *Mardi.* In this new work on whaling he felt obliged as he had, after *Mardi,* with *Redburn* and *White-Jacket,* "to refrain from writing the kind of book I would wish to."

He would give the truth of the thing, spite of this, yes. His head was lifted to Dana as it was to his father-in-law seven months earlier. He did his work clean. *Exs: Redburn* and *White-Jacket.* "In writing these two books I have not repressed myself much—so far as *they* are concerned; but have spoken pretty much as I feel."

There was only one thing in the spring of 1850 which he did not feel he could afford to do: "So far as I am individually concerned, & independent of my pocket, it is my earnest desire to write those sort of books which are said to 'fail.' "

In the end, in *Moby-Dick*, he did. Within three months he took his head again. Why?

Through May he continued to try to do a quick book for the market: "all my books are botches." Into June he fought his materials: "blubber is blubber." Then something happened. What, Melville tells:

> I somehow cling to the strange fancy, that, in all men hiddenly reside certain wondrous, occult properties—as in some plants and minerals—which by some happy but very rare accident (as bronze was discovered by the melting of the iron and brass at the burning of Corinth) may chance to be called forth here on earth.

When? Melville is his own tell-tale: he wrote these words in July, 1850. They occur in an article he did for Duyckinck's magazine. He gave it the title HAWTHORNE AND HIS MOSSES, WRITTEN BY A VIRGINIAN SPENDING A JULY IN VERMONT.

The subject is Hawthorne, Shakespeare and Herman Melville. It is a document of Melville's rights and perceptions, his declaration of the freedom of a man to fail. Within a matter of days after it was written (July 18 ff.), Melville had abandoned the account of the Whale Fishery and gambled it and himself with Ahab and the White Whale.

The *Mosses* piece is a deep and lovely thing. The spirit is asweep, as in the book to come. The confusion of May is gone. Melville is charged again. *Moby-Dick* is already shadowed in the excitement over genius, and America as a subject for genius. You can feel Ahab in the making, Ahab of "the globular brain and ponderous heart," so much does Melville concern himself with the distinction between the head and the heart in Hawthorne and Shakespeare. You can see the prose stepping off.

The germinous seeds Hawthorne has dropped in Melville's July soil begin to grow: Bulkington, the secret member of the crew in *Moby-Dick*, is here, hidden in what Melville quotes as Hawthorne's self-portrait—the "seeker," rough-hewn and brawny, of large, warm heart and powerful intellect.

Above all, in the ferment, Shakespeare, the cause. The passages on him—the manner in which he is introduced, the detail with which he is used, the intensity—tell the story of what had happened. Melville had read him again. His copy of THE PLAYS survives. He had bought it in Boston in February, 1849. He described it then to Duyckinck:

> It is an edition in glorious great type, every letter whereof is a soldier, & the top of every 't' like a musket barrel.
>
> I am mad to think how minute a cause has prevented me hitherto from reading Shakespeare. But until now any copy that was come-atable

to me happened to be a vile small print unendurable to my eyes which
are tender as young sperms.

But chancing to fall in with this glorious edition, I now exult over
it, page after page.

The set exists, seven volumes, with passages marked, and comments
in Melville's hand. The significant thing is the rough notes for the composition of *Moby-Dick* on the fly-leaf of the last volume. These notes involve
Ahab, Pip, Bulkington, Ishmael, and are the key to Melville's intention
with these characters. They thus relate not to what we know of the Moby-
Dick that Melville had been working on up to July but to *Moby-Dick* as he
came to conceive it at this time.

Joined to the passages on Shakespeare in the Mosses piece, the
notes in the Shakespeare set verify what *Moby-Dick* proves: Melville and
Shakespeare had made a Corinth and out of the burning came *Moby-Dick*,
bronze. . . .

A "MOBY-DICK" MANUSCRIPT

It is beautifully right to find what I take to be rough notes for *Moby-Dick*
in the Shakespeare set itself. They are written in Melville's hand, in pencil,
upon the last fly-leaf of the last volume, the one containing *Lear*, *Othello*
and *Hamlet*. I transcribe them as they stand:

> Ego non baptizo te in nomine Patris et
> Filii et Spiritus Sancti—sed in nomine
> Diaboli.—madness is undefinable—
> It & right reason extremes of one,
> —not the (black art) Goetic but Theurgic magic—
> seeks converse with the Intelligence, Power, the
> Angel.

The Latin is a longer form of what Melville told Hawthorne to be
the secret motto of *Moby-Dick*. In the novel Ahab howls it as an inverted
benediction upon the harpoon he has tempered in savage blood:

Ego non baptizo te in nomine patris, sed in nomine diaboli.

I do not baptize thee in the name of the father, but in the name of the
devil.

The change in the wording from the notes to the novel is of extreme
significance. It is not for economy of phrase. The removal of Christ and
the Holy Ghost—Filii et Spiritus Sancti—is a mechanical act mirroring
the imaginative. Of necessity, from Ahab's world, both Christ and the

Holy Ghost are absent. Ahab moves and has his being in a world to which They and what They import are inimical: remember, Ahab fought a deadly scrimmage with a Spaniard before the altar at Santa, and spat into the silver calabash. The conflict in Ahab's world is abrupt, more that between Satan and Jehovah, of the old dispensation than the new. It is the outward symbol of the inner truth that the name of Christ is uttered but once in the book and then it is torn from Starbuck, the only possible man to use it, at a moment of anguish, the night before the fatal third day of the chase.

Ahab is Conjur Man. He invokes his own evil world. He himself uses black magic to achieve his vengeful ends. With the very words "in nomine diaboli" he believes he utters a Spell and performs a Rite of such magic.

The Ahab-world is closer to *Macbeth* than to *Lear*. In it the supernatural is accepted. Fedallah appears as freely as the Weird Sisters. Before Ahab's first entrance he has reached that identification with evil to which Macbeth out of fear evolves within the play itself. The agents of evil give both Ahab and Macbeth a false security through the same device, the unfulfillable prophecy. Ahab's tense and nervous speech is like Macbeth's, rather than Lear's. Both Macbeth and Ahab share a common hell of wicked, sleep-bursting dreams. They both endure the torture of isolation from humanity. The correspondence of these two evil worlds is precise. In either the divine has little place. Melville intended certain exclusions, and Christ and the Holy Ghost were two of them. Ahab, alas, could not even baptize in the name of the Father. He could only do it in the name of the Devil.

That is the Ahab-world, and it is wicked. Melville meant exactly what he wrote to Hawthorne when the book was consummated:

I have written a wicked book, and feel as spotless as the lamb.

Melville's "wicked book" is the drama of Ahab, his hot hate for the White Whale, and his vengeful pursuit of it from the moment the ship plunges like fate into the Atlantic. It is that action, not the complete novel *Moby-Dick*. The *Moby-Dick* universe contains more, something different. Perhaps the difference is the reason why Melville felt "spotless as the lamb." The rough notes in the Shakespeare embrace it.

"Madness is undefinable." Two plays from which the thought could have sprung are in the volume in which it is written down: *Lear* and *Hamlet*. Of the modes of madness in *Lear*—the King's, the Fool's—which is definable? But we need not rest on supposition as to what Melville drew of madness from *Hamlet*, or from *Lear: Moby-Dick* includes both Ahab and

Pip. Melville forces his analysis of Ahab's mania to incredible distances, only himself to admit that "Ahab's larger, darker, deeper part remains unhinted." Pip's is a more fathomable idiocy: "his shipmates called him mad." Melville challenges the description, refuses to leave Pip's madness dark and unhinted, declares: "So man's insanity is heaven's sense."

The emphasis in this declaration is the key to resolve apparent difficulties in the last sentence of the notes in the Shakespeare volume:

> It & right reason extremes of one,—not the (black art) Goetic but Theurgic magic—seeks converse with the Intelligence, Power, the Angel.

I take "it" to refer to the "madness" of the previous sentence. "Right reason," less familiar to the 20th century, meant more to the last, for in the Kant-Coleridge terminology "right reason" described the highest range of the intelligence and stood in contrast to "understanding." Melville had used the phrase in *Mardi*. What he did with it there discloses what meaning it had for him when he used it in these cryptic notes for the composition of *Moby-Dick*. *Mardi*:

> Right reason, and Alma (Christ), are the same; else Alma, not reason, would we reject. The Master's great command is Love; and here do all things wise, and all things good, unite. Love is all in all. The more we love, the more we know; and so reversed.

Now, returning to the notes, if the phrase "not the (black art) Goetic but Theurgic magic" is recognized as parenthetical, the sentence has some clarity: "madness" and its apparent opposite "right reason" are the two extremes of one way or attempt or urge to reach "the Intelligence, Power, the Angel" or, quite simply, God.

The adjectives of the parenthesis bear this reading out. "Goetic" might seem to derive from Goethe and thus *Faust*, but its source is the Greek "goetos," meaning variously trickster, juggler and, as here, magician. (Plato called literature "Goeteia.") Wherever Melville picked up the word he means it, as he says, for the "black art." "Theurgic," in sharp contrast, is an accurate term for a kind of occult art of the Neoplatonists in which, through self-purification and sacred rites, the aid of the divine was evoked. In thus opposing "Goetic" and "Theurgic" Melville is using a distinction as old as Chaldea between black and white magic, the one of demons, the other of saints and angels, one evil, the other benevolent. For white or "Theurgic" magic, like "madness" and "right reason," seeks God, while the "black art Goetic" invokes only the devil.

Now go to *Moby-Dick*. In the Ahab-world there is no place for "converse with the Intelligence, Power, the Angel." Ahab cannot seek it, for understood between him and Fedallah is a compact as binding as Faust's with Mephistopheles. Melville's assumption is that though both Ahab and Faust may be seekers after truth, a league with evil closes the door to truth. Ahab's art, so long as his hate survives, is black. He does not seek true converse.

"Madness," on the contrary, does, and Pip is mad, possessed of an insanity which is "heaven's sense." When the little Negro almost drowned, his soul went down to wondrous depths and there he "saw God's foot upon the treadle of the loom, and spoke it." Through that accident Pip, of all the crew, becomes "prelusive of the eternal time" and thus achieves the converse Ahab has denied himself by his blasphemy. The chapter on THE DOUBLOON dramatizes the attempts on the part of the chief active characters to reach truth. In that place Starbuck, in his "mere unaided virtue," is revealed to have no abiding faith: he retreats before "Truth," fearing to lose his "righteousness." . . . Stubb's jollity and Flask's clod-like stupidity blunt the spiritual. . . . The Manxman has mere superstition, Queequeg mere curiosity. . . . Fedallah worships the doubloon evilly. . . . Ahab sees the gold coin solipsistically: "three peaks as proud as Lucifer" and all named "Ahab!" Pip alone, of all, has true prescience: he names the doubloon the "navel" of the ship—"Truth" its life.

"Right reason" is the other way to God. It is the way of man's sanity, the pure forging of his intelligence in the smithy of life. To understand what use Melville made of it in *Moby-Dick* two characters, both inactive to the plot, have to be brought forth.

Bulkington is the man who corresponds to "right reason." Melville describes him once early in the book when he enters the Spouter Inn. "Six feet in height, with noble shoulders, and a chest like a coffer-dam." In the deep shadows of his eyes "floated some reminiscences that did not seem to give him much joy." In the LEE SHORE chapter Bulkington is explicitly excluded from the action of the book, but not before Melville has, in ambiguities, divulged his significance as symbol. Bulkington is Man who, by "deep, earnest thinking" puts out to sea, scorning the land, convinced that "in landlessness alone resides the highest truth, shoreless, indefinite as God."

The rest of the *Pequod's* voyage Bulkington remains a "sleeping-partner" to the action. He is the secret member of the crew, below deck always, like the music under the earth in *Antony and Cleopatra*, strange. He is the crew's heart, the sign of their paternity, the human thing. And by that human thing alone can they reach their apotheosis.

There remains Ishmael. Melville framed Ahab's action, and the parts Pip, Bulkington and the rest of the crew played in the action, within a narrative told by Ishmael. Too long in criticism of the novel Ishmael has been confused with Herman Melville himself. Ishmael is fictive, imagined, as are Ahab, Pip and Bulkington, not so completely perhaps, for the very reason that he is so like his creator. But he is not his creator only: he is a chorus through whom Ahab's tragedy is seen, by whom what is black and what is white magic is made clear. Like the Catskill eagle Ishmael is able to dive down into the blackest gorges and soar out to the light again.

He is passive and detached, the observer, and thus his separate and dramatic existence is not so easily felt. But unless his choric function is recognized some of the vision of the book is lost. When he alone survived the wreck of the *Pequod,* he remained, after the shroud of the sea rolled on, to tell more than Ahab's wicked story. Ahab's self-created world, in essence privative, a thing of blasphemies and black magic, has its offset. Ahab has to dominate over a world where the humanities may also flower and man (the crew) by Pip's or Bulkington's way reach God. By this use of Ishmael Melville achieved a struggle and a catharsis which he intended, to feel "spotless as the lamb."

Ishmael has that cleansing ubiquity of the chorus in all drama, back to the Greeks. It is interesting that, in the same place where the notes for *Moby-Dick* are written in his Shakespeare, Melville jots down: "Eschylus Tragedies." Ishmael alone hears Father Mapple's sermon out. He alone saw Bulkington, and understood him. It was Ishmael who learned the secrets of Ahab's blasphemies from the prophet of the fog, Elijah. He recognized Pip's God-sight, and moaned for him. He cries forth the glory of the crew's humanity. Ishmael tells *their* story and *their* tragedy as well as Ahab's, and thus creates the *Moby-Dick* universe in which the Ahab-world is, by the necessity of life—or the Declaration of Independence—*included. . . .*

SHAKESPEARE CONCLUDED

Melville was no naïve democrat. He recognized the persistence of the "great man" and faced, in 1850, what we have faced in the 20th century. At the time of the rise of the common man Melville wrote a tragedy out of the rise, and the fall, of uncommon Ahab.

In the old days of the Mediterranean and Europe it was the flaw of a king which brought tragedy to men. A calamity was that which "unwar strook the regnes that been proude." When fate was feudal, and a great man fell, his human property, the people, paid.

A whaleship reminded Melville of two things: (1) democracy had not rid itself of overlords; (2) the common man, however free, leans on a leader, the leader, however dedicated, leans on a straw. He pitched his tragedy right there.

America 1850 was his GIVEN:

"a poor old whale-hunter" the great man;
fate, the chase of the Sperm whale, plot (economics is the administration of scarce resources);
the crew the commons, the Captain over them;
EQUALS:

tragedy.

For a consideration of dominance in man, read by all means the chapter in *Moby-Dick* called THE SPECKSYNDER, concerning emperors and kings, the forms and usages of the sea:

through these forms that certain sultanism of Ahab's brain became incarnate in an irresistible dictatorship.

For be a man's intellectual superiority what it will, it can never assume the practical, available supremacy over other men, without the aid of some sort of external arts and entrenchments, always, in themselves, more or less paltry and base.

Nor will the tragic dramatist who would depict mortal indomitableness in its fullest sweep and direct swing, ever forget a hint, incidentally so important in his art, as the one now alluded to.

More, much more.

Melville saw his creative problem clearly:

He had a prose world, a NEW.
But it was "tragedie," old.
Shakespeare gave him a bag of tricks.
The Q.E.D.: Moby-Dick.

The shape of *Moby-Dick*, like the meaning of its action, has roots deep in THE PLAYS. Melville studied Shakespeare's craft. For example, *characterization*. In at least three places Melville analyzes *Hamlet*. There are two in *Pierre*. One enlarges upon the only note he writes in his copy of the play: "the great Montaignism of Hamlet." The third and most interesting passage is in *The Confidence Man*. There Melville makes a distinction between the making of "odd" and the creation of "original" characters in literature. Of the latter he allows only three: Milton's Satan, Quixote, and Hamlet. The original character is

like a revolving Drummond light, raying away from itself all round it—everything is lit by it, everything starts up to it (mark how it is with Hamlet).

Melville likens the effect to "that which in Genesis attends upon the beginning of things." In the creation of Ahab Melville made the best use of that lesson he knew how.

Structure, likewise. *Moby-Dick* has a rise and fall like the movement of an Elizabethan tragedy. The first twenty-two chapters, in which Ishmael as chorus narrates the preparations for the voyage, are precedent to the action and prepare for it. Chapter XXIII is an interlude, THE LEE SHORE; Bulkington, because he is "right reason," is excluded from the tragedy. With the next chapter the book's drama begins. The first act ends in the QUARTER-DECK chapter, the first precipitation of action, which brings together for the first time Ahab, the crew, and the purpose of the voyage—the chase of the White Whale. All the descriptions of the characters, all the forebodings, all the hints are brought to their first manifestation.

Another interlude follows: Ishmael expands upon MOBY-DICK and THE WHITENESS OF THE WHALE.

Merely to summarize what follows, the book then moves up to the meeting with the *Jeroboam* and her mad prophet Gabriel (chp. LXXI) and, after that, in a third swell, into the visit of Ahab to the *Samuel Enderby* to see her captain who had lost his arm as Ahab his leg to Moby-Dick (chp. C). The pitch of the action is the storm scene, THE CANDLES. From that point on Ahab comes to repose, fifth act, in his fate.

In this final movement Moby-Dick appears, for the first time. It is a mistake to think of the Whale as antagonist in the usual dramatic sense. (In democracy the antagonisms are wide.) The demonisms are dispersed, and Moby-Dick but the more assailable mass of them. In fact the actual physical whale finally present in *Moby-Dick* is more comparable to death's function in Elizabethan tragedy: when the white thing is encountered first, he is in no flurry, but quietly gliding through the sea, "a mighty mildness of repose in swiftness."

Obviously *Moby-Dick* is a novel and not a play. It contains creations impossible to any stage—a ship, the *Pequod;* whales; Leviathan; the vast sea. In the making of most of his books Melville used similar things. In *Moby-Dick* he integrated them as he never had before nor was to again.

The whaling matter is stowed away as he did not manage the ethnology of *Typee* nor was to, the parables of *The Confidence Man.* While the book is getting under way—that is, in the first forty-eight chapters—Melville allows only four "scientific" chapters on whaling to appear. Likewise, as the book sweeps to its tragic close in the last thirty chapters, Melville rules out all such exposition. The body of the book supports the bulk of the matter on the Sperm whale—"scientific or poetic." Melville carefully controls these chapters, skillfully breaking them up: the eight different vessels the *Pequod* meets as she moves across the oceans slip in and cut between the considerations of cetology. Actually and deliberately the whaling chapters brake the advance of the plot. Van Wyck Brooks called them "ballast."

Stage directions appear throughout. *Soliloquies,* too. There is a significant use of the special Elizabethan soliloquy to the skull in Ahab's mutterings to the Sperm whale's head in THE SPHINX (chp. LXX). One of the subtlest *supernatural effects,* the "low laugh from the hold" in the QUARTER-DECK scene, echoes Shakespeare's use of the Ghost below ground in *Hamlet.*

Properties are used for precise theater effect. Ahab smashes his quandrant as Richard his mirror. Of them the Doubloon is the most important. Once Ahab has nailed the coin to the mast it becomes FOCUS. The imagery, the thought, the characters, the events precedent and to come, are centered on it. It is there, midstage, Volpone, gold.

Of the soliloquies, Ahab's show the presence of *Elizabethan speech* most. The cadences and acclivities of Melville's prose change. Melville characterized Ahab's language as "nervous, lofty." In the soliloquies it is jagged like that of a Shakespearean hero whose speech like his heart often cracks in the agony of fourth and fifth act.

The long ease and sea swell of Ishmael's narrative prose contrasts this short, rent language of Ahab. The opposition of cadence is part of the counterpoint of the book. It adumbrates the part the two characters play, Ishmael the passive, Ahab the active. More than that, it arises from and returns, contrapunto, to the whole concept of the book revealed by the notes in Melville's copy of Shakespeare—the choric Ishmael can, like the Catskill eagle, find the light, but Ahab, whose only magic is Goetic, remains dark. The contrast in prose repeats the theme of calm and tempest which runs through the novel. Without exception action rises out of calm, whether it is the first chase of a whale, the appearance of the Spirit Spout, the storm, or the final chase of Moby-Dick precipitously following upon the THE SYMPHONY.

As the strongest literary force Shakespeare caused Melville to approach tragedy in terms of the drama. As the strongest social force America caused him to approach tragedy in terms of democracy.

It was not difficult for Melville to reconcile the two. Because of his perception of America: Ahab.

It has to do with size, and how you value it. You can approach BIG America and spread yourself like a pancake, sing her stretch as Whitman did, be puffed up as we are over PRODUCTION. It's easy. THE AMER-ICAN WAY. Soft. Turns out paper cups, lies flat on the brush. N.G.

Or recognize that our power is simply QUANTITY. Without considering purpose. Easy too. That is, so long as we continue to be IN-GENIOUS about machines, and have the resources.

Or you can take an attitude, the creative vantage. See her as OB-JECT in MOTION, something to be shaped, for use. It involves a first act of physics. You can observe POTENTIAL and VELOCITY separately, have to, to measure THE THING. You get approximate results. They are usable enough if you include the Uncertainty Principle, Heisenberg's law that you learn the speed at the cost of exact knowledge of the energy and the energy he loss of the exact knowledge of the speed.

Melville did his job. He calculated, and cast Ahab. BIG, first of all. ENERGY, next. PURPOSE: lordship over nature. SPEED: of the brain. DIRECTION: vengeance. COST: the people, the Crew.

Ahab is the FACT, the Crew the IDEA. The Crew is where what America stands for got into *Moby-Dick*. They're what we imagine democracy to be. They're Melville's addition to tragedy as he took it from Shakespeare. He had to do more with the people than offstage shouts in a *Julius Caesar*. This was the difference a Declaration of Independence made. In his copy of the play Melville writes the note

TAMMANY HALL

in heavy strokes beside Casca's description of the Roman rabble before Caesar:

> If the tag-rag people did not clap him and hiss him, according as he pleas'd and displeas'd them, as they use to do the players in the theatre, I am no true man.

Melville thought he had more searoom to tell the truth. He was writing in a country where an Andrew Jackson could, as he put it, be "hurled higher than a throne." A political system called "democracy" had led men to think they were "free" of aristocracy. The fact of the matter is Melville couldn't help but give the "people" a larger part because in the life around him they played a larger part. He put it this way:

> this august dignity I treat of, is not the dignity of kings and robes, but that abounding dignity which has no robed investiture.

> Thou shalt see it shining in the arm that wields a pick and drives a spike; that democratic dignity which, on all hands, radiates without end from

God; Himself! The great God absolute! The center and circumference of all democracy! His omnipresence, our divine equality!

If, then, to meanest mariners, and renegades and castaways, I shall hereafter ascribe high qualities, though dark; weave round them tragic graces; if even the most mournful, perchance the most abased, among them all, shall at times lift himself to the exalted mounts; if I shall touch that workman's arm with some ethereal light; if I shall spread a rainbow over his disastrous set of sun; then against all mortal critics bear me out in it, thou just Spirit of Equality, which hast spread one royal mantle of humanity over all my kind!

Remember Bulkington.

To MAGNIFY is the mark of *Moby-Dick*. As with workers, castaways, so with the scope and space of the sea, the prose, the Whale, the Ship and, OVER ALL, the Captain. It is the technical act compelled by the American fact. Cubits of tragic stature. Put it this way. Three forces operated to bring about the dimensions of *Moby-Dick*: Melville, a man of MYTH, antemosaic: an experience of SPACE, its power and price, America; and ancient magnitudes of TRAGEDY, Shakespeare.

It is necessary now to consider *Antony and Cleopatra*, the play Melville pencilled most heavily. Rome was the World, and Shakespeare gives his people and the action imperial size. His hero and heroine love as Venus and Mars, as planets might.

> His legs bestrid the ocean; his rear'd arm
> Crested the world.

So Cleopatra dreamed of Antony. Melville marked her words. He marked Antony's joyful greeting to Cleopatra after he has beaten Caesar back to his camp:

> O thou day o' th' world!

And Cleopatra's cry of grief when Antony dies:

> The crown o' th' earth doth melt.

Antony and Cleopatra is an East. It is built as Pyramids were built. There is space here, and objects big enough to contest space. These are men and women who live life large. The problems are the same but they work themselves out on a stage as wide as ocean.

When Enobarbus comments on Antony's flight from Actium in pursuit of Cleopatra, we are precisely within the problems of *Moby-Dick*:

> To be furious
> Is to be frighted out of fear, and in that mood

> The dove will peck the estridge. I see still
> A diminution in our captain's brain
> Restores his heart. When valour preys on reason
> It eats the sword it fights with.

In exactly what way Ahab, furious and without fear, retained the instrument of his reason as a lance to fight the White Whale is a central concern of Melville's in *Moby-Dick*. In his Captain there was a diminution in his heart.

From whaling, which America had made distinctly a part of her industrial empire, he took this "poor old whale-hunter," as he called him, this man of "Nantucket grimness and shagginess." Out of such stuff he had to make his tragic hero, his original. He faced his difficulties. He knew he was denied "the outward majestical trappings and housings" that Shakespeare had for his Antony, his Lear and his Macbeth. Melville wrote:

> Oh, Ahab! what shall be grand in thee, must needs be plucked at from the skies, and dived for in the deep, and featured in the unbodied air!

He made him "a khan of the plank, and a king of the sea, and a great lord of leviathans." For the American has the Roman feeling about the world. It is his, to dispose of. He strides it, with possession of it. His property. Has he not conquered it with his machines? He bends its resources to his will. The pax of legions? the Americanization of the world. Who else is lord?

Melville isolates Ahab in "a Grand-Lama-like exclusiveness." He is captain of the *Pequod* because of "that certain sultanism of his brain." He is proud and morbid, willful, vengeful. He wears a "hollow crown," not Richard's. It is the Iron Crown of Lombardy which Napoleon wore. Its jagged edge, formed from a nail of the Crucifixion, galls him. He worships fire and swears to strike the sun.

OVER ALL, hate—huge and fixed upon the imperceptible. Not man but all the hidden forces that terrorize man is assailed by the American Timon. That HATE, extra-human, involved his Crew, and Moby-Dick drags them to their death as well as Ahab to his, a collapse of a hero through solipsism which brings down a world.

At the end of the book, in the heart of the White Whale's destruction, the Crew and Pip and Bulkington and Ahab lie down together.

All scatt'red in the bottom of the sea.

NEWTON ARVIN

The Early Novels:
"Typee," "Omoo,"
"Redburn," "White-Jacket"

It was no mere accident that [the school of writing embodied by Richard Henry Dana and Alexander Kinglake in their travel books *Two Years Before the Mast* and *Eothen* was the one which] furnished Melville his springboard as an artist. He did not begin at once, like most of them, as a writer of tales, sketches, or novels for the periodicals or the booksellers' libraries of the era; he did not begin as a successor of Sterne or Godwin or Scott, of Mrs. Radcliffe or Hoffmann. He began as one more writer of travel narrative, and the books from which he took off were not *Tristram Shandy* or *Waverly* but Mungo Park's *Travels in the Interior of Africa,* the Rev. C. S. Stewart's *Visit to the South Seas,* and of course the book he called "my friend Dana's unmatchable *Two Years Before the Mast.*" Saying this is something like saying that George Eliot began as a writer of critical and philosophical articles for the *Westminster Review;* no other writer of just that sort has gone on to write books like *Middlemarch,* and none of the other writers of "travels" or "journals" or "narratives" went on to write books like *Moby Dick.* But George Eliot's whole work is pervaded by the attitudes of the moralist and critic, and Melville, for his part, was always to be an imaginative writer for whom the facts of movement through space, of change of site, of physical unrestingness

From *Herman Melville.* Copyright © 1950 by William Sloane Associates, Inc. Greenwood Press, Inc.

and the forward push were basic. The voyage or quest was not simply a subject or an occasion for him; it was an archetypal pattern of experience to which his whole nature instinctively turned, and he was to lose half his strength not when he lost contact with the earth but when he stood still upon it.

Typee and Omoo, to be sure, were books that he wrote, if not off the top of his mind, at any rate off its less profound levels, and it is idle to look for great depths or difficulties in them; to do so would be to miss their special quality of spontaneity and youthfulness. Yet there are intimations of complexity in them, and in a purely literary sense, easy though they seem, they are curiously many-faceted. They owe something, in a general way, to the whole tradition of travel literature since the modern age of discovery began, and particularly to the voyages of the eighteenth century, to the writers of the age of Cook and Carteret and Bougainville, whose aim was always to be lucid, impersonal, informative; to suppress *themselves* and to convey the facts, however novel or strange, with the most reasonable and enlightened objectivity. A love of information for its own sake was one of the aspects of Melville's complex mind, as every reader of *Moby Dick* knows; and when, in *Typee,* he describes the process of making tapa or the operations of the system of tabu, or when, in *Omoo,* he dilates on the botany and the economy of the coco-palm, his tone and manner are not easily distinguishable from those in which Captain Cook or Bougainville or Langsdorff had expatiated on exactly similar subjects. Melville's first two books have been quoted by anthropologists since his time, by Sir James Frazer for example, as having at least some claim to trustworthiness, despite Melville's very small comprehension of the language of Taipi or Tahiti. The fact is that, whenever his imagination was at work most freely and naturally, it sought for and found the factual, prosaic counterpoise to the inwardness and ideality that were its essential expression; and *Typee* and *Omoo* owe much of their vitality to their apparently unpoetic ballast of facts.

A transformation, however, had taken place in the literature of travel since the eighteenth century, just as it had done in literature generally, and such books could no longer be written sustainedly in the old manner, any more than novels could be written in the manner of Diderot or Smollett. The dry, clear, sober impersonality of the older writers had given place to a more and more frankly personal and subjective style, whimsical, humorous, lyrical, sentimental, or poetic; Melville began writing in a period that had formed its taste on such lighthearted and charming books as Heine's *Pictures of Travel,* Irving's *Alhambra,* Kinglake's *Eothen,* and Gautier's *Travels in Spain*. Information of a kind does indeed appear in books like these, but what really counts in them is not that but feeling, fancy, atmosphere, and the effort to evoke as many as brilliant pictures as possible. The sense of the painterly has usurped the place of the older interest in fact.

Even in a writer like Mungo Park, at the turn of the nineteenth century, one detects already a strain of personal feeling and even a sense of the pictorial that is by no means merely "eighteenth century"; and Mungo Park was almost certainly one of Melville's literary masters. There are deeply moving passages in Park's *Travels*, but what happened to travel writing after his time becomes evident when one turns to Melville abruptly from a writer of his sort. Here is a passage, quite typical of Park's ordinary narrative style, from his account of a night spent at an African town in the kingdom of Kajaaga:

> I found a great crowd surrounding a party who were dancing by the light of some large fires, to the music of four drums, which were beat with great exactness and uniformity. The dances, however, consisted more in wanton gestures than in muscular exertion or graceful attitudes. The ladies vied with each other in displaying the most voluptuous movements imaginable.

Compare with this—in its quiet, taciturn failure to realize a potentially quite wonderful picture—compare with it Melville's description in *Omoo* of the dancing girls at Tamai or, better yet, this description in *Typee* of a fishing party returning from the beach at night:

> Once, I remember, the party arrived at midnight; but the unseasonableness of the hour did not repress the impatience of the islanders. The carriers dispatched from the Ti were to be seen hurrying in all directions through the deep groves; each individual preceded by a boy bearing a flaming torch of dried cocoa-nut boughs, which from time to time was replenished from the materials scattered along the path. The wild glare of these enormous flambeaux, lighting up with a startling brilliancy the innermost recesses of the vale, and seen moving rapidly along beneath the canopy of leaves, the savage shout of the excited messengers sounding the news of their approach, which was answered on all sides, and the strange appearance of their naked bodies, seen against the gloomy background, produced altogether an effect upon my mind that I shall long remember.

Naturally this is not yet Melville in his great evocative vein, and Stevenson was later to outdo him, just here, in finish and precision of brush stroke, but the passage will serve as a fair example of Melville's painterliness in *Typee* and *Omoo*. Like some other passages in those books, it hints to us—with its romantic chiaroscuro, its violent contrast of deep shadow and high flaring lights, the uncanniness of its moving figures, and its dependence on words like "wild," "startling," "strange," and "gloomy"—hints to us that Melville, in looking at the scenes that passed before him and in reinvoking them, had learned something from such Gothic writers as Mrs. Radcliffe and "Monk" Lewis, and that through them, perhaps also independently, his landscape sense had been formed by the Baroque painters they were always echoing, by Claude Lorrain and Salvator Rosa. Salvator in the Marquesas might have done the nocturne of the fishing party. Baroque, at any rate, most of Melville's landscapes and seascapes certainly are, as well as many of the other scenes he composes like pictures. The hours he spent as a boy poring over the portfolios of prints Allan Melville had brought home had worked a permanent influence on his imagination.

His first two books abound in pictorial effects that can only be described as in some sense romantic; wild and fearful like the gorges, ravines, and chasms of Nuku-Hiva through which he and Toby make their painful way in *Typee*; solemn, deeply shaded, and awe-inspiring, like the tabu groves in Taipi-Vai; uncannily beautiful like another fishing party by torchlight, in *Omoo*, in the sullen surf off Moorea; or in a wholly different vein— the vein of Claude rather than of Salvator—pastoral, Arcadian, richly reposeful, like the first breathless glimpse of the Paradisal valley of Taipi. Already in these early, experimental books, with varying degrees of success, Melville knows how to cover a gamut of painterly and emotional effects that ranges all the way from the broad and serene to the wild, the grim, and even the grotesque. And indeed it is evident that these contrasts of tone and feeling, especially marked in *Typee*, are conscious and artful, not merely inadvertent, and that they express a native feeling for structure and style that already suggests how much farther Melville may go as an imaginative writer than any of the narrators he is emulating. *Two Years Before the Mast* is a greater book than either *Typee* or *Omoo*, in its strong, sustained austerity of style as well as in its grandeur of feeling; but Melville's books are the unmistakable products of a far more complex and ductile mind than Dana's, and potentially, of course, of a richer creative power. Dana's great book suggests no artistic mode beyond itself; *Typee* and *Omoo* hint constantly at the freer and more plastic form of fiction.

When they first appeared, indeed, they were taxed, or credited, by many readers with being *pure* fiction, and some of these readers, at least, were more imaginative than those who took them for sober fact. It is not only that we now know how long a bow Melville was drawing in both books, especially *Typee*; how freely he was improvising on the mere actualities of his experience; that is an external and mechanical sort of check.

The books themselves need only to be read responsively in order to uncover their real quality—their real and equivocal quality of narrative that is constantly vibrating between the poles of "truthfulness" and fantasy. The proportion of sober truthfulness in *Omoo* is doubtless greater than in *Typee*, and the free, fanciful strains in it take the form of playfulness, gay exaggeration, and grotesqueness rather than, as they mostly do in *Typee*, of a heightened "anxiety," on the one hand, and a deliberate idyllism, on the other. But in both books Melville is far too much the born artist not to keep bathing the plain truth in a medium of imaginative intensity.

A few weeks after *Typee* was published . . . Toby Greene unexpectedly turned up in Buffalo to testify to the veracity of those chapters for which he could vouch, but we must not take his evidence too literally. Melville's story of what happened after he and Toby plunged into the interior of Nuku-Hiva, of the hardships and sufferings they underwent before they arrived in Taipi—this story bears on the face of it the hallmarks of poetic sublimation. Plenty of travelers have undergone greater ordeals than Melville's was at its worst, and one has only, again, to read Mungo Park's account of some of his solitary vicissitudes in order to observe how calmly and even barely the thing can be done. There is nothing calm or bare and certainly nothing austere in Melville's narrative. It is frankly and volubly a tale of tribulation: it abounds in the imagery of physical and mental misery. At the outset Melville and Toby are drenched by a downpour of tropical rain; they find themselves trapped in a thicket of dense, resistant reeds; they are baked by the heat of midday; they scramble up a steep cliff and crawl along a ridge on their bellies to evade detection; they are confronted by a series of "dark and fearful chasms, separated by sharp-crested and perpendicular ridges," up and down which they painfully clamber; they spend the nights in gloomy ravines, shivering with the chill and dampness; and at last they make their way down into the valley by falling, rather than descending, from ledge to ledge of a horridly high, steep precipice. Throughout, they suffer from hunger and raging thirst; Melville, from a painful injury to his leg; and both of them, from "frightful anticipations of evil." We move, in all this, not over the solid terrain of even a romantic island but amidst a dream-imagery of deadly apprehensiveness, baffled and dismayed by obstacle after obstacle, and oppressed continually by a dread of what is before us. Such writing is far less reminiscent of *Two Years* than it is of Mrs. Radcliffe or Poe.

The note of nightmarish foreboding, in any case, is struck recurrently in *Typee*, where it reaches a culmination of intensity in the last chapters, with Melville's gruesome discoveries and his horror lest he should be powerless to escape. It alternates, however, like a theme in music, with the strongly contrasted note of contentment and peace; the contentment and peace of daydreaming. The conflict between wishful revery and the anxiety that springs from a feeling of guilt, in short, goes on throughout the book. In *Omoo*, on the other hand, perhaps because it was written in a period of emotional freedom and effervescence, there is no such inner drama and no such stylistic musicality. The contrasts of tone in the book are furnished partly by the simple alteration between personal narrative and impersonal informativeness, but also by the relatively prosaic setting-off of the hardships and exasperations of life aboard the *Julie* (Melville's name for the *Lucy Ann*) or in the Calabooza Beretanee against the heady pleasures of freedom and vagrancy. The play of fantasy in *Omoo* takes the form not of nightmarishness or even of daydreaming but of an easy and emotionally liberating current of humorous narrative, always slightly in excess, as one sees with half an eye, of the sober autobiographical facts. It usually has the satisfactory effect of throwing a ludicrous light on the representatives of order and authority—captains and mates, consuls and missionaries, resident physicians and native constables. There is still, as a result, an emotional release in reading *Omoo*, as in reading any such book; we take our own revenge on respectability by contemplating the discomfiture of the feeble Captain Guy and the bullying consul Wilson, or by listening to the wily sermon of the Chadband whom Melville describes himself as hearing in the church at Papeete.

It is true that, compared with the billows of almost demoniac humor on which *Moby Dick* is so incredibly sustained, the humor of *Typee* and even of *Omoo* seems gentle and rather tame. Yet one feels at once that it is the expression of a genuinely humorous fancy. One feels it in such accounts as that of the popgun war in *Typee* or of Long Ghost's jolly philanderings in *Omoo*. One feels it even verbally in such remarks as that Captain Guy was "no more meant for the sea than a hairdresser," or the observation on the ugliness of the ship's carpenter on the *Julia:* "There was no absolute deformity about the man; he was symmetrically ugly." One feels this youthful humor chiefly, however, in the individual characters in whom both books abound, and who are treated with a freedom far closer to fiction than to mere reminiscence. The difference is easily evident when one puts one of Dana's characters—say the young Hawaiian, Hope, or the English sailor, George P. Marsh, a decayed gentleman—side by side with characters like Melville's Kory-Kory or Long Ghost. Dana's portraits have the sobriety and the realism of Copley's in another medium; Melville's come closer to suggesting Cruikshank or Phiz. For the rest, in the period when he was writing *Typee* and *Omoo*, it was mostly the amusing, even lovable oddities and humors of human character that engaged him, not its darknesses and depravities. There are shadows of some intensity here and there; in the brutal Captain Vangs and in the dark, moody, vindictive Maori harpooneer, Bembo; but mostly the scene is animated by such gently comic personages as fussy old Marheyo in Taipi, or the grotesque-looking Kory-Kory, or the poor landlubber sailor, Ropey, on the *Julia*.

Most of them are mere sketches, lightly and hastily drawn; and the most fully realized feminine character, the exquisite Fayaway, is not so much drawn as vaguely and dreamily evoked in wishful water colors. Only one personage among them all is painted at full length; this is the demoted ship's surgeon, Long Ghost, who is the real protagonist of *Omoo* (Melville himself is the protagonist of *Typee*), and who embodies the complete footlooseness, the perfect irresponsibility, which Melville, on one side of his nature, would have liked to attain. A ruined gentleman, well-read and well-mannered, but lazy, mischievous, reckless, amorous, and rascally, Long Ghost appears in the forecastle of the *Julie* as if he were a personal materialization of all Melville's longings for a really unbraced and ungirded freedom. So long as the mood lasts, Long Ghost sticks by his side, a perfect companion, indeed another self, but at length the mood passes, the fundamental seriousness in Melville reasserts itself, and about to join the crew of the *Leviathan* he takes leave both of the waggish doctor and, to all intents and purposes, of the beachcomber in himself.

The gesture has an almost allegorical quality. Lighthearted and unprofound as on the whole they are, *Typee* and *Omoo* have an undertone of serious meaning. Taken together they tell the story of a quest or pilgrimage—a pilgrimage not, certainly, "from this world to that which is to come," but from the world of enlightened rationality, technical progress, and cultural complexity backward and downward and, so to say, inward to the primordial world that *was* before metals, before the alphabet, before cities; the slower, graver, nakeder world of stone, of carved wood, of the tribe, of the ritual dance and human sacrifice and the prerational myth. It was a pilgrimage that led to no all-answering oracle or consummatory revelation; in that sense it was a failure. But it was a pilgrimage that Melville's deepest needs had driven him to make, and he did not return from it empty-handed. There are passages in *Typee* especially that tell us how really intense, how far from merely fashionable, was his animus against "civilized barbarity," against "the tainted atmosphere of a feverish civilization." He returned to civilization in the end, but he had had a long gaze at a simpler, freer, gayer, and yet also statelier mode of life, and this was to serve him, in memory, as a stabilizing and fortifying image. His own creative power, moreover, at its height, was primeval and myth-making in a sense that, in his day, was of the rarest: it could never have been set free, just as it was, if he himself had not made his descent into the canyon of the past. In touching the body of Fayaway, Melville had regained contact with the almost vanished life of myth.

His instincts had guided him rightly when they sent him wandering into the young Pacific world, and they guided him rightly when they drove him away from it again and back to civilized society, to resume a burden he had temporarily laid down—the burden of consciousness, of the full and anguished consciousness of modern man. He had taken a long plunge into the realm of the preconscious and the instinctual, the realm of heedless impulse and irreflective drift; he had been refreshed, indeed remade, by it; but he had found there no ultimate resolution of his difficulties. Not in avoiding the clash between consciousness and the unconscious, between mind and emotion, between anxious doubt and confident belief, but in confronting these antinomies head-on and, hopefully, transcending them—in that direction, as Melville intuitively saw, lay his right future as an adult person. The alternative was a lifetime of raffish vagrancy with the seedy Long Ghost, and a kind of Conradian dilapidation at the end. In the last chapter of *Omoo,* saying good-bye to his companion, he insists on Long Ghost's taking half the Spanish dollars which the captain of the *Leviathan* has given him as an advance; a generous but also a proper payment for the wisdom he has acquired in Long Ghost's society. A new cruise awaits him, on another vessel; and in fact, when Melville finished the writing of *Omoo,* he had come to the end of one expedition, in the intellectual and literary sense, and was ready to set out again in a quite different direction. . . .

In both the intellectual and the literary senses *Mardi* had turned out, despite its undeniable qualities, to be a great detour for Melville; in the end it brought him back to his own route but in an oblique and rather wasteful way. His mind was still developing too rapidly and too intensely for him to be long content with the kind of skepticism, impatient and even intemperate, which *Mardi* ended by expressing. There is a lesser skepticism and a larger one, and the skepticism of this book is not yet the latter. In its form and texture, too, *Mardi* was evidently not what Melville was struggling to arrive at; he made no second use of its characteristic manner, and years later he was to voice his true feeling about the book when he remarked that the worst thing he could say about Richter's *Titan* was that "it is a little better than *Mardi.*" His central problem as a writer was to find a fictional style in which there would be a particular kind of dynamic balance between fact and form, between concept and symbol, between the general

and the particular—"the whole problem is there," as Gide once observed—
and Melville had by no means found his solution in transcendental allegory
of the Early Romantic type or even in the ancient mode of satirical burlesque
he had inherited from Rabelais and Swift. Just how flimsy Yillah and Hautia
are as vehicles for Melville's meaning is evident when one reflects for a
moment on the essential unnaturalness and unspontaneity, for him, of the
flower images that accompany them, the un-Melvillean verbenas and ver-
vain; and as for the Rabelaisian tour of the archipelago of Mardi, it grows
more and more perfunctory and essayistic as the book wears on.

Manqué though it was, however, Mardi had been written, we may
be sure, at the cost of a heavy drain on Melville's psychological resources,
and he was not yet ready to move on to another effort of comparable scope
and difficulty: time would have to elapse before his highest energies could
accumulate their full weight and force. Meanwhile it was a question of
lowering his sights a degree or two, and what he did when he went on to
write Redburn and White-Jacket had superficially the air of a return upon
himself, a lapse back to the vein he had already worked in Typee and Omoo,
the vein not of metaphysical allegory but of unpretentious reminiscent
narrative, vibrating again between the poles of literal autobiography and
free fictional improvisation. Redburn and White-Jacket take us back once
more to the ship and the sea voyage, to "real" ships and "real" seas: in the
one case, to the deck of an American merchant vessel making an ordinary
trip across the North Atlantic; in the other, to the deck of an American
man-of-war on its cruise from the port of Callao in Peru, around the Horn,
back to its home port on the eastern seaboard. Both books abound in
information, in factuality, in solid objects and practical activities, and in
all this they recall Typee and Omoo. But the movement Melville was describing, it need hardly be said, was not a retrograde but a spiral one, and
Redburn and White-Jacket, though they have lost the youthful charm of the
earlier books, are denser in substance, richer in feeling, tauter, more complex, more connotative in texture and imagery. Whatever imperfections
they may have, they give us the clear sense that the man who wrote them
was again on his own track.

The prose, for one thing, is that of a much more mature person and
more expert writer. One easily sees how much ground Melville has gained,
partly as a result of writing Mardi, when one turns from almost any page
of the first two books to almost any page of the later ones. Here is a
characteristic passage from Omoo:

> Toward morning, finding the heat of the forecastle unpleasant, I ascended
> to the deck, where everything was noiseless. The Trades were blowing
> with a mild, steady strain upon the canvas, and the ship heading right

> out into the immense blank of the Western Pacific. The watch were asleep. With one foot resting on the rudder, even the man at the helm nodded, and the mate himself, with arms folded, was leaning against the capstan.
>
> On such a night, and all alone, revery was inevitable. I leaned over the side, and could not help thinking of the strange objects we might be sailing over.

Certainly the nocturnal picture here is pleasantly rendered; the effect of contrasted motion and stillness (the advancing ship, the nodding helmsman, and the like) is quickly and agreeably achieved; the rhythms are easy; the forward movement of the sentences is steady and effortless; the plain, low-pitched diction surges a little, at one moment, to a kind of grandeur in the phrase, "the immense blank of the Western Pacific." But rhythmically the passage achieves little more than easiness; the language is almost neutral and without idiosyncrasy; and the sense of a missed opportunity in the last sentence is acute. There are finer passages in *Typee* and *Omoo*, but virtually nowhere in those books does Melville write as he repeatedly writes in *Redburn* or *White-Jacket*. Is it possible, in such a passage as the following, from *Redburn*, to mistake the gain in rhythmical variety and intricacy, in sharpness of diction, in syntactical resource, in painterly bravura and the fusing of image and emotion into a unity of strangeness, beauty, and dread? It is part of the chapter in which Melville describes his ascent of the mainmast to loosen a skysail at midnight:

> For a few moments I stood awe-stricken and mute. I could not see far out upon the ocean, owing to the darkness of the night; and from my lofty perch the sea looked like a great, black gulf, hemmed in, all round, by beetling black cliffs. I seemed all alone; treading the midnight clouds; and every second, expected to find myself falling—falling—falling, as I have felt when the nightmare has been on me.
>
> I could but just perceive the ship below me, like a long narrow plank in the water; and it did not seem to belong at all to the yard, over which I was hanging. A gull, or some sort of sea-fowl, was flying round the truck over my head, within a few yards of my face; and it almost frightened me to hear it; it seemed so much like a spirit, at such a lofty and solitary height.

It is not only the spectral sea-fowl here, flying round the masthead in the darkness, which tells one that, in the progress from *Typee* to *Moby Dick*, Melville has already passed the middle point.

If this holds for *Redburn* stylistically, it holds no less truly for its substance and spirit. The outward subject of the book is a young boy's first voyage as a sailor before the mast; its inward subject is the initiation of innocence into evil—the opening of the guileless spirit to the discovery of "the wrong," as James would say, "to the knowledge of it, to the crude experience of it." The subject is a permanent one for literature, of course, but it has also a peculiarly American dimension, and in just this sense, not in any other, *Redburn* looks backward to a book like Brockden Brown's *Ormond* as well as forward to *The Marble Faun* and to so much of James himself. Wellingborough Redburn sets out from his mother's house in a state of innocence like that before the Fall, a state like that of Brown's Constantia Dudley or James's Maisie Farange, but he has hardly gone a mile from home before the world's wickedness and hardness begin to strip themselves before him. Man, Redburn quickly finds, is a wolf to man. On the river boat his shabby indigence elicits no compassion from the comfortable passengers, but only coldness and disdain. He reaches the city and is very soon victimized by a rascally pawnbroker, a pawnbroker who might have stepped out of *David Copperfield* or *Cousin Pons*. He takes himself aboard the *Highlander* and begins at once to be sworn at, pushed around, humiliated, and persecuted by mates and sailors alike; and the dapper Captain Riga, who had appeared so friendly in his cabin while the ship lay at anchor, now, when poor unsophisticated Redburn attempts to address him as man to man, flies into a rage and flings his cap at him.

Blows and hard words are mostly Redburn's lot on the *Highlander*, yet he suffers not only from the inhumanity of men but from the spectacle of their depravity generally. His feelings about the sailors vacillate, it is true; as individuals he finds some of them generous and friendly; but taking them in the lump, he is conscious chiefly of their drunkenness, their profanity and obscenity, their indurated cynicism and sneering misanthropy. All this accumulated evil, indeed, is focused so concentratedly in the figure of one man, the sailor Jackson, as to raise him to something like heroic stature, the stature at any rate of one of Schiller's Majestic Monsters. The first of Melville's full-length studies of "depravity according to nature," Jackson is stricken, symbolically, with a fatal disease—the penalty for his "infamous vices," as Redburn learns—but this does not keep him from being a pitiless bully and exercising an unchallenged and almost preternatural sway over the rest of the crew, who thus, in their pusillanimity, pay tribute to the principle of pure evil in him. He for his part feels nothing but malevolence toward them; nothing but malevolence toward Redburn, if only because he is young, handsome, and innocent; and indeed "he seemed to be full of hatred and gall against everything and everybody in the world." His enmity toward the boy sets the rest of the crew against him too, and Redburn begins to feel a compensatory hatred growing up in himself against them all; but meanwhile, day by day, his ears are assailed by the bitter talk of a man who is "spontaneously an atheist and an infidel," and who argues through the long night watches that there is "nothing to be believed; nothing to be loved, and nothing worth living for; but everything to be hated, in the wide world."

There is a touch of Svidrigailov or old Karamazov in this Jackson, and there is a touch of the Dostoyevskian also in Redburn's feeling that there was "even more woe than wickedness about the man." He is so impressive a figure, one sees, partly because so much of Melville's own bitterness and disbelief entered into his composition. Jackson is easily first among the personal embodiments of evil in this book, but in addition to him and to all the personages, and more overpowering than any of them, there is the infernal city of Liverpool, a near neighbor of the City of Destruction itself. That older allegory is bound to occur to one's mind in thinking of *Redburn* and Liverpool, but even so it was not until the nineteenth century that the great city, any great city, the great city *an sich*, could become just the kind of symbol it did become of human iniquity. In imagining Liverpool as he did, Melville was wholly at one with the deepest sensibility of his age, and in his wonderful series of Hogarthian evocations— in the dark, begrimed, polluted streets, the great prisonlike warehouses, the squalid dwellings, the loathsome haunts of vice and crime, and the beggars, the quacks, the crimps, the peddlers who populate these infested purlieus like moral grotesques—in all this there is a power quite comparable to that with which Balzac's Parisian Inferno is rendered, or Baudelaire's *fourmillante cité*, the London of *Bleak House* and *Our Mutual Friend*, or the Dublin of *Ulysses*. Melville's Liverpool, too, like his Lima, is a City of the Plain.

In such a setting as this there is no mere enigma even in the one chapter of *Redburn* in which Melville seems to be indulging in deliberate mystification—the chapter in which he represents Redburn as being carried off to London on an unexplained errand by his new friend Harry Bolton and taken by him to "Aladdin's Palace." This is an Orientally luxurious pleasure-house of some ill-defined sort, where they spend a melodramatic night, and where Harry appears to lose most of his remaining funds at the tables. Aladdin's Palace is the opulent counterpart of the "reeking" and "Sodom-like" dens in Liverpool where Redburn's shipmates indulge their squalid vices; the walls of one room are hung with pornographic paintings to which Melville suggests various learned parallels, but most of these he himself invented as he composed the passage; and their real purpose, like that of the whole chapter, is to dramatize the horrified Redburn's feeling that "this must be some house whose foundations take hold on the pit,"

and that "though gilded and golden, the serpent of vice is a serpent still."
He fails to see another stick or stone of London, and one more drop is thus
added to his cup of disappointment; but his experience of evil has been
extended in still another direction, and by the engaging Harry, too. The
conflict between wishfulness and revulsion is evident enough. For the rest,
though the chapter is not without a genuine vein of dreamlike intensity,
it is vitiated as a whole by the kind of unnaturalness into which Melville
so easily fell with such themes.

Meanwhile, *Redburn* abounds in the imagery not only of moral evil
but of disease, disaster, and death. The voyage itself, here as elsewhere, is
a metaphor of death and rebirth, of the passage from childhood and innocence to experience and adulthood; the crossing, to and fro, of a sea in
the waters of which one dies to the old self and puts on a new. As if to
enforce this intention irresistibly, the *Highlander's* voyage outward and the
voyage home are both initiated by a scene of violent death. During the
first long night watch that Redburn stands with his mates on the voyage
out, he is terrified when all at once a sailor, suffering from delirium tremens,
dashes up the scuttle of the forecastle and flings himself to his death over
the bows of the vessel. The boy Redburn is then poetically identified with
this sailor when he is made to occupy the dead man's bunk. Still more
ghastly than this is the discovery, in the first dogwatch of the voyage
homeward, that a Portuguese sailor who had been thrown, apparently dead
drunk, into a bunk as they left port, is literally dead, and that his corpse
is now flickering with a hideous phosphorescence. Neither incident, it
appears, occurred on the actual voyage that the young Melville made; both
are inventions, and all the more eloquent for being so.

Inventions, too, no doubt, are at least some of the other disastrous
episodes of the voyage and of the stay in Liverpool: the collision between
the *Highlander* and another vessel, in the darkness, which just fails to be
fatal; the sighting of a dismantled, waterlogged schooner in the Irish Sea,
with dead men lashed to the taffrail, the victims of storm and starvation
(an echo, possibly, of *Arthur Gordon Pym*, but not an improvement on it);
the murder of a prostitute at a bar in Liverpool by a drunken Spanish sailor;
and the epidemic that, on the homeward voyage, destroys many of the
inmates of the overcrowded, unwholesome steerage, and throws the refined
cabin passengers into a cowardly panic of terror and selfishness. In these
last scenes, as nowhere else in his work, Melville resorts to the symbolism
of plague and pestilence that had proved, or was to prove, so expressive
for a long series of modern writers, from Defoe and Poe to Thomas Mann;
and though for him, as for most of them, the literal pestilence has a moral

or spiritual reference, it is characteristic that for him, almost alone among such writers, it has a democratic and humanitarian reference also.

All these elements in *Redburn*, at any rate, are "symbolic" in the sense that, at their best, they are imagined and projected with an intensity that constantly pushes them beyond mere representation, and that makes them reverberate with a more than prosaic force in the reader's own imagination. Nothing like this had been true of *Typee* or *Omoo:* if there are symbols in those books, they are there only in the loose sense in which one would find them in any piece of writing that lifted itself even a little above the level of a mere record. The sense of symbol in *Redburn* is unmistakably more acute than in anything of Melville's that preceded *Mardi*, and moreover there are two or three points in the book at which one sees Melville moving toward an even franker and more direct form of symbolism, one which he himself would doubtless have called "allegorical," but which is far from being allegorical in the sense in which Yillah and Hautia had been. It is a question now, not of bodying forth emotional and intellectual experience in deliberately poetic characters and fables, of elaborating dramatic symbols that have obvious analogies in the realm of thought and feeling. It is a question of endowing ordinary objects, ordinary incidents, with a penumbra of feeling and suggestion that imparts to them a symbolic character. One might describe these as antiromantic or shrunken symbols; they have something of the quality of what is called witty imagery, and they were to become more and more idiosyncratic for Melville.

One of them, here, is the old-fashioned glass ship which Redburn's father had brought home from France and which the boy's imagination had hovered over until the object converted his vague longings into a definite purpose of going to sea. On the very day on which he actually left home for his voyage, the little glass figurehead of a warrior had fallen from the bows of the ship into the waves below it, and there he still lies: "but I will not have him put on his legs again, till I get on my own." In very much the same vein of feeling is the old guidebook to Liverpool which, as we have seen already, had proved so helpful to Redburn's father in his perambulations about the city, but which now proves as misleading and even pervertive as every guidebook is that has had its day. Most striking of all, however, and happiest in its imaginative quality is the old gray shooting-jacket that Redburn's elder brother gives him as he sets out from home; the moleskin shooting-jacket with big horn buttons, long skirts, and many pockets, that brings down upon Redburn so much derision from fellow-passengers, shipmates, and Englishmen; which shrinks day by day, particularly after a rain, until he finds it more and more uncomfortable to wear;

and which comes to be for him an obsessive emblem of his lost gentility and social humiliation. Redburn's shooting-jacket puts one in mind of that other shabby garment, the old clerk's overcoat in Gogol's famous tale, and indeed, in his characteristic preoccupation with clothing, especially shabby and uncomfortable clothing, Melville suggests the Russians more than any other English or American writer quite does. For the "insulted and injured" there is of course a natural metaphor in old, cheap, and ill-fitting clothes.

Bitter as the feeling in this is, however, and despite the underlying gravity of the symbolism generally, *Redburn* is anything but a lugubrious book as a whole, and it has probably never made any such impression on its readers: the current of animation and vivacity on which it is sustained is purely inspiriting; if this is "pessimism," it is pessimism of the most tonic sort. The book abounds in self-pity, certainly, but distinctions have to be made even here, and there is a kind of self-pity that is more bracing than what passes for restraint and austerity: on the whole, the self-pity in *Redburn* is clearly of that order. Melville's feeling, moreover, for light and shade did not fail him in the writing of *Redburn* as it had done in the writing of *Mardi*. There is the familiar ballast of prosaic information, for one thing—the chapter, for example, on the furniture of the quarter-deck—and there is a good deal of Melville's characteristically smiling and low-toned humor. The account of Max the Dutchman, who has a sober and respectable wife in New York and an equally sober and respectable one in Liverpool, and whose wardrobe is kept in order by the launderings of both spouses—Max the Dutchman is in Melville's happiest vein. He had always had a taste for the burgherlike humor of the little Dutch masters—Teniers, Brouwer, Jan Steen—and in passages like this he approximates it, though in a softened form. In its richness of emotion and variety of tone, *Redburn* generally is the most likable of Melville's secondary books; and it is only because he was so rebelliously conscious how much higher he was capable of going that Melville could have spoken of it contemptuously as "beggarly *Redburn.*"

Taken as a whole, *White-Jacket*, which he now went on to write, is something of a drop in quality after *Redburn;* it bears somewhat the same relation to that book as *Omoo* bears to *Typee*. Neither *Redburn* nor *White-Jacket*, and especially not the latter, was written with the concentrated conviction of Melville's whole nature: increasingly he was resentful of the necessities that forced him to write in what seemed to him an inferior strain. Both these books, he said in a letter, he had done simply as jobs, for the sake of making money, as other men are forced to saw wood, and at a time when what he earnestly desired was to write "those sort of books which are said to 'fail'." This, naturally, is a biographical fact, not a critical one, and we cannot be affected by Melville's own feeling in judging either *Redburn* or *White-Jacket;* but the biographical fact has an explanatory interest nevertheless. The earnest desire Melville expressed in his letter was soon to be fulfilled; meanwhile, he seems to have been writing at a murderous rate of speed, and *White-Jacket* itself appears to have been dashed off in the incredible space of two and a half months. It is little wonder that, in writing it, Melville should have lifted from other books not only information (as he had always done) but whole scenes and episodes, without always justifying the theft by improving on what he took. In at least one case he did so, but the symptoms of hurry and fatigue are all too evident elsewhere.

Hitherto he had intuitively succeeded in finding pretty much the true balance between narrative and factuality, between the imaginative and the informative, and in *White-Jacket* he continues to alternate the two—but now in what seems a relatively perfunctory and even wearied manner. The current of personal narrative is simply not full enough or strong enough to buoy up and float along the solid and sometimes rather lumpish blocks of straight exposition and description—straight information about the American navy generally and the individual battleship in particular. Not quite for the first time, but for the first time oppressively, one is conscious of the slight streak of pedantry that was always latent in Melville's passion for facts, and that when his imagination was not deeply engaged betrayed him into dullness and jejuneness. In proportion to the whole, one hears too much, in *White-Jacket,* about the gundeck and the berthdeck, the starboard watch and the larboard watch, the quarter-deck officers and the warrant-officers, and so on. In matters of organization and routine such as these Melville was not genuinely interested, or was interested only with the least creative facet of his imagination, and the result is that he largely fails to endow these things with imaginative life.

The book suffers too, more than the earlier books had done, from the humanitarian note that dominates it as it dominates no other work of Melville's. It is hardly worth saying that, on ethical grounds, one cannot fail to share Melville's indignation. Whatever the personal basis for it, he could not have taken firmer ground than he did when he cried out against "the social state in a man-of-war," the atrocious evil of flogging, and the like. All of it does the utmost credit to Melville's humanity. What was amiss was not this, certainly, but for the time being Melville's sense of form, his literary instinct. In speaking of *White-Jacket* one is tempted to paraphrase Flaubert's remark about *Uncle Tom's Cabin* and Negro slavery, and to ask: "Is it necessary to make comments on the iniquities of the Navy? Show them to me; that is enough." *White-Jacket* is not a novel, to be sure, but it is not a mere pamphlet either; it is an imaginative work of a very special and precarious sort, and it would have gained incalculably if Melville had made his protests far less insistent and less explicit, and if he had dramatized them much more. At least one of the flogging scenes, for example, seems terribly true, but none of them is comparable in repellent power to the one scene with which Dana, in *Two Years*, contents himself; and Melville dilutes the force of his protest partly by his repetitions of the shocking image and partly by his detailed comments on the evil. His moral passion, as so often happens, had asserted itself overaggressively at the expense of his inventive and dramatic gift.

It did not keep him, however, from continuing in *White-Jacket* the search for a right symbolic method that he had carried on in the two books that came before it. This search now led him, confusedly enough, in two directions, one of them a sterile, one a fruitful direction. It was an unhappy inspiration, as it was very probably an afterthought, that induced him to transform the man-of-war itself into the particular kind of symbol that the subtitle, "The World in a Man-of-War," indicates. From time to time as the book advances there are hints that the battleship *Neversink* is a kind of Microcosm of the universe; in one of the later chapters it is specifically remarked that "a man-of-war is but this old-fashioned world of ours afloat"; and finally Melville appends a short epilogue in which the analogy between a battleship and the Macrocosm is explicitly enforced. Just as the *Neversink* sails through the sea, so the earth sails through the air, "a fast-sailing, never-sinking world-frigate, of which God was the shipwright." But the port from which the Macrocosm sails is forever astern; unlike most battle-ships, that frigate sails under sealed orders, "yet our final haven was pre-destinated ere we slipped from the stocks at Creation." There are parallels, too, between the social arrangements on a man-of-war and the state of society itself, and though "we the people," like the common seamen in the Navy, suffer many abuses, the worst of our evils we blindly inflict on ourselves.

There are fine touches in this epilogue, like the strangely Kafkaesque suggestion that an abused sailor would appeal in vain, during this life, "to the indefinite Navy Commissioners, so far out of sight aloft." Yet on the whole the macrocosmic symbolism of the man-of-war world is as infelicitous in its way as the allegory of *Mardi* is in its. It is not only hackneyed in itself—the thought of Longfellow's Ship of State is dangerously near at hand—but treated just as Melville treats it, it is far too simply pictorial and its ethical bearing is made far too ponderously explicit. What is it indeed but a curiously belated, anachronistic example of what the sixteenth and seventeenth centuries would have called an Emblem—a highly pictorial allegory with a significance that is frankly and unequivocally enforced? Ships under full sail on calm or stormy seas appear from time to time in the sometimes charming cuts that illustrate the old emblem books, and there is an allegorical ship, allegorical of the soul and its destiny, in the third book of Quarles's *Emblems*. Melville felt a natural affinity, as some other writers of his time did, for the literature of the Baroque era, and sometimes it proved to have a genuinely quickening influence on him. But the emblem in a nineteenth-century literary setting was as inappropriate as a sixteenth-century woodcut would have been as an illustration; it was not in those terms that Melville's problem would find its proper solution.

He was much closer to his own true vein in inventing the symbol that gives the book its title, the white jacket that, in lieu of a genuine pea jacket or grego, he represents his young hero, or rather "himself," as concocting out of an old duck shirt before the *Neversink* sets sail from Callao. He does so in order to protect himself from the boisterous weather they are sure to encounter as they round Cape Horn. "An outlandish garment of my own devising," the jacket is ample in the skirts, clumsily full about the wristbands, and of course white—"yea, white as a shroud." He darns and quilts the inside of it in the hope of making it truly waterproof; but, in spite of this, in rainy weather it proves to be as absorbent as a sponge, and thus "when it was fair weather with others, alas! it was foul weather with me." It is such an ungainly, eccentric garment that it brings down constant ridicule on the wearer's head, and worse than that, evokes a kind of superstitious hatred on the part of the other sailors. On one occasion they take White-Jacket himself to be the ghost of the cooper, lost overboard the day before, when they see him lying on the main-royalyard in the darkness; as time goes on, some of them are convinced that other deaths in the crew can be laid to the jacket, and White-Jacket himself begins to feel that the accursed garment has "much to answer for."

He has tried to persuade the first lieutenant to let him have some black paint to cover it with, but in vain. And this is a great part of his misery, for most monkey jackets are of a dark hue and keep their wearers from being too easily visible, especially at night. When, on the other hand, an officer wants a man for some particularly hard job, "how easy, in that mob of incognitoes, to individualize 'that white jacket,' and dispatch him on the errand!" White-Jacket tries to free himself of the wretched thing by swapping it with a messmate and even by putting it up at auction, but no one will have it, and he begins to imagine that he will never be free of it until he rolls a forty-two-pound shot in it and commits it to the deep.

This thought, however, is too much like the thought of his own death, and he refrains. But when the cruise is almost over, the jacket very nearly proves to be his death after all. White-Jacket is sent up the mainmast one night to reeve the halyards of a stun-sail, and while he is trying to do this he loses his balance and, entangled about the head by his jacket, falls rushingly from the yard-arm into the sea. Down he plunges, down into the deathlike waters of the deep. After some seconds, however, he shoots up again to the surface, and attempts to strike out toward the ship, but the fatal jacket, looped about him as it is, almost destroys him. He saves himself only by cutting himself out of it with a knife and ripping it up and down "as if I were ripping open myself." It sinks slowly before his eyes, and White-Jacket returns to life. He does so because he has in fact ripped open an aspect of himself, thrown it off, and allowed it to sink in the sea; the aspect of himself that is mere uniqueness and differentness, mere protective-unprotective self-assertion, easy to identify and individualize in any mob, and white, fatally white, as white as a shroud.

It is a magnificent symbol of the lesser Self, the empirical Self, the Ego; a far finer symbol for its purpose than that of the man-of-war for its, and it is so partly because it is homely and unhackneyed, partly because it is inexplicit, and partly because, though it has an interpretable meaning, that meaning remains elusive and slightly equivocal. The jacket was probably sheer invention on Melville's part, though he alleged in a letter to Dana that it was a real jacket. It does not matter in the least. In its setting the thing has the air of the only kind of reality that counts. Sheer invention, however, so far as Melville's external experience went, is certainly the great scene just alluded to, in which the jacket plays so nearly fatal a role. In literal fact no such mishap befell Melville on the *United States*. The ship's log is silent on the affair, and besides it has long been known that the whole scene is a rewriting of a passage in a little volume called *A Mariner's Sketches* by an old Yankee sailor named Nathaniel Ames, which had been published in Providence twenty years earlier.

It was a passage that was bound to catch Melville's attention as he read the book: the nightmarish image of falling to one's destruction from a high place had appeared before in his own writing, and what psychiatrists call hypsophobia was as characteristic for him as it was for Poe. He had reached the head of Taipi-Vai, according to his own story, by a series of horrifying falls from ledge to ledge of a dreamlike precipice; and in *Redburn*, in the passage already quoted, he represents his horror of "falling—falling—falling" when he is sent up to loosen the skysail. Harry Bolton on the voyage home suffers so terribly from this phobia that he refuses ever to climb the mast a second time, though he is permanently disgraced for it. And even earlier in *White-Jacket*, Melville or his fictional persona has nearly fallen to his death from the main-royalyard when the superstitious sailors below him suddenly lower the halyards. It takes no great penetration to detect in this recurring image the unconscious impulse to suicide, and the great scene in *White-Jacket* owes its inescapable power, as the scene of White-Jacket's near-floggling does, to the fact that, though it never occurred in the physical world, it did certainly occur in the inner one. The self-destructiveness in Melville expressed itself thus as well as in other ways.

Meanwhile, for all its limitations, *White-Jacket* has stretches of admirable writing in it, of which this scene of the fall from the yard-arm is one. It is already a famous case, but it remains an especially illuminating one, of Melville's genius for transmuting an uninspired model into something greatly expressive. Nathaniel Ames's own account of his fall from the futtock shrouds—oddly enough, it was on the same frigate, the *United States*—though it has several touches of strong realistic truth, is essentially as pedestrian as one would expect it to be if one heard it from the lips of the old seaman himself. Melville transformed it as Shakespeare sometimes transformed Holinshed or North's Plutarch: keeping the facts and the narrative order and even some of the details of feeling, but imparting rhythmicality, and a wonderfully connotative one, to what had had no rhythm at all; working small miracles of linguistic expressiveness ("the strong shunning of death shocked me through"); and intensifying the whole emotional value of the incident through an accompaniment of powerful images—"the speechless profound of the sea," "the maelstrom air," and "some inert, coiled fish of the sea." When he finds in Ames a matter-of-fact sentence like this:

> I kept going down, down, till it appeared to me that the seven fathoms and a half, (the depth of water at our anchorage,) had more than doubled since we let go our anchor;

Melville remakes it thus:

> The blow from the sea must have turned me, so that I sank almost feet foremost through a soft, seething, foamy lull. Some current seemed hurrying me away; in a trance I yielded, and sank deeper down with a glide. Purple and pathless was the deep calm now around me, flecked by summer lightnings in an azure afar.

Much of the effect of this extraordinarily hypnotic passage is due to the delicate skill with which Melville avails himself of phonetic color—the color, here, of labials and sibilants especially and the closed sound of long e—

but much also to the subtly responsive rhythms (conveying the delicious sense of movement downward through a liquid medium, in such gently protracted phrases as "through a soft, seething, foamy lull"), as well as to the synaesthetic use of a word like "lull" for an experience of the sense of touch, and the sudden shift from the sense of motion to the perception of color in the fine words, "purple" and "azure."

Admittedly this whole scene of the descent into the sea and the re-emergence from it is a rare peak in Melville's early prose; it is the finest writing in the ornate style that he did before *Moby Dick,* and one can account for it only by remembering that it sprang from a profound inward experience of life and death in conflict. But it is not the only passage of brilliant narrative writing in *White-Jacket,* despite the dead calm of many chapters. In an entirely different key, the key of relaxed and indulgent humor, the scene called "A Man-of-War College," in which the school-master of the *Neversink* lectures to his flock of restless midshipmen on the refinements of naval strategy, is written with admirable ease and charm. In still another and a darker style, that of indignant, satirical caricature, Melville never went beyond the great scene of "The Operation"; the scene in which the pompous and unfeeling surgeon of the *Neversink,* Dr. Cad-wallader Cuticle, performs an unnecessary amputation upon an injured foretopman, under which the wretched man dies. There is an inevitable suggestion of Smollett both in the name and in the character of the surgeon, as there is in the whole chapter; yet after all Melville did not write with the particular kind of harsh, brilliant, indefatigable speed and vigor one associates with the author of *Roderick Random.* Indeed, the passage has an essentially different quality from any of the scenes aboard the *Thunder* in that novel, a quality not so much of choleric energy as of mingled pity and detestation, revulsion and ruthlessness, humor and hatred. It would be easy, too, to say that Melville was writing in much the same style in which, for example, Rowlandson drew when he made his monstrous print of "The Amputation"; but the real feeling in Melville is in fact no more that of Rowlandson—broad, gross, and grotesque—than it is that of Smollett. It is a feeling in which anger at the spectacle of cruelty is underlain by a still stronger sorrow at the spectacle of evil generally.

On these more intangible grounds *White-Jacket* represents no retreat from or palliation of the insights expressed in *Redburn.* One must confess, in fact, that the later book is the more richly counterpointed, in a moral sense, of the two. The World in a Man-of-War is, at the one extreme, quite as black a world as that in a merchant vessel or a great seaport; it is a world, on the whole, "charged to the combings of her hatchways with the spirit of Belial and all unrighteousness." A world of which the ferocious Articles of War form the domineering code could hardly be other than a basically brutal and un-Christian one, and brutal and un-Christian, with its ultimate dedication to purposes of bloodshed and destruction, the microcosm of the *Neversink* is. What follows morally is what could be predicted: overbearing arrogance on the part of most of the officers, genteel rascality on the part of others, petty insolence even in the boyish midshipmen, and cringing subservience or sullen vindictiveness on the part of many of the sailors—for Melville, committed as he is to the rank and file as over against their superiors, cannot and will not represent the human reality as different from what he has found it in experience. He does not spare himself the task, painful though he obviously finds it, of hinting at "other evils, so direful that they will hardly bear even so much as an allusion"; evils that involve some of the common seamen in "the sins for which the cities of the plain were overthrown."

The portrait of Bland, the knavish master-at-arms, though it is less completely dramatized than that of Jackson, is at least as subtle analytically; and his well-bred, unvulgar, "organic" scoundrelism is both more inexplicable and more profound than Jackson's understandable blackguardliness. Yet morally speaking, despite all this, *White-Jacket* has a higher *relievo* and a more complex truth than *Redburn*. There is the moral relief of goodness in *Redburn* but it is too largely associated with passiveness and even effeminacy; Redburn himself remains too much the mere victim, embittered but not very resistant, and Harry Bolton is a more extreme case than he. The stage in *White-Jacket* is occupied by a much more richly representative cast of characters. Not all the officers are bullies or martinets. Mad Jack, a junior lieutenant, is a paragon of generous, manly seamanship, and Colbrook, the handsome and gentlemanly corporal of marines, has the extraordinary courage to intercede for White-Jacket when he comes so close to a flogging. Some of the midshipmen are "noble little fellows," and as for the common seamen, there is the self-respecting old Ushant, there is Nord the silent and meditative, and above and beyond all there is of course the "incomparable" and "ever-glorious" Jack Chase, the heroic captain of the maintop, a far more masculine image of virtue than the pathetic Harry. It is quite in keeping with his love for Jack Chase, moreover, that we should feel the vein of iron in White-Jacket as we never quite feel it in Redburn. Melville, as he wrote the book, had at least for the time recovered from the despairing mood of *Mardi* and from the largely resentful mood of *Redburn*. White-Jacket, it is true, would have gone to his death rather than submit to a flogging, but he would have done so in an act of protest; and in a later scene, when death by water would have come so easily, he has the still greater courage to cut himself out of his fatal garment and return to life.

HERSHEL PARKER

The Metaphysics of
Indian-Hating

Even the closest student of *The Con-
fidence-Man* admits that it "still keeps many, or most, of its secrets." A
reader can still share the sense of discovery which informed this paragraph
by Sedgwick:

> There is interpolated in *The Confidence-Man* a strange story, the point of
> which, I believe, has escaped notice. I refer to the story of Colonel
> Moredock, the Indian-hater, followed by a discussion of the genus "Indian-
> hater" and the metaphysics of Indian-hating. The allegory here is so
> transparent that it needs no comment. The point to which it leads
> is important; to my way of thinking it is the most important thing in
> the book.

But today the critic of the Indian-hater section cannot be as confident as
Sedgwick that the point has escaped notice. Both Elizabeth Foster and
Nathalia Wright have agreed that the section is the crux of the book, and
the "transparent" allegory has evoked a good deal of comment. In this
paper I will survey the arguments of the three major critics of the Indian-
hater chapters, John W. Shroeder, Roy Harvey Pearce, and Miss Foster,
and point out some unresolved difficulties. Then, often working from their
findings, I will interpret the story in terms of the opposing elements of the
allegory and in relation to a theme recurring in all of Melville's novels.
The Indian-hater story, as I read it, is a tragic study of the impracticability

From *Nineteenth-Century Fiction* 18 (September 1963). Copyright © 1963 by The Regents
of the University of California.

of Christianity, and, more obviously, a satiric allegory in which the Indians are Devils and the Indian-haters are dedicated Christians, and in which the satiric target is the nominal practice of Christianity.

If Shroeder has not "let more light into this book than any other critic," as Miss Foster says, certainly his use of literary cross-references "to locate the events of *The Confidence-Man* geographically and spiritually" is the most illuminating criticism besides her own. Briefly as Shroeder treats the Indian-hater chapters, he indicates convincingly the diabolic nature of the Indians and the god-like character of the Indian-hater. Colonel Moredock, says Shroeder, "has succeeded in locating Evil in its real home; there is no distortion in his vision of spiritual reality." But I would quarrel with Shroeder's conclusion that the only hope in this "dark book" is that "the triumph of the confidence-man is opposed and objectified, though apparently not negated, by an adversary of heroic proportions"—that is, by Moredock. And I suggest that Shroeder, while accurately formulating the terms of the allegory, has missed the ironic inversion of accepted values which is the basis of Melville's gigantic satire.

Pearce's article amounts to a general contradiction of Shroeder's conclusions. He denies that the Indians "are symbols of satanism," and argues from Melville's attitude toward real Indians that he does not use the Indian symbolically in *The Confidence-Man*. Pearce submits "that there is nothing but distortion in the Indian-hater's vision of spiritual reality," and denies that Moredock "functions as a kind of hero." The artistic function of Melville's version of the Indian-hater story—a version in which hatred is called a "devout sentiment" and the hater is praised—"is to be too violent a purge, a terrible irony." In Pearce's reading there is hope neither in the blind confidence of some of the passengers of the Fidèle nor in Moredock's blind hatred: "The blackness is complete."

Although agreeing with Pearce that the Indian-hater is in no sense a hero, Miss Foster finds that "in the Indian-hater chapters the Indian embodies allegorically a primitive, or primal, malign, treacherous force in the universe." Unlike Pearce, she distinguishes between Melville's attitude toward real Indians and his use of them as symbols. She takes exception to Pearce's "blackness": "Melville, though a pessimistic moralist in this novel, is not, I take it, a despairing one. Like many another moralist and writer of comedy, he is concerned to point out the dangers of both extremes." Reading the section as one of Melville's warning qualifications of "the cynicism and materialism of the main argument," she concludes that Melville "gives us an unforgettable picture of a society without faith or charity. . . . This is the alternative if we jettison charity—a world of solitary, dehumanized Indian-haters."

Despite Miss Foster's tactful mediation between Shroeder and Pearce and despite her own interpretation, major problems remain. Neither Pearce nor Miss Foster has adequately explored the implications of Shroeder's evidence that the Indians are diabolic. Nor has enough been made of the likelihood that in an allegory as carefully structured as *The Confidence-Man* the antagonist of the satanic Indians might be in some way religious. Then, Pearce's disgust at the praise accorded Moredock (disgust shared by any reader of the Indian-hating story as a literal narrative) has not been reconciled with Shroeder's claim that Moredock is the heroic adversary of the Confidence Man. The solution lies, I suggest, in taking the episode as allegory, as Shroeder and Miss Foster do, and in carefully identifying the elements of that allegory. Melville's opposition of the Indian-hater and the Indian constitutes, I believe, a consistent allegory in which Christianity is conceived as the dedicated hatred of Evil at the cost of forsaking human ties, and in which most of the human race is represented as wandering in the backwoods of error, giving lip-service to their religion but failing to embody it in their lives. The allegory is a grotesquely satiric study of the theme which Miss Foster calls the most obvious in the novel, "the failure of Christians to be Christian," and in the vein of *Mardi* and *Pierre* it is a study of the practicability of Christianity as Jesus preached it.

Both Shroeder and Miss Foster offer evidence for the identification of the allegorical significance of the Indians. Demonstrating that snakes in *The Confidence-Man* are associated with the Devil as in Genesis, *Paradise Lost,* and Hawthorne's works, Shroeder argues cogently that the coupling of the Indian and the snake at the outset of the Indian-hater story is a deliberate guide to the diabolic nature of the Indians. Never definitely calling the Indians Devils, Miss Foster observes that in Mocmohoc "readers will have recognized a type of the Confidence Man." She also suggests the possibility that "the Indian is something not so much sub-human as extra-human," and that by giving Indian containers for their wine bottles and cigars to the cosmopolitan and Charlie (the ordinary Mississippi confidence man who tells the Moredock story), "Melville meant to remind the reader that they are the Indians of the argument." The same function, I would add, is served by Melville's having the cosmopolitan ironically call his pipe a "calumet"—a peace pipe. Miss Foster agrees that Shroeder "demonstrates beyond question the diabolic and mythic nature" of the Confidence Man, but she does not pursue the allegorical associations of the Indians with Devils. Yet if the Confidence Man is associated with snakes and *is* the Devil, while Indians are associated with snakes and at least one Indian is "a type of the Confidence Man," then in Melville's allegorical geometry the Indians are Devils also.

Recognizing the Indians as types of the Devil of Christian literary tradition, we should reasonably expect the Devil's antagonist to be an earnest Christian. But Moredock, who dedicates his life to killing, hardly fits the ordinary conception of a follower of Jesus. The cosmopolitan (the last avatar of the Confidence Man) makes the obvious objection in professing himself unable to believe that a man so loving to his family could be so merciless to his enemies. Pearce in a similar spirit rejects Shroeder's interpretation of Moredock as the man who has located Evil in its real home. But repugnant as it is, the logic of the opposition demands that we see Moredock as a Devil-hating Christian, though one who does not live up to all of Jesus' commands. The outrageous irony that has escaped notice is that it is when Moredock is murdering Indians that he is Christian and when he is enjoying the comforts of domestic life that he is apostatizing.

Before seeing how the dedication to Indian-hating is described in terms of dedication to Christianity, one must dispose of the cosmopolitan's ironic objection that some parts of Charlie's story do not hang together: "If the man of hate, how could John Moredock be also the man of love?" Considering the familiarity with the Bible which he displays elsewhere, the cosmopolitan should be aware that there is ample biblical authority for being both a man of hate and a man of love. In Amos 5:15 the duality is stated baldly: "Hate the evil, and love the good." Psalm 139, from which Melville quotes earlier, is also explicit about the duty to hate: "Do not I hate them, O Lord, that hate thee? and am not I grieved with those that rise up against thee? I hate them with perfect hatred: I count them mine enemies." In this tone Melville's Father Mapple cries: "Woe to him whom this world charms from Gospel duty! Woe to him who seeks a pour oil upon the waters when God has brewed them into a gale!" Father Mapple in his peroration is as implacable as Moredock: "Delight is to him, who gives no quarter in the truth, and kills, and burns, and destroys all sin though he pluck it out from under the robes of Senators and Judges." There is a darker side of Christianity, as Melville is careful to remind us by the cry of "church militant!" when the Methodist minister shakes the one-legged man till his timber-toe clatters "on the deck like a nine-pin," by the mention of Torquemada, the Spanish inquisitor general, and by the references to Jesuits, to Loyola, and to a "a victim in *auto-da-fé.*"

Once we accept Melville's ironic view of Christianity as the practice of Devil-hating, we are ready to follow the similarity of the dedication to Indian-hating to the dedication to Christianity. Keeping in mind the word "Metaphysics" in the title of Chapter xxvi, we can see the significance of the religious references like "guilty race," "monk," and "cloistered" in

Melville's description of how the Indian-hater *par excellence* comes to his resolution:

> An intenser Hannibal, he makes a vow, the hate of which is a vortex from whose suction scarce the remotest chip of the guilty race may reasonably feel secure. Next, he declares himself and settles his temporal affairs. With the solemnity of a Spaniard turned monk, he takes leave of his kin; or rather, these leave-takings have something of the still more impressive finality of death-bed adieus. Last, he commits himself to the forest primeval; there, so long as life shall be his, to act upon a calm, cloistered scheme of strategical, implacable, and lonesome vengeance.

Later in the conversation Charlie's allusion to Matthew 19 (or Mark 10) emphasizes the similarity of the dedication of the Indian-hater to the way Jesus would have one begin a life as His follower. The whole of the passage just quoted from should be read in the light of Jesus' words to the rich young man, and to His disciples after the young man has gone sorrowfully away, especially the command to dispose of worldly possessions and the reward promised to "every one that hath forsaken houses, or brethren, or sisters, or father, or mother, or wife, or children, or lands, for my name's sake." Moreover, there is a parallel to the Christian's being, as Paul says (Romans 6:2), "dead to sin."

Throughout Charlie's story theological terms are employed to describe the "devout sentiment" of Indian-hating. We are told that there is

> a species of diluted Indian-hater, one whose heart proves not so steely as his brain. Soft enticements of domestic life too often draw him from the ascetic trail; a monk who apostatizes to the world at times. . . . It is with him as with the Papist converts in Senegal; fasting and mortification prove hard to bear.

According to Charlie, Judge Hall "would maintain that there was no vocation whose consistent following calls for such self-containing as that of the Indian-hater *par excellence*." Here Melville is using "vocation" in its literal and theological sense of "calling." Where in Melville's source the real James Hall says that Moredock watched the murderers of his mother for more than a year before attacking them, Melville alters the account to stress Moredock's solitude, for "upwards of a year, along in the wilds" after his dedication. Melville has already made the judge declare that the backwoodsman is "worthy to be compared with Moses in the Exodus." Now he emphasizes Moredock's role as religious leader by making him on one occasion seek the murderes "at the head of a party pledged to serve him for forty days." Here Melville has added to Hall's account the biblical number for times of purgation and preparation—forty. It is Melville (or his storyteller Charlie) who gives Moredock a retributive spirit that speaks like God's "voice calling through the garden." In Charlie's story Moredock's manner of being benevolent is in accord with Jesus' command in the Sermon on the Mount (Matthew 6:3): "But when thou doest alms, let not thy left hand know what thy right hand doeth." And, apropos of Moredock's refusal to seek high political office, Judge Hall (according to Charlie) says that the Colonel

> was not unaware that to be a consistent Indian-hater involves the re-nunciation of ambition, with its objects—the pomps and glories of the world; and since religion, pronouncing such things vanities, accounts it merit to renounce them, therefore, so far as this goes, Indian-hating, whatever may be thought of it in other respects, may be regarded as not wholly without the efficacy of a devout sentiment.

Leaving such vanities behind, the dedicated Indian-haters inhabit the moral wilderness which, as Miss Wright says, is "the symbolic scene of mature experience throughout Melville." The Indian-hater *par excellence* is nearly fabulous, a soul "peeping out but once an age." The lesser Indian-hater like Moredock either backslides to domestic life or, desperate from the loneliness which his ascetic vow has imposed, "hurries openly towards the first smoke" and embraces the Indian Devil. For as the pamphlet in *Pierre* has it, efforts at the absolute imitation of Christ may often involve the idealist in "strange, *unique* follies and sins." Those still less devoted, the inhabitants of the fringes of the moral wilderness, the backwoods, are "diluted Indian-haters" who give nominal allegiance to the religious ideals realized (if at all) only by the Indian-hater *par excellence.* They teach their children the traditional hatred of the Indian as Eve teaches her children enmity to the serpent, and they join in community disapproval of the adversary without ever applying the religion of Indian-hating, or Devil-hating, to their ordinary lives. To repeat Sedgwick's phrase, almost without irony, the allegory is transparent.

With the basic allegory of Indian Devils and Devil-hating Christians established, the story can be interpreted coherently. We are spared Pearce's revulsion at the literal story and can appreciate the grisly humor in Melville's outrageous distortion of our habitual way of thinking of Christianity. For in a book in which the Devil comes aboard the world-ship to preach Christianity as an April Fool's joke, it is apt that the best haters be the best Christians. The story of the Weavers and the Wrights can be recognized as not simply a piteous tale of frontier betrayal and violence, but as a warning against making a "covenant" with the Devil. The "moral indig-nation" of the Indians who claim to be maligned is wryly comic, especially since the "Supreme Court" to which is left the question of whether Indians should be permitted to testify for themselves is, within the allegory, the Last Judgment. Any reading of the section with the terms of the allegory in mind will reveal other elements in Melville's mordantly comic study of the discrepancy between the Christianity that Jesus preached and that which nominal Christians practice.

It is not surprising that the reviewers of The Confidence-Man in 1857 did not understand the allegory. As Miss Foster shows, Melville in the mid-1850's habitually concealed his darker meanings from a public unwilling or unable to face them. Among modern readers the point of the story has not "escaped notice" by being uncharacteristic of Melville, for "the failure of Christians to be Christian" is satirized in every novel from Typee to Billy Budd, and the tragic theme of the impracticability of Christianity is dramatized at length in Mardi and Pierre. Perhaps readers of the Indian-hater chapters have been, in the pamphlet's word, too "horological" to acknowledge biblical authority for single-minded hatred of Evil, or to acknowledge the Christlikeness of forsaking family and property for religion. The final irony may be that for modern readers able to accept Melville's darkest meanings Christianity is so "diluted" that they have become insensitive to his satire and, more appallingly, have lost his apprehension that the impracticability of Christianity is tragic.

GUY CARDWELL

Melville's Gray Story: Symbols and Meaning in "Benito Cereno"

The Symbols in this story offer special difficulties, because many of them carry shifting, multiple values instead of values that are constant even though imprecise. Moreover, the entire congeries of major symbols is so interrelated and is so organic a part of the tale that a reinterpretation of one symbol may require a reinterpretation of all.

The unusual difficulties offered by the symbols are, then, a product of Melville's habit of mind and of the use to which he puts the symbols as organizing instruments, influencing both emotional and logical structure. Melville was an inveterate seeker after absolutes; but his quest, unsatisfied, ended characteristically in skepticism or in irony. This combination of intense probing and final uncertainty naturally expressed itself in symbols that satisfy Freud's definition: they suggest things that cannot be phrased; they lead us into dim, branched approaches to imperfectly seen truths. And, when a reader feels that he has laid hands on a symbol and has wrenched from it the secrets of the unlikes that it relates, a shift in the narrative or the introduction of a paired symbol may force a reversal of understanding or a widening of signification to embrace the opposite of what at first seemed to be the import.

As shall be seen, reversal or widening of signification is an essential feature of the story; it is occasioned by the structure and is at the same

From *Bucknell Review* 8 (May 1959). Copyright © 1965 by D. C. Heath & Co.

time an integral feature of the partly reflexive or "spatial" organization. Because the formal organization is in part perceived instantaneously rather than merely cumulatively and sequentially, the devoted reader develops a series of partly contradictory conceptions of form and meaning. If the interpretation offered in this essay is an accurate one, revelations succeed one another in this order: elements of the superficial narrative fall into place as they would in an ordinary detective story; symbols are comprehended by a kind of explosive insight, and the world is seen as sharply divided between good and a most puissant evil; dissatisfaction with this understanding develops, and a new, more plausible conception takes shape. In the end the symbols play a part in making cohesive, powerful and existentially complex a story that, as it is ordinarily interpreted, could well be called sprawling, insipid, and naive.

The symbols throughout "Benito Cereno" are deeply imbedded in the story at the simplest narrative level; but they acquire some of their most permanent significances in retrospect to accord with the reader's latest understanding of the action. This does not mean that some symbols do not maintain several meanings from the beginning or that others do not come into the story stable and ready-made, as univocal as symbols are likely to be. Melville uses, for example, the ship as microcosm; land as the known; sea as the unknown. He uses, too, the puzzling knot; the sword of authority; the flawed bell; the lock and key.

Such conventional symbols retain their factual authority and convey expected meanings but are comparatively uninteresting. Three distinct sets of extensively elaborated symbols are enormously more important and require close scrutiny. They are responsible for much that is exciting, moving, and troublesome in the story. First, there is the color symbolism. The outstanding example of Melville's color symbolism is, of course, the "Whiteness of the Whale" in *Moby-Dick*; but he frequently worked with both black and white. In "The Whiteness of the Whale" he stresses ambiguity, moving from instances in which whiteness charms to instances in which whiteness horrifies. Horror of whiteness is irrational, but natural: a dumb brute recognizes the demonism of the world. "Though in many of its aspects this visible world seems formed in love, the invisible spheres were formed in fright."

The most frequently mentioned color in "Benito Cereno" is black, but the contrast with white is implicit when not stated. At first view the *San Dominick* looks like a whitewashed monastery appropriately peopled with dark-cowled Black Friars. The sternpiece shows a dark satyr in a mask, pressing his foot on the prostrate neck of a writhing figure, likewise masked. Dark festoons of sea-grass sweep slimily over the ship's name. Don Benito sulks "in black vapors." The whiteness of Don Benito Cereno and the blackness of Babo are dramatized in a shaving scene: Don Benito's "usual ghastliness was heightened by the lather; the lather was made whiter by the contrasting sootiness of the Negro's body." Later, as Captain Amasa and Don Benito are ushered in to luncheon by a mulatto, they engage in a biologist's debate on the quality of being part white, part black. A climactic use of black will be mentioned later.

A second major symbolic interest is in nature, both human and external. Partly enigmatic references abound. As he observes the crew and captain of the Spanish ship, Delano's suspicions lead him to make pithy observations on treachery and loyalty, the nature of blacks, on primitive virtues, and on the benignity of sun, sea, wind, and sky. Reassured by the kindly aspect of nature he smiles at mocking phantoms. Negroes, throughout much of the story, are represented as natural, simple, and good. Whites, particularly Don Benito—who is ill, moody, and out of tune with nature— apparently are not to be trusted. Delano gazes approvingly at a slumbering Negress, sleeping like a doe in the shade of a woodland rock, her fawn sprawling at her lapped breasts, ineffectually rooting.

But even in this last idyllic scene the reader may find some ambiguity. The animal imagery has ominous overtones, and Delano reflects that Negresses are unsophisticated as leopardesses, loving as doves. Some of the Negroes sleep under the inverted longboat, and it becomes a "sort of den" for them. A row of black, savage hatchet polishers makes the good captain uneasy; he admires, but again uneasily, a giant mute black, Atufal, who stalks about in his chains.

After the climatic discovery of the drama that has been acted out on board the *San Dominick,* all that the reader has accepted as the truth about nature and the innocence of natural man must be ironically reversed. Atufal is not really chained. Babo's loving service to Don Benito is a colossal hypocrisy. The Negresses are parties to the plot and are as murderous as the males. In the battle for the *San Dominick* the slaves' red tongues loll wolflike from black mouths. The reader, cleverer and more skeptical than Delano, now looks back with ironic condescension to Delano's simple remorse that he should have harbored suspicions that might betray "an atheist doubt of the ever-watchful Providence above."

At this point, it is expedient to treat together religious symbols and the three chief characters in the story: Don Benito, Babo, and Delano. At first glance it seems that Don Benito offers no difficulties after one reaches the nominal climax. At this false climax, the moment when Babo's cruel role becomes apparent, one comprehends the factual narrative as a unit and is prepared (one believes) to make use of clues to the symbolic strata.

One sees Don Benito as the suffering hero, and a carefully magnified one. Aboard that floating monastery, the *San Dominick,* he endures torment at the hands of black Babo. In the ship which rolls hearse-like, in the coffined cabin, he follows his leader, as the scrawled legend at the bow—*Seguid vuestro jefe*—has it. His immediate leader is the skeleton of the trusting, betrayed Aranda, hung out as a figurehead, but powerful religious conno-tations are present, as they aften are in Melville. At the end of the story, Don Benito and Captain Amasa philosophize in a dramatic passage on evil and the effects of illusion. The melancholy Don Benito declares that neither time nor nature can make him forget the past; mild trade winds but waft him to his tomb. Then Captain Delano cries out, "You are saved . . . what can cast such a shadow upon you?" and Benito answers:

"The Negro."

These last two are, for the time, the chief operative words in the story, seeming to sum up with magnificent suggestiveness the action and the meaning of the action. They are a burning glass that concentrates what appears to be the total meaning of the experience. The two words (*el negro*—the black) compact all the imagery associated with blackness into a sum-mation of horror at evil rampant, masked as goodness, successful in the world, though tripped, occasionally, by chance. Each instance of the word *black* or of the idea of blackness in the story now becomes an integrating agent, a variation on a connective theme. Finally, pursued by the stare of Babo's black head, Don Benito's white body is carried from the monastery on Mount Agonia to the vaults where lies the body of Don Alexandro Aranda. Don Benito does, "indeed, follow his leader." (There is inciden-tally, no Mount Agonia. Melville could as well have written "Grotto of the Agony." Don Benito, "the Benedictine," is the Christlike man follow-ing the Master.)

Everything that we now know about Don Benito sheds light on Babo. The two exchange places, like figures on a Swiss weather prophet. Babo is no longer the affectionate servitor of a capricious master capable of slashing his slave's cheek over a trifling matter. He (his name suggests baboon, perhaps too readily, to most readers) is now seen as evil incarnate, blackness made manifest. Babo's is the mind that plots mutiny and murder; Babo's is the hand that aims a dirk at the heart of the good, the Christlike man. That Melville should comment on his physical likeness to a begging friar of St. Francis is a grotesque irony, for the Gray Friars led lives in closest possible imitation of Christ; and Babo could have howled with the mad Ahab in *Moby-Dick,* "*Ego non baptizo te in nomine patris, sed in nomine diaboli!*"

At this stage in our reading of the story—and this is where the critics have unfortunately stopped—Captain Amasa Delano is the good-hearted, good-natured, obtuse (as the scholars often call him) Yankee from Duxbury. Stanley Williams and Richard Chase hold that in the presence of evil Delano is uncomprehending, philosophically and ethically immature. As Chase, applying with ruthlessly procrustean surgery the experience-innocence formula, puts it, Delano is tragically blind, a successful (that is, ignorantly Adamic) American gentleman who can never, in any final sense, be saved. His opposite, Don Benito, a son of the old European culture, though sapped of will, is spiritually enlightened by his commerce with evil and the long dark past.

By interpretation of this kind the story falls for nearly all critics into a coherent, orderly pattern of meaning. Don Benito is pure good; Babo is pure evil; and Delano is the genial, insensitive observer. Melville sees the essential nature of the world clearly, and sees it as a perfect dichotomy.

It is true that throughout the long first division of the narrative Delano serves as a center of revelation whose slowness to understand the action is suitable to the deliberate unfolding of a mystery story; but this interpretation simply will not do. It is too neat, too glib, too shallow, and too entirely unlike Melville. A little reflection and our minds stubbornly refuse to canonize Don Benito; we cannot believe that Delano is altogether blind; and we have some sympathy, too, for Babo. In brief, troubled retrospection produces emotions and ideas that will not fit within this apparently tight, final framework.

Fortunately, Melville helps us towards a new interpretation. In two places, and in two places only, he goes behind his characters in "Benito Cereno." In the first of these instances, in his fourth paragraph, he writes that, to Captain Delano's surprise, the incoming vessel "showed no colors":

> Considering the lawlessness and loneliness of the spot, and the sort of stories, at that day, associated with those seas, Captain Delano's surprise might have deepened into some uneasiness had he not been a person of a singularly undistrustful good nature, not liable, except on extraordinary and repeated incentives, and hardly then, to indulge in personal alarms, any way involving the imputation of malign evil in man. Whether, in view of what humanity is capable [sic], such a trait implies, along with a benevolent heart, more than ordinary quickness and accuracy of intellectual perception, may be left to the wise to determine.

This is either an involved, unfavorable reflection on the captain's acuteness or a moderately plain directive, and it can hardly be an adverse reflection. If it is a directive, we have voyaged on tranced, metaphysical sets where the simple, innocent, but not unintelligent Captain Delano is our certified ontologist and axiologist, a philosophical, not a mechanical, center of revelation.

Delano's worth as a mentor obviously depends on his fundamental insights: he does not make too much of evil in man; he is modestly optimistic about man's capabilities. He is not a dialectician, but his silences carry meaning. (Expressive muteness appears often in this story. Atufal carries out his assigned role without a word; Babo's hand, controlling Don Benito, is "mute as that on the wall"; captured, Babo is silent; gibbeted, he meets a "voiceless end.") When Don Benito discourses with Captain Delano on Appearance and Reality and ends in the perfect conviction that Evil is too much for us, we are not surprised that the generous captain should be silent. He has offered consolations—Time and Nature—and he is not given to the refined development of theory.

When we arrive at this view of Delano, the name of his vessel, the *Bachelor's Delight,* is no longer a puzzling, discordant item. In *Moby-Dick* Melville has already introduced a *Bachelor* and a *Delight.* There the *Bachelor,* "glad ship of good luck," her last cask of oil wedged in, was joyously homeward-bound. Her captain had heard of the white whale but did not believe in him. The *Delight,* "most miserably misnamed, lost five men to the whale, and her captain thought of the harpoon not yet forged that would kill him. Delano, then, may be related to both the *Bachelor* and the *Delight:* he was acquainted with horror but did not *usually* impute malign evil.

If we seek, we can find additional detailed evidence that Delano was neither the epitome of moral blindness nor an amiable but mechanical figure. What, for example, are his social judgments? How does he view the Negroes, Don Benito, and nature? He pities Spaniards and blacks, although he perceives that suffering has brought out the less good-natured qualities of the Negroes. He considers Negroes to be generally cheerful and tactful. He takes to them, not on theoretical, abolitionist grounds, but naturally, "not philanthropically, but genially, just as other men to Newfoundland dogs." They are, he notes, like animals, both loving and savage. Does this impress us as a foolish stereotype or plain good sense? Are only blacks like animals? We note that a white sailor has the look of a grizzly bear. If these attitudes and opinions seem sensible to us, how do they square with what we know of Melville's conception of human nature? Reviewing Parkman's *Oregon Trail* in 1849, Melville wrote:

> We are all of us—Anglo-Saxon, Dyaks, and Indians—sprung from one head, and made in one image.

And wherever we recognize the image of God, let us reverence it, though it hung from the gallows.

In the second passage in which he goes behind his characters, as a preliminary to the shaving scene, Melville comments on the good humor and harmoniousness of the Negro's disposition, extending this observation with the comment:

> When to all this is added the docility arising from the unaspiring contentment of a limited mind, and that susceptibility of blind attachment sometimes inhering in indisputable inferiors, one readily perceives why those hypochondriacs, Johnson and Bryon—it may be something like the hypochondriac, Benito Cereno—took to their hearts, almost to the exclusion of the entire white race, their serving men, the negroes, Barber and Fletcher.

Mixed with the ironic comparison of captive Don Benito's attitude to that of Johnson and Byron is the writer's own conception of Negro character. Injection of historical instances, Barber and Fletcher, takes the reader outside the story and upholds the recommended, generally favorable stereotype against Benito's helpless horror.

What of Don Benito? Throughout the first division of the story Delano sees in Don Benito both a tortured, sensitive soul and a neurotic representative of a decayed aristocracy. The revelation of Babo's plot hardly serves to cancel out this impression. Don Benito has no "sociality," a trait that the good captain admires. If he represents experience as contrasted with Captain Delano's innocence, it is an experience which debilitates, forcing the sickly Spaniard to a final retreat from reality.

Is it significant that *benito* means "a Benedictine" and the Benedictines are Black Monks? Black Friars, as the Negroes are described early in the tale, and a Black Monk together aboard the ruined *San Dominick* seeing nothing but evil in each other! Delano finds wholesome and reassuring the glimpses he has of his jolly whaleboat, his link with the *Bachelor's Delight*, a well-known world where optimism and despair are mixed in normal proportions and kindly authority preserves a friendly order.

Captain Delano, then, is not simply the obtuse observer, a detective-story character who watches the plot unfold. He is in a serious sense the perceiving center, and in his innocent perceptiveness he reveals kinship to Jack Chase and Billy Budd. With Delano as our guide we see that the world is not neatly dichotomized, does not fall into a simple Manichean dualism. As in "The Encantadas," "Often ill comes from good, as good from ill." As in the "Maldive Shark," one may find "asylum in the jaws of the Fates." Gray—mixed black and white—is now the thematic color of

"Benito Cereno." We see now why it is that at the opening of the story Amasa Delano rises shortly after a gray dawn to examine the strange sail coming into the dun bay; why the sea is sleeked like waved lead, the sky forming a gray surtout; why the *San Dominick* sails through shreds of fog over leaden swells; why gray fowl flit through gray vapors: "Shadows present, foreshadowing deeper shadows to come."

One major puzzling element in the story remains. Why did Melville include the long, mainly unchanged extract from Captain Delano's published account of his affair with the Spanish ship? It involves considerable repetition of what has been told before, and it changes the tone of the story. A recapitulation, some clarifying, some relaxing of tension are clearly in order even if "Benito Cereno" is read as an overly ornate detective story, a kind of television melodrama that divides its characters into unequivocally good guys and bad guys. But when the story is read in this way, the length of the extract must seem tediously excessive to the most tolerant critic. It becomes easy to charge Melville with ineptitude in handling his source (and some ineptitude there may be, a failure in exclusiveness). It becomes easy, too, to suggest that Melville simply failed to rework properly materials he had thought of expanding to book length or to say that he padded the story by one-fourth because he was paid space rates by *Putnam's*. But as soon as "Benito Cereno" is read as a gray story, the long extract is seen in new perspective.

We have been in the world of the mystery thriller, but that is not the world in which Melville intends to leave us. The extract adds verisimilitude in a very important way: as the brief reference to Barber and Fletcher persuades us that genuine affection may exist between Negroes and Englishmen, so the long extract imposes the sanction of reality upon the total meaning of the story. By expanding the story to include the world of fact, Melville forces the reader to contemplate its web of ideas in the light of corollary, existential problems. Among the problems would inevitably be questions about the nature of freedom and slavery. In 1855 these questions were urgently in the minds of all his readers. They had been dealt with frequently, most popularly only four years earlier by Mrs. Stowe.

"Benito Cereno" is not to be thought of as an anti-antislavery piece, and by our final interpretation Melville shows no signs of wishing to emulate Mrs. Stowe in reverse, that is by creating a Christlike white man to match against her black, martyred Uncle Tom. Don Benito is not a deeply perceptive martyr: the hypochondriac dies of his own inadequacy, of his inability to face or transcend the horror of life. On the other hand, by the interpretation urged here, "Benito Cereno" speaks to the burning issue of slavery as, knowing Melville, we would expect it to.

The relationship between master and slave in Latin America was not so different from that in the United States as to encourage Melville to suppose the whites all good, the blacks appropriate symbols of evil. (Slavery and the slave trade carried their typical ills with them to both continents. Some of the images that Melville attaches to the *San Dominick* remind us that the Brazilians called slave ships from Angola *tumbeiros,* floating coffins.) The fictional world and the real world come into close congruence when, in the extract from Delano's narrative, Melville represents white Spaniards as attempting to stab shackled slaves after the capture of the *San Dominick.* "Benito Cereno," we see, is by the man who at a time when calmness was needed pleaded for understanding treatment of the South in his supplement to *Battle-Pieces* (1866) but classed himself among those "who always abhorred slavery as an atheistical iniquity." It is by the man who, in a more heated moment, wrote in *Mardi* (1849):

> "Pray, heaven!" cried Yoomey, "they may yet find a way to loose their bonds without one drop of blood. But hear me, Oro! were there no other way, and should their master not relent, all honest hearts must cheer this tribe of Hamo on: though they cut their chains with blades thrice edged and gory to the haft!"

Comparison of the extract with Captain Delano's original *Narrative of Voyages and Travels* reveals that Melville went to great trouble to revise his source. Although the moral meaning of the source is comparable to the moral meaning of the story, the source is too crassly candid and too naively pessimistic to suit Melville. In the source, Don Benito, himself, is caught in the act of stabbing a shackled slave; he proves to be dishonest in money matters and practices gross ingratitude towards Delano. In the source Delano takes a crudely pessimistic, juvenile view of life's moral mysteries; he cannot find it in his soul that he has ever deserved the miseries of the ingratitude he has experienced.

Modified, made more complex and mature, the moral view of Delano in the source becomes that which Melville distils into the story. The sins and confusions that the living Yankee captain recognized in life are drawn by Melville into his tale. For life's ultimate moral mysteries he had no solution, but he struggled to bring us into their presence. In the end, to select merely one example, the wound on Babo's face is not a horrid, Gothic detail, nor is it evidence of iron-willed satanism. Though self-inflicted, it may betoken cruelties visited on Babo's race by the whites. Beyond this, it may be emblematic of those psychic wounds that each man inflicts on himself or on his fellow. Babo's character is like all character, deeply mysterious. Nature, human and external, is neither Locke's state of unmixed peace and good will nor Hobbes' *bellum omnium contra omnes.*

Read for the second time, "Benito Cereno" is, like a Greek tragedy, an exercise in dramatic irony. On first reading the irony is retrospective: the revelation of the entire ironic situation breaks upon the reader after the action of the story is completed. Consequently, the fundamental, weighty ironies of the story have little to do with maintaining interest and integrating the story structurally for first readers. But these ironies do lend unifying strength to the structure when viewed retrospectively.

Admittedly, Melville made unusual demands on his readers. We must deal with shifting symbols, reflexive structure, and ambiguity of moral vision. Admittedly he placed a sudden and heavy burden on a slender framework, the conventional mystery-and-key organization. There is, moreover, the "technical" difficulty that Melville's key opens a succession of obstinate doors and that our task as readers is unfinished until we stand beyond the last one. Then apparently disjointed or senseless parts fall into their due places. Then we contemplate the ambivalence of a writer who took a mixed (if not undecided) view of reality. This view of reality is at least akin to that of our century and excites our sympathy. If not profoundly tragic, it is, nonetheless, far removed from the common optimism of Melville's time, whether transcendental or scientific.

R. W. B. LEWIS

Melville After "Moby-Dick":
The Tales

"Failure is the true test of greatness,"
Herman Melville remarked in his essay on Hawthorne (1850). He was
speaking of the artist's need to risk defeat by constantly attempting more
demanding and original creative enterprises; and, like Faulkner in our day,
Melville always honored the daring failure over the safe success. "If it be
said," he contended (half anticipating Faulkner's remark about Hemingway), "that continual success is a proof that a man wisely knows his powers,
it is only to be added that, in that case, he knows them to be small."
Melville must have known his own powers to be great ones: he was, at the
very moment, in the midst of his most powerful work and spectacular critical
failure, *Moby-Dick*. But just as he had a zest for the overreaching artistic
effort, so Melville grew to have a special psychological affinity with defeat,
almost a bias toward it. "Praise be to God for the failure!" is the motto of
one of his slighter stories; and in *The Encantadas* he located his symbol of
worshipable humanity "not in the laureled victor, but in this vanquished
one," Hunilla, the Chola widow. It is in a context of such affinities and
beliefs that the writing here examined is to be measured.

For the most part, the stories and poems written after *Moby-Dick*
represented new directions for Melville's imagination, new challenges to
his shaping power; and they were written during what are generally regarded
as Melville's long years of failure, neglect, and silence—following the large

From *Trials of the Word: Essays in American Literature and the Humanistic Tradition*. Copyright
© 1965 by R. W. B. Lewis. Yale University Press.

misunderstanding of *Moby-Dick* and the critical catastrophe of *Pierre* (1852). Some of the items were no doubt, as Melville said about his book-length poem *Clarel* to an English admirer, "Eminently adapted for unpopularity," given the habits and expectations of the American reading public in Melville's lifetime. But, while the imagery of defeat and of physical wreckage and spiritual ruin abounds, Melville's work after *Pierre* and in media other than the novel comprises an extraordinarily successful achievement. It is a body of work, moreover, that expresses a steadily deepening tone of authority—even, perhaps, of metaphysical and religious authority. In those buried years, Melville came to speak in all eloquence with what Scott Fitzgerald would call "the authority of failure."

Still, it is useful to approach that achievement and that authority from the moment of Melville's encounter with Nathaniel Hawthorne. They met in 1850, not long after Melville, in the immensity of his enthusiasm for *Mosses from an Old Manse*, contributed the essay on Hawthorne to the *Literary World*. Most of what Melville had to say in that essay—his metaphysical expostulations, his insight into Shakespearean tragedy, his passion for paradox as the great vehicle of truth, his search for the robustly native American writer, his sense of the fellowship of creative genius the world round—this tells us, of course, a good deal more about Melville's view of life and of art than about Hawthorne's. But as a result of "Hawthorne and his Mosses," there developed between the two men the most illuminating relationship in the history of American literature; not the less illuminating because it was strained and flawed and doomed to brevity; and not less because, although each had much to teach the other (Melville felt that "this Hawthorne has dropped germinous seeds into my soul"), the writers were in fact moving in almost exactly opposite directions.

Melville's letters chart the course of this curious friendship. "When the big hearts strike together," he wrote Hawthorne, "the concussion is a little stunning." But Melville had a more avid taste than did Hawthorne for intellectual and emotional concussion; as, one feels sure, he did for the "ontological heroics" he speaks of looking forward to enjoying with the older man. On Melville's side, the relationship reached its peak of intensity in the almost uncontrollable and mystical excitement with which he acknowledged Hawthorne's reception (evidently both discerning and sympathetic) of *Moby-Dick*. At that instant, Melville felt Hawthorne to be a "divine magnet" to whom "my magnet responds"; he felt that "the Godhead is broken up like the bread at the Supper," and that he and Hawthorne were the pieces. Hawthorne did not have the temperament to reply in kind; and in the following year, when Melville was being so savagely belabored in the press for *Pierre*, the friendship seems to have gone stale—perhaps, as one or two critics have suggested, because neither Hawthorne nor anyone else could have supplied Melville with the kind of protection and comfort he thought he needed. The last extant letter is dated November 1852; and shortly thereafter Hawthorne went abroad for a long stay. The two men met at least once again in 1856, when Melville stopped off for a few days with the Hawthornes in Liverpool; but Melville was to believe that they had been "estranged in life / And neither in the wrong." Such was the burden of Melville's "Monody," a poem that is almost certainly Melville's obituary both to Hawthorne and to their friendship.

But, as I have said, these two enormously gifted spirits were moving in opposite directions from the moment they met; and it was only Melville's constant fascination with the mating of opposites that made any friendship at all possible between them. To begin with, Melville, in 1850, had five novels behind him (*Typee, Omoo, Mardi, Redburn,* and *Whitejacket*); he was occupied with *Moby-Dick* and after that with *Pierre;* but his novelistic aspirations were becoming ever more thwarted, and within a couple of years his energies and interests would turn decisively toward the shorter form, toward the story or tale or novella. In 1850, Hawthorne, on the other hand, was done with the shorter form; he had behind him a number of masterful stories and tales, and his endeavors in this vein had reached their climax and end in that very great novella *The Scarlet Letter;* he had, indeed, already advanced into the field of long fiction and had almost completed the first of his "novels," *The House of the Seven Gables.* By the time (in August 1852) that Melville urged Hawthorne to make a tale similar to Hawthorne's own "Wakefield," out of the "Agatha anecdote," the proposal was in every sense anachronistic. Hawthorne was right, in his evasive but kindly way, to suggest instead that Melville should undertake the thing. And Melville did, though without success; it was his first invasion of the short story, and it led swiftly enough to *Bartleby* and *The Encantadas.*

More importantly, Melville and Hawthorne congenitally moved in opposite directions of mental and imaginative inquiry: as one sentence in Melville's letter about "Agatha" reminds us. Concluding his ruminations, Melville tells Hawthorne: "You have a skeleton of actual reality to build about with fulness & veins & beauty." The remark bespeaks Melville's customary method: that of beginning with the actual, the bare bones of the case, often with the personally experienced, and then enlarging by the resources of art toward fullness and beauty. His writing at its best seems to be palpably thickening and stretching, as the actual gives birth to some breath-taking glimpse into the generalized condition of man. Melville's characteristic accomplishment (for example, in *The Encantadas*) was to move from a sort of journalistic immediacy to an exposure of some grave and permanent principle or element that must be at work (even if perniciously at work) in human experience; his creative torment was the awareness, which he often dramatized, that the effort so to expand, to enlarge, was incalculably difficult. Such, however, was neither Hawthorne's accomplishment nor his torment. Although he did of course draw upon the actual and his own experience, nonetheless, and especially in his shorter fiction, Hawthorne habitually began with some perennial human impulse and then sought for the concrete terms by which he might embody it. Hawthorne, in a word, really did approach the allegorical mode, though little that he wrote can be classed as pure allegory; but Melville, for all his allegorical hints and leanings, approached rather the form of the fable. All the difference between them can be suggested by comparing Hawthorne's "Wakefield" (which Melville so admired) and Melville's *Bartleby*. Both are accounts of self-impelled isolates; Wakefield is "the Outcast of the Universe," and Bartleby seems "alone, absolutely alone in the universe." But Hawthorne's capital letters point to a fixed type of human situation that he is, primarily, trying to illustrate; while much of the odd charm of *Bartleby* is its tantalizing escape from fixity. Bartleby remains a mystery just because he is irredeemably an individual, not finally and fully explicable by any general theory of human conduct, toward which the creative effort nonetheless inclines.

Hawthorne must have taught Melville a good deal about the formal possibilities of fiction; and his talent for the dark insinuation must have encouraged Melville in his desire (as he says about Shakespeare in the Hawthorne essay) to express the "deep far-way things in him," to probe "the very axis of reality." Hawthorne's fiction also provided Melville with the major example in America of the poetic resource by which such probing could be attempted—the resource of the complex symbol. On his part, Hawthorne was perhaps reminded by Melville of the inestimable value of the particular, the potent vitality of the immediate: certainly, *The Blithedale Romance*, the only work of fiction that Hawthorne began and completed during the years in question, is by all odds his most "realistic" work, the one most rooted in the actual. But then they moved on, in literally and physically opposite directions—Hawthorne away from the obscurity of a customs house into the bright light of quite considerable popularity; Melville away from his own considerable popularity toward the obscurity of his own eventual job as a customs inspector—and between them there fell a silence.

When Melville said in *The Encantadas* that he worshiped humanity not in the figure of the victor but in the figure of the vanquished, he was giving precise statement to the tragic sense that possessed him in the 1850s. It is a sense that communicates more directly to our own age of wholesale wreckage and defeat—when the laurels go so often and so resoundingly to the worst of men and of causes—than it did to the confident America of Melville's time. Melville, like Albert Camus (who said, via Dr. Rieux in *The Plague*, that "I feel more solidarity with the vanquished than with the saints"), found human dignity in the little dark corners of life; not among the powerful and successful, but among the oppressed, the afflicted, the defeated; among the victims of God or of nature or, simply of "things." In the character of Captain Ahab, Melville had offered a titanic image of magnificent defeat; but in the tales of the fifties, the focus was rather on the touching and forlorn.

Bannadonna, the arrogant Renaissance architect in *The Bell-Tower*, pursues his tragic course in the classical manner; he is the person of exceptional abilities and overweening pride who brings upon himself his own violent destruction. Ironically, this was the only short story of Melville's reprinted during his lifetime—reprinted twice, in fact, and once under the general title of *Little Classics: Tragedy*. Melville's genuinely classic conception of tragedy would find expression in his Civil War poetry; but in the years immediately following *Pierre*, he evinced an unclassical involvement with pathos. More representative than Bannadonna, at this time, are persons like Bartleby, "a bit of wreck in mid-Atlantic"; or Hunilla, with her tearless bleak endurance; or Jimmy Rose, transformed at a stroke from a wealthy man-about-town to a sandwich-filching parasite—"poor, poor Jimmy—God guard us all—poor Jimmy Rose!"; or the blank-looking girls in the infernal papermill, with their pallid cheeks and pale virginity; or Benito Cereno, almost literally shocked to death by his encounter with evil. Vanquished ones like these characterize Melville's collection of short stories, *The Piazza Tales* in 1856, and make incarnate in their variously pathetic ways Melville's then current estimate of life.

Instances of physical collapse or decay are often associated with these cases of human misfortune. The fall of the tower of Bannadonna in an earthquake is sheer melodrama; but elsewhere we observe the "sad disrepair" of Don Benito's ship, the *San Dominick*, which looks as though put together and launched from Ezekiel's valley of dry bones, and the awe-inspiring barrenness of the cindery Encantadas which seem to be Ezekiel's valley itself. We can watch Melville, in his letter to Hawthorne about the

proposed "Agatha anecdote," lingering with mournful affection over a projected account of the slow decay of Agatha's mailbox and the post on which
it stands:

> To this *post* they must come for their letters. And, of course, daily young
> Agatha goes—for seventeen years she goes thither daily. As her hopes
> gradually decay in her, so does the post itself and the little box decay.
> The post rots in the ground at last. Owing to its being little used—hardly
> used at all—grass grows rankly about it. At last a little bird nests in it.
> At last the post falls.

The passage does, indeed, reflect Melville's continuing taste for Gothic
moldering, along with his alertness to what he called "the linked analogies"—between the concrete (the post and the box) and the soul of man
(Agatha's hopes). But, at the same time, the lines quoted suggest another
significant aspect—namely, the source and the nature of Melville's idea of
defeat.

It is easy enough to say that Melville's sensitivity to failure in the
mid-fifties was the direct consequence of his own "failure" as a novelist,
after several years of considerable "success." What is important is Melville's
view of just what had happened, of where the failure lay. In his view, the
point was not only that his last two novels had failed to sell widely—though
this was a fact of great seriousness to him (dollars, as he said, always damned
him). It was not only that American critics did not like his work, or
neglected it—though Melville shared with many another American writer
a much higher regard for British than for American critics and reviewers.
What had really happened, Melville evidently believed, was something
rather different. What had failed was an effort at communication. A recurring motif during these years, accordingly, is the motif of the undelivered
letter or the misapprehended sign.

In *Benito Cereno*, both the wretched Spanish nobleman and members
of his crew attempt to convey by sign language the reality of their desperate
situation; and good Captain Delano fails consistently to receive their messages. Closer to the "Agatha" passage above and probably carried over from
its rhetoric is the picture of the island "post-office" in *The Encantadas*:

> It may seem very strange to talk of post-offices in this barren region, yet
> post-offices are occasionally to be found there. They consist of a stake
> and a bottle. The letters being not only sealed, but corked. They are
> generally deposited by captains of Nantucketers for the benefit of passing
> fishermen, and contain statements as to what luck they had in whaling
> or tortoise-hunting. Frequently, however, long months and months, whole

years glide by and no applicant appears. The stake rots and falls, presenting
no very exhilarating subject.

A still less exhilarating subject and the most memorable example of this
theme occur at the end of *Bartleby*, when the narrator reports the rumor
that Bartleby had at one time worked as a subordinate clerk in the Dead
Letter Office in Washington. What could be more terrible for a man prone
to hopelessness like Bartleby, the narrator asks, than the business of "continually handling these dead letters, and assorting them for the flame. . . .
On errands of life," he adds, appalled, "these letters speed to death."

So Melville's letters of life—his novels—had in his view of the
matter sped to death, undelivered, unread by the addressee, the public;
destined only to be destroyed. Melville felt that he had somehow failed to
deliver the messages that shaped themselves so urgently in his imagination;
and for a writer as profoundly personal and expressive as Melville, a failure
of this kind was apt to be devastating. He could not—like Henry James
and to some extent like Hawthorne—rest in satisfied contemplation of his
own created objects; nor, once those objects were, metaphorically, destroyed, could he assuage his spirit in contemplation of the ideal that the
object had made concrete—as he admires Hawthorne for seeming to say
in "The Artist of the Beautiful." But what he could do, and what in these
stories he did do, was to convert his sense of the failure of communication
into a central fictional theme; and to make expert shorter fiction out of
the failure of his longer fiction. It was a courageous undertaking indeed;
and it has been properly celebrated by Hart Crane, in his poem "At Melville's Tomb," as the artistic effort by which Melville is to be identified:

> Often beneath the waves, wide from this ledge
> The dice of dead men's bones he saw bequeath
> An embassy. Their numbers as he watched,
> Beat on the dusky shore and were obscured.

Crane had to explain to his editor that his intention had been to relate
the bones of dead mariners, men who failed to reach the shore alive, with
"certain messages undelivered," certain experiences not finally communicated; both the bones and the messages beat on the dusky shore and get
obscured. The passage is complex; but it testifies in its oblique way to an
essential aspect of Melville, as well as to the sureness of Crane's understanding of it.

To formulate success and failure in terms of communicaiton is,
needless to say, to find the focus of human experience in the question of

community—that is, of the relation between the individual and community. The tales of the fifties contain some of the most extreme and disturbing images of isolation that modern literature has recorded; and they are the more disturbing because, Bannadonna apart, these luckless men and women are not cut off from humanity through pride, like Ahab ("and Ahab stands alone among the millions of the peopled earth"), or through some sinful act, like Coleridge's mariner. They are rather the victims of a calamity: of a flaw in the psychological mechanism, like Bartleby; of an altogether "absurd" accident, like Hunilla; of the brutality of other men, like Benito Cereno. And, conversely, the one story in the group that breathes an air of perfect contentment is itself an image of perfect community—the account of an evening spent in a London men's club, *The Paradise of Bachelors*. This semi-fictional fusing of several dinners at the Elm and the Erechtheum Clubs in December 1854 is Melville's worldly, even lip-smacking counterpart to James's "The Great Good Place"; and it offers a Melvillean ideal of genial masculine companionship: "It was the very perfection of quiet absorption of good living, good drinking, good feeling, and good talk. We were a band of brothers. Comfort—fraternal, household comfort, was the grand trait of the affair." One should probably not make too much of the celibate aspect of the English Paradise; for what Melville rejoices in is less the absence of women—of the heterosexual element—than the absence of families ("You could plainly see that these easy-hearted men had no wives or children to give an anxious thought"). And, beyond that, the situation so handsomely set forth is a mode of sexless companionship, in the basic meaning of "companionship" as a deep sharing of nourishment, of both physical and spiritual bread. It is the antithesis of the situation of Bartleby and the others.

In the course of his sketches of isolation and defeat, Melville observes and dramatizes a variety of responses among those for whom there is no Erechtheum Club available. At one extreme is Don Benito, who summons up the courage to plunge out of his confinement and rejoin humanity in the friendly boat of Amasa Delano (a moment reminiscent of the scene Melville selected for special praise in *The House of the Seven Gables*, "where Clifford . . . would fain throw himself forth from the window to join the procession"); but thereafter the Spaniard yields to the horror of his experience and slides helplessly toward death. At quite another extreme is the Chola widow, that "lone shipwrecked soul," whose isolation is absolute, whose plight is the most hideous—and whose fortitude is the most enduring. Somewhere in between is the canny, unashamed adjustment of Jimmy Rose, who emerges from his spell of self-concealment after the disaster, "to crawl through life, and peep among the marbles and ma-hoganies for contumelious tea and toast"; and Bartleby, who, bit of un-salvageable wreckage that he is, yet continues to utter his brief refusal, who says, "No," to the end—not, "No! in thunder," as Melville imagined Hawthorne saying, but, "No," in a soft intractable undertone.

It has been sufficiently suggested, I trust, that these portraits of the vanquished and victimized are not themselves instances of *artistic* failure or of *literary* defeat. On the contrary, the tales of the fifties represent a very far reach in shorter American fiction: though we have to remove them some distance from the enormous shadow of *Moby-Dick* before their qualities become visible. *Jimmy Rose* may be not much more than an anecdote, though it is carried beyond its slender limits by a surprisingly appropriate verbal vigor. Even *The Bell-Tower*, while "literary" in a bad sense of the word, keeps stirring the edges of our imagination by the hint of a meaning (about cultural history, about race and sex) much more interesting than the moral so heavily insisted on. *The Tartarus of Maids* is a story of perhaps exaggerated reputation that threatens to bore us with the strained comedy of its sexual and anatomical allegory; but, again, the narrative tends to slip out of its frame of contrived fantasy to touch some ultimate in human, and especially in feminine, degradation, some final reduction of the female in a mechanized world to a sexless and, as it were, devaginated thing. These are stories that reward our best attention; once read, they refuse to be dislodged from their little niches in our memory. But three other stories do more than that: they add to our store of imaginative understanding and of beauty; once read, they become part of the way we look into life and appraise it. These, of course, are *Bartleby*, *The Encantadas*, and *Benito Cereno*.

About *Bartleby*, the least ought to be said; for it is a fable, almost a parable, something that depends, for our satisfaction, on remaining intact. It provides an image in steady slow motion of the gradual extinction of spirit, of the dissolution of all but the fact of will in a single human psyche—not the will *toward* anything, not active desire, but the faculty itself. Bartleby is a voluntary phantom, the dim underside of Captain Ahab. His thinning actuality is perceived in its contrast with the Dickensian fullness of urban life, the Wall Street office, the two volatile clerks and the impish call-boy, the busy activities of the legal profession, and the prudent and well-intentioned narrator. Seen from that vantage point of cozy normality and unquestioning conformity, Bartleby flickers with ever-decreasing light and ever-increasing mystery. The narrator's final exclamation ("Ah, Bartleby! Ah, humanity!") suggests that in the declining person of Bartleby he—and Melville—had identified some type of human character and experience; but all that has been identified is the mystery of life. The story's mild paradox is that it is the narrator's failure to make contact with Bartleby ("It was his soul that suffered, and his soul I could not reach") that leads him to a sense of common humanity; he feels "a fraternal melancholy." A glimpse of fraternity is thus stimulated by the discovered absence thereof; what is shared is an awareness of darkness; and at the end all we know is that we know nothing.

The Encantadas offers the inquiring reader a more strenuous problem of judgment. If Bartleby is all compact, The Encantadas is all meandering sketchiness; and nothing is less clear, at first sound, than its exact tone. A contemporary reviewer referred to the work as "a series of charming descriptions," as though it were a contribution to pastoral literature; but we shall not be far wrong if we take it, instead, as a sustained and conscious exercise in the antipastoral mode. The pastoral is an account of the world in its unfallen state, as nostalgically imagined after the fact of the fall (the definition can arguably hold even for the Virgilian pastoral); but Melville's key contention here is that "In no world but a fallen one could such lands exist." The Encantadas is not—as was so much American writing contemporary with Melville—an artistic transformation of the actual and fallen world; it is an extension of it. It surveys a certain terrain and certain objects and experiences to conclude, as Cardinal Newman once concluded after surveying human history, that the data collected showed the human race must be "implicated in some terrible and aboriginal calamity."

Melville searches the islands for signs of the absolute consequences of just such an aboriginal calamity; as Charles Darwin, by a suggestive coincidence, had earlier explored the same islands for material to use in his study of the biological rise of man. Indeed, Melville's sketches of the Galapagos archipelago (a thick cluster of islands some six hundred miles west of Ecuador) are at once a scientific description, in the Darwinian manner, and an adumbration of the moral and social world that is the so-called civilized home of modern man. That home is kept present to our minds by the story's allegorical tendency (we should not use a stronger word), which is indicated throughout by the quotations from Melville's favorite allegorical poem, The Faerie Queene, and finds its most vivid expression in the hallucination at the end of Sketch First, when a "scene of social merriment" seems to fade into a scene of lonely, haunted woods, and the representative of the Encantadas, a gigantic tortoise, crawls across the ballroom floor. Not only the tortoise with his reminder of mortality, but equally the heroic Hunilla, the Calibanesque Oberlus, the pirates and ghosts and lizards, the "runaways, castaways, solitaries, gravestones etc.": all these beings (Melville suggests) inhabit not only the faraway Galapagos, as a matter of scientific fact; they also inhabit—metaphorically—our modern civilization, they inhabit our drawing rooms, they inhabit our personalities.

The power of *The Encantadas*, in short, derives—as so often with Melville—from its linked analogies, from the creative relation between the abundant concrete and the range of moral and psychological and metaphysical implication. No work of Melville's is so close in its narrative strategy to *Moby-Dick*, a book that was once also praised for being, so to speak, a charming description of whaling voyages. In *Moby-Dick*, we have the leisurely and thorough account of whaling, its history and geography and folklore, the exact dimensions of the various species of whales and their heads and members, the techniques of harpooning; so, in *The Encantadas*, we attend to the skimpily known history of the islands, the reports of visiting frigates, the names and dates of the chief authorities, a survey of the landscape and of plant and animal life, the blurry reports of settlements, uprisings, and freebooting. Like *Moby-Dick*, too, the shorter work—while, similarly, throwing off a steady shower of allegorical sparks—gathers dramatic momentum and bursts into a sudden new vitality toward the end. The dramatic focus of *The Encantadas* is the successive appearances and stories of the Chola Widow Hunilla and the Hermit Oberlus in Sketches Eighth and Ninth, a pairing of images in a sort of dyptich. The opposite possibilities they represent have already been stated fairly flatly at the opening of Sketch Second, where, speaking of the tortoise, Melville remarks that "dark and melancholy as it is up the back, [it] still possesses a bright side: . . . Enjoy the bright . . . but be honest, and don't deny the black. Neither should he, who cannot turn the tortoise from its natural position . . . for that cause declare the creature to be one total inky blot" (compare this with the "Try-Works" meditation in *Moby-Dick*). Hunilla and Oberlus were in fact actual human beings, one a Peruvian and the other an Irishman; they come to us as living individuals; but within the prepared atmosphere of allegory they also enlarge into symbols of the human potential—that of grandeur amid defeat and that of bestial degradation. Hunilla, utterly alone except for her dogs and the transient brigands by whom she has been periodically assaulted, embodies what there is of spiritual brightness in the grim hell of the actual; Oberlus has become an animal and an isolate by choice.

Opposition, to speak colloquially, was Melville's middle name; and contrariety is no less central in *Benito Cereno*. Here we have one of modern literature's great enactments of the greatest of all oppositions, to the perennial eye of the poet: that between appearance and reality—concretely, between the apparent situation on board the *San Dominick,* the apparent relation between black man and white man, between slave and master, obedience and command; and the reality of all that. Melville's handling of his story—wherein the slow-witted, kindhearted American, Amasa Delano, boards the Spanish ship, explores it, talks with the Captain and his Negro "servant" Babo, and departs without ever gaining more than the most fleeting impression of the truth—has been much praised. The protective innocence of Delano has been analyzed, and the depths of Babo (the slave who has in fact seized command by means of horrifying violence) have been sounded with various psychological instruments. Melville's exploitation of the element of color in this story has likewise been admired; and his creative techniques studied by comparing the novella to its easily available source in Delano's *Narrative of Voyages and Travels.* But another aspect is still worth considering—that is, whether and how the central opposition is "resolved."

Superficially, the resolution occurs when the narrative of the apparent situation—presented through the undiscerning eyes of Amasa Delano—is followed by the narrative of what had really happened, in the deposition made by the ailing Don Benito at the court in Lima, during the trial of the Negroes. That legal document has caused critical trouble and has resulted, for example, in a hostile verdict on *Benito Cereno* by Newton Arvin, in the best critical study of Melville yet written. The charge is that the deposition is a dry letdown after the murky excitements of the longer section that precedes it, and that in any case Melville had shirked his artistic responsibility by bringing in the (actual) court testimony and laying it down flat in his pages. As to the letdown, the deposition will probably prove engrossing enough, if read without prejudice. But as to the artistic problem, the documentary pages may well comprise one of Melville's happiest strokes. For Melville's point in thus juxtaposing these two so different narrative modes and voices is this: *that neither version of the events contains the truth.* No reader doubts that Delano's version is false, that he got everything wrong way round; but we should recognize, I think, that Benito Cereno's version is equally flawed by an inadequacy of perception, equally remote from the whole reality of the adventure. The remoteness, in the second case, is conveyed precisely by the language of the deposition—by those abstractions of the legal vocabulary that evade all contact with the blood and stuff of experience. We are presumably intended to accept the Spaniard's statements of the external facts, the process of revolt and of massacre, the names and numbers of those that killed or were killed. But for Melville facts were not truth and, wrongly handled, could be an obstacle to truth. The Spaniard was quite unequipped by his aristocratic temperament to grasp the motives at work, the raging desire of the Negroes for freedom, the murderous animosity that slavery begot in them; as Captain Delano was unequipped by his temperament to grasp the force and presence of evil. Neither narrative, accordingly, rises to the truth of the affair; and yet this is a curious instance of two wrongs making a right—or, rather, of two falsehoods making a truth between them. As our minds play back and forth between the two versions, we find each making us more and more aware of what is false in the other. And so the truth comes finally into view, as contained in the continuing tension between alternate versions, in a subtly and knowingly unresolved duplicity.

Another complaint against *Benito Cereno* is an alleged lack of political morality on Melville's part: as though he had failed to indicate sympathy with the Negroes' lust for freedom; as though he were blind to the evil of slavery. But it is Don Benito who is blind to that evil, not Melville. Melville was profoundly aware not only of the slavery issue but of its ambiguities and complexities, and his awareness is conveyed in a doubleness of narrative mode whereby moral guilt and moral myopia are subtly distributed to all participants in the drama. It can be noted, meanwhile, how frequent is the theme of insurrection in the tales of the fifties; the notion of revolt pressed hard upon Melville's imagination. In addition to the bloody uprising of the slaves in *Benito Cereno*, we recall the mutiny of the lawless mariners against the Dog-King, in Sketch Seventh of *The Encantadas*. Bartleby himself is a sort of passive, unconquerable *homme révolté*. And though, in the uncannily prophetic climax of *The Bell-Tower*, it is the machine that mysteriously turns on the man and destroys him, Melville supplied a motto for the story that points to the analogy intended and relates *The Bell-Tower* unexpectedly and very closely to *Benito Cereno*: "Like negroes, these powers own man sullenly; mindful of their higher master; while serving, plot revenge." More generally still, Melville—as I have been stressing on almost every page—was singularly attuned to conflict as the very definition of experience; to opposition and ambiguity intensifying betimes into frightful collision, and with neither side (to adopt his remark about Hawthorne and himself) altogether in the wrong. No American writer was better prepared to measure the full significance of the quarrel over slavery that led to rebellion and, in 1861, grew into armed conflict with the outbreak of the national Civil War.

But if he was prepared to take its measure, he was only partially prepared to express his understanding of the conflict in the literary genre to which he was now turning—the genre of lyric and narrative poetry. After the failure of *Pierre*, Melville had applied himself to the shorter fictional form; now, after another effort in the longer mode (*The Confidence-Man*, 1857) and another critical and financial failure, he abandoned prose fiction completely and wrote nothing but poetry until, more than thirty years later, he came back to prose for the last time to write that rusty masterpiece, *Billy Budd*.

PAUL BRODTKORB, JR.

Ishmael: The Nature and Forms of Despair

"Call me Ishmael," we are told. But that name is equivocally stated, despite the abruptly imperative form of its declaration. The narrator precisely does *not* say that his name *is* Ishmael; or even that he is called Ishmael as a kind of nickname. "Call me Ishmael," he says, and immediately the diction of affable informality followed by the shock of the biblical name which is both formal and highly unlikely puts us in the presence of someone who for reasons of his own would rather not say who he really is.

If "Ishmael" is self-adopted, it is, with all its allusiveness, doubtless a more accurate designation of him than its sayer's real name, for it clearly signifies his sense of himself and his world. But because behind the show of affability a real name is withheld, Ishmael remains to some extent a stranger, and a man in a false position; and because he does, as soon as the self-bestowed name is spoken, the shadow of nothingness is upon the book.

That shadow lengthens when we note the contradictory details that slips of memory betray the narrator into. The playful but ultimately serious hyperbole, intended to win us over; the authoritative reporting of unknowable or imaginary events; the fanciful lies, such as the Town-Ho's story—these darken the shadow. "Ishmael," we soon discover, is a storyteller in every sense; he tells us a fish story that, like most fish stories, is partly true and partly false.

Yet he is not especially anxious to conceal this from us. On the contrary, "storyteller" is the first and continuing guise in which he presents himself. At times he explicitly discusses the problems of a storyteller in creating atmosphere and plausibility. At other times he shows himself manipulating the truth:

> "Do tell, now," cried, Bildad, "is this Philistine a regular member of Deacon Deuteronomy's meeting? I never saw him going there, and I pass it every Lord's day."
> "I don't know anything about Deacon Deuteronomy or his meeting," said I, "all I know is, that Queequeg here is a born member of the First Congregational Church. He is a deacon himself, Queequeg is."
> "Young man," said Bildad sternly, "thou art skylarking with me—explain thyself, thou young Hittite. What church dost thee mean? answer me."
> Finding myself thus hard pushed, I replied. . . .
>
> (XVIII)

Caught out in a lie, Ishmael eludes Bildad's wrath by enthusiastic embroidery of his story's loose ends. In content and circumstances, the incident is typical of Ishmael's lies, the facts of which if based on actuality are already highly interpreted by self-interested exegesis. More important, however, is what this sort of incident—the Town-Ho's story, though a more disinterested, virtuoso lie, is similar in this respect—suggests about the audience of an Ishmaelean lie: Ishmael lies to those who invite his mockery. He lies to the earnest ones of the earth: the owners, aristocrats, and authorities; the stern, the righteous, or the self-satisfied; all who because of the pompous security they command are gullible. He lies, in short, to the Bildads who in being false comforters take false comfort. He lies because he strongly suspects either that their truths are lies also; or that they use their truths like lies, for their own ends.

Similarly, Ishmael lies to us: the comfortable readers of adventure stories like *Typee, Omoo,* and *Moby Dick* who kill our boredom by distorting what boredom means. We are all in false positions, his attitude seems to say; and it says this at the same time that it says that *his* false position, because it is consciously chosen in full awareness of the alternatives, is more responsible and therefore, perversely, truer than the received and unexamined false positions of others; and in this attitude we may understand a major basis of Ishmael's respect for Ahab, whose defiant despair creates a personal truth so passionately thought-out and passionately willed that often reality crucially seems to conform to it. Like Kierkegaard, Ishmael is despairingly left with the idea that for man, in many complicated ways, subjectivity is truth; or, rather, the only truth is in subjectivity.

One result of all this is that for the pragmatic reader the prevalence of Ishmaelean lies, once recognized, must permeate with nonbeing everything that Ishmael says. Because anything is potentially untrue, the single and final reality of the events of the Pequod's last voyage is to be found in Ishmael's not wholly trustworthy mind. For such a reader, *Moby Dick's* foundations in the actuality that Ishmael pretends to report are very shaky ones: he can never lose his awareness that he is reading a *novel,* not something solid like the history or biography that Captain Veres prefers; moreover, he is reading a peculiarly self-subverting novel that pretends to be true (but clearly isn't) autobiography, which in turn disconcertingly combines features of epic, romance, and Menippean satire. Nowhere is there dry land. Nothing can be trusted to be what it seems, and the reader, if only for self-preservation, must have "doubts of all things earthly" (LXXXV). In a curious way, the reader is forced even against his will to share Ishmaelean attitudes.

But the situation is perhaps not so desperate. Consider the case of Bulkington, the account of whom provides a reassuring example of Ishmael's manipulation for his own purposes of reality. Bulkington is the man "who in mid-winter just landed from a four years' dangerous voyage . . . unrestingly" pushes "off again for still another tempestuous term" (XXIII) as the helmsman of the outsetting Pequod. "A huge favorite" (III) with his previous shipmates aboard the Grampus, Bulkington is a natural leader of men, and a man of singular physique and mentality.

Yet after his appearance as the Pequod's helmsman in the "six-inch chapter" called "The Lee Shore," he inexplicably disappears: "So far as this narrative is concerned," Ishmael says of him, he will be "but a sleeping-partner" (III). Given Bulkington's initial presentation, his noble integrity and intelligence, he ought to have had, like Chekhov's pistol, a major function in the drama: leading the men against Ahab, or, if convinced that Ahab is right, becoming a source of strength for his captain. Yet Bulkington, who ought to be as weightly as his name and body, disappears. Perhaps he died early in the voyage, so that he was absurdly unable to assume the role implied for him; but even this is not recorded. Why not?

The formal answer seems to lie in what *is* given of Bulkington's role: he is the helmsman at the outset of the voyage, and thereafter a "sleeping-partner." A helmsman directs the ship; a sleeping-partner is commonly a partner whose existence is kept secret from the general public, and who takes no overt part in the enterprise with which he is involved even though his capital may dominate it. Ishmael admits (or makes it up out of nothing) Bulkington's existence to us but thereafter suppresses his presence, which finally exists as a "deep" memory embodied in the "six-inch chapter" which is his "stoneless grave" (XXIII). Because that memory is an explanation of Bulkington's motivation, his motivation is what, for purposes of the narrative, Bulkington becomes; as sleeping-partner, that is what he *is*. The motivation attributed to him is a kind of eternal drive toward knowing the truth: up until his last voyage always voyaging, on this last voyage Bulkington faced conclusively his own "ocean-perishing," and facing this final human reality has, according to Ishmael, allowed Bulkington to see "glimpses . . . of that mortally intolerable truth; that all deep, earnest thinking is but the intrepid effort of the soul to keep the open independence of her sea; while the wildest winds of heaven and earth conspire to cast her on the treacherous, slavish shore." Because his motivation here resembles that of both Ishmael and Ahab, comprehending the latter's will to absolute, ultimate knowledge as well as the former's compulsive mental integrity that must admit all contradictory speculation; and because this motivation is what Bulkington *is*; and because his Being-in-this-mode is the helmsman of the outsetting Pequod, thereafter becoming a sleeping-partner whose secret capital is part of the Pequod's value, Bulkington's literary existence is as a kind of animating and directive principle of the voyage. His being expresses that "the highest truth" resides only in the condition of "landlessness"—which is to say that it either (as Ahab thinks) may be found within landlessness, or (as Ishmael suspects) may be landlessness itself. Like Ishmael, Bulkington finds no final answers, but experiences the spirit in which the questions must be framed; like Ahab, he dies and becomes a grim "demigod," whose "apotheosis" is the chapter, as Ahab's is the book.

Bulkington is *used* by Ishmael allegorically. In this use he finds the role wherein, as far as the narrative is concerned, lies his chief reality. If Bulkington's literary existence is given us for the sake of what it means to Ishmael, and if that meaning "is" his spiritual presence, then his *actual* presence must be suppressed; for any one of his three probable roles in actuality would have conflicted with his Ishmael-conferred meaning: if Bulkington supported Ahab, he became the partisan of a delimited portion of the principle he reflects; if he fought Ahab, he similarly denied validity to what by virtue of Ishmael's initial presentation of him is part of himself, as well as competing with the white whale for the office of Ahab's antagonist (Bulkington would have been a more effectual human antagonist than Starbuck; but in Ishmael's intention only Moby Dick could be worthy of meeting Ahab conclusively); and, last, if Bulkington absurdly died before his natural leadership could play out its role, the direction and principle of the voyage would be too contrarily and specifically obliterated. For all such reasons, it does not matter that about Bulkington, Ismael lies.

Ishmael's handling of Bulkington suggests, in fact, that we are not in danger of losing our bearings on his manipulated version of the Pequod's voyage because his major manipulations of reality—his hyperbole, irony, and lies—are in each case open to teleological analysis and, over all, are performed in the service of his vision of the meaning of the truth. In short, Ishmael is simply a writer of fiction. As such, his truth is born of his lies; and given the nature of his truth, it could exist only by virtue of them.

Ishmaelean truth, as Ishmael's total vision of the world manifests it, is the truth of relativity: "There is no quality in this world that is not what it is merely by contrast," he says early in the book (XI); "nothing exists in itself." If things exist only in relation to other things, and assume their qualities by virtue of contrast with other qualities, then just as truth must exist by virtue of lies, Being by virtue of nonbeing, so the self must exist by virtue of the not-self: "O Nature, and O soul of man!" says Ahab, "how far beyond all utterance are your linked analogies! not the smallest atom stirs or lives on matter, but has its cunning duplicate in mind."

Such an ontology must assume an epistemology in which mind and matter are similarly interdependent. The reality of life, Ishmael tells us in the very first chapter of his book, is physically "ungraspable." It exists as an "image" of a "phantom" of itself seen by the water-dreaming Narcissus (who is all of us) in the shifting water-world, which, before it is depths, is reflecting surfaces. Life as man knows it is a phantom image that is experienced superficially and elusively in a momentary present; it is dependent on an unsuspected source which both projects and ambiguously (in the end, mistakenly) perceives it, a relation which prevents it from being directly confronted. The future's attempt to grasp the phantom's solidity must destroy the reality as well as its image. Reality, in other words, is so evasive because at the same time that the seen does not exist apart from the seer, it is nevertheless different from him; and because both terms exist only in tenuous relationship, consciousness cannot be escaped in order to grasp any objective presence. To mistake this, like Narcissus and Ahab, is to risk death.

Meaning, in such a relationship, is as inescapable as it is elusive; and, whatever else it may be, it is first of all *human* meaning, conferred by man in the process of living. Meaning is inescapable because it is generated in the act of perception itself; the very clarity of outline of an object belongs to the meaning that is present in the object's perception. Meaning is human meaning because it existentially "is" only as the doubloon's value "is": conferred by man. Indeed, the doubloon chapter's chief function is to slow down the normal act of perception for the reader's edification: confronting the doubloon, each onlooker notices some details but not others, sees analytically or synthetically, perceives obverse or reverse, notes contexts or not, and in so doing creates partial and finite static value out of what must remain eternally itself and mute—a static value out of a coin which, nailed to the midpoint, is an integral part (the "navel," says Pip) of a ship that moves on a sea that moves on a world itself whirling through the shifting skies. If Ishmaelean man must confer meaning on *things*, the things are processional and the meaning is dictated by the changeable limits of his self-structured experience and the evanescent dominance of his moods. Meaning is an integral part of reality, but reality does not exist apart from consciousness. Reality and meaning *are* the relation of man and world; they are the quality of his concern with the things of his world: a coffin may "be" a coffin, but "by a mere hap" of man's purposeful concern it may also be a sea-chest, then a life buoy—ultimately, in its potentiality it "is" all three at once, for Ishmaelean Being is becoming and is therefore always touched with possibility; with, that is, nothingness.

On such assumptions is founded the assertion that the highest truth is to be found in landlessness alone; that it is "shoreless, indefinite as God" (XXIII). It is why at sea each gam suggests a potential, *established* view of the whale, even unto the status of national attitudes; because, in the end as in the beginning, the overwhelming, unarguable facticity of the whale can be elucidated *only* in terms "of what has been promiscuously said, thought, fancied, and sung of Leviathan, by many nations and generations, including our own" (from the "Extracts" supplied by a sub-sub-librarian).

It is the reason, also, that Ishmael himself resembles the mutability and shiftiness he experiences as his world; because there is nothing on which he can solidly base his existence in a universe of infinite possibility that at the same time is infinite repetition, a world both fated and free and therefore dreadful, Ishmael can only be these contrarieties, a modern Narcissus. Thus we are never told Ishmael's real name: to name is implicitly to define, but because he can see nothing certain he can will nothing with his total being; therefore, for us as for himself, he can *be* nothing definite. Unlike Ahab, he has no aspirations to sainthood.

As character, Ishmael is a sailor; as narrator, a storyteller. The sort of book this uncommon sailor writes follows from the self-world relation which is his reality. It is a book not surprisingly grounded, often, in despair, an emotion whose forms are as protean and dialectical as those of boredom and dread.

Theologically, despair is the despair of God's power to save one's soul. In doubting that power, God as God is doubted, as is the nature of ultimate truth. Certainly, Ishmael has many moments when his despair is overt and resembles the theological, as in the passage in which he experiences death as absolute disappearance, or in his rejection of Christian hope in chapter XCVI: "All is vanity. ALL. This wilful world hath not got hold of unchristian Solomon's wisdom yet." However, Ishmael's theological doubts do not express themselves always in such melancholy tones. Quite evidently well-acquainted with the Bible, Ishmael admits to being a former believer ("I was a good Christian; born and bred in the bosom of the infallible Presbyterian Church," X) just before he humorously turns idolator with Queequeg. He cherishes "the greatest respect towards everybody's religious obligations, never mind how comical" (XVII). "Hell," he says cheerfully, "is an idea first born on an undigested apple-dumpling; and since then perpetuated through the hereditary dyspepsias nurtured by Ramadans" (XVII). No longer having doctrinal beliefs, he must needs be tolerant: "Heaven have mercy on us all—Presbyterians and Pagans alike— for we are all somehow dreadfully cracked about the head, and sadly need mending" (XVII). Without doctrine, he is, as he himself admits, a kind of pagan, "a savage, owning no allegiance but to the King of the Cannibals; and ready at any moment to rebel against him" (LVII). Beyond that, he is uncommitted, *even to paganism:* "Doubts of all things earthly, and intuitions of some things heavenly; this combination makes neither believer nor infidel, but makes a man who regards them both with an equal eye" (LXXXV); neither believer nor infidel, because no mere label will do.

Ishmael's minimal beliefs make him perhaps more prone to superficial mood swings than more solidly grounded citizens. Like "all sailors of all sorts" he is "more or less capricious," even "unreliable" (XLVI); he has lived in "the outer weather" and inhaled its "fickleness." Yet this very fickleness is a sign of the persistence of the despair that underlies it, a despair which is to be measured not only in specifically negative theological moments, but in the extent to which defeated hope pervades Ishmael's book.

The poet, says Emerson, meaning the term more broadly than versifier, is the sayer, the namer. Ishmael is a poet who names what he knows to be dreadfully nameless: he tells us of Timor Tom, New Zealand Jack, Don Miguel, and Moby Dick—all of them "famous whales" (XLV); but, if the final presence of Moby Dick may serve as index, the homeliness of these names falls absurdly short of defining the exotic wonder of their bearers' presences. What he does with individual whales, Ishmael does with the class of whales: a man who repeatedly protests his disbelief in the adequacy of systems, with humorous despair he offers us a "book" system of whale classification punningly based on the whale's most obvious feature—its sheer volume; a system in which his absurd and arbitrary ("Be it known that, waiving all argument, I take the good old fashioned ground that the whale is a fish," XXXII) terms must do "nothing less" than essay "the classification of the constituents of a chaos." Wishing to anatomize the idea of whaleness, he does so, literally, piece by piece, with actual whales; yet what his vision records is so contradictory he is repeatedly forced to confess that he can find no rational explanation to make everything cohere. Emotions as well as reason falter before the whale, as Ishmael shows us the creature in every light so that our fear, awe, wonder, sympathetic concern (in, for example, the episode involving baby whales in "The Grand Armada"), even our pity (for the frightened old bull whose sore Flask pricks) are aroused, and though each emotion will do for a time, no feeling is in itself sufficient to comprehend both the temporal and spatial magnitude of the phenomenon, as well as its occasionally intimate appearances. To go whaling is to go mentally adventuring among the exotic wonders of the water-world, but there is emptiness in the experience; and even at the beginning of his book, the narrator's despair intrudes each time he records his hopeful exhilaration anticipatory of adventure, yet systematically subverts it with foreshadowings of separation and death ("From that hour I clove to Queequeg like a barnacle; yea, till poor Queequeg took his last long dive," XIII) so that underlying the exuberance and ferocity of the pursuit is a constantly deepening sense of futility. Such despair proceeds from the narrator's knowledge of the voyage's end, but it has become pervasive because of his deeper consciousness of endings.

Each increase in consciousness, says Kierkegaard, involves increased despair; yet the possibility of despair is man's advantage over animals. Ishmael says he is a savage; being a savage implies, as with Queequeg, "unconsciousness" (XIII), a being able to be always equal to oneself. The civilized man because of his wider conceptual awarenesses can be of several minds, therefore not equal to himself; and to the extent that this describes Ishmael, Ishmael is not a savage. His savagery is "true" only in certain aspects and those only intermittently or qualifiedly. With him, as with Ahab or the whale, again no simple formula will do.

Ishmael shares, for example, the patience of savages:

> Now, one of the peculiar characteristics of the savage in his domestic hours, is his wonderful patience of industry. An ancient Hawaiian war-club or spear-paddle, in its full multiplicity and elaboration of carving, is as great a trophy of human perseverance as a Latin lexicon. . . .
> As with the Hawaiian savage, so with the white sailor-savage. With the same marvelous patience, and with the same single shark's tooth,

of his one poor jack-knife, he will carve you a bit of bone sculpture, not quite as workmanlike, but as close packed in its maziness of design, as the Greek savage, Achilles's shield; and full of barbaric spirit and suggestiveness. . . .

(LVII)

Such artist-savages make material worthless in itself into things of value as, patiently, they literally fill their time with meaning. In telling his story, of course, so does Ishmael; with the difference that unlike the unreflective savages he describes he is conscious not only of what he is doing but of the contexts in which he is doing it. He is conscious, too, that the chief meaning with which he fills up time is built of uncertainty, contradiction, and irony, barbarically spirited and suggestive without doubt, but hardly clear in detail. The precision of savage art is not attainable for Ishmael because his mind must comprehend more things, all of which he "tries," achieving what he can (LXXIX): a kind of "careful disorderliness" (LXXXII). Even the attempt to be a *primitive* artist is futile, because although he has the patience he does not have the unconsciousness.

Despair shows some of its dialectical capacity in its grounding of Ishmaelean humor, the major purpose of which is to articulate discrepancies between the actual and the ideal. Repeatedly, the point of Ishmael's humor is a demonstration of the incomprehensibly angular absurdities of himself or others projected against the implicit possibilities of human grace, thereby drawing attention to missed connections in the universe. Early in the book Ishmael had said:

a good laugh is a mighty good thing, and rather too scarce a good thing; more's the pity. So, if any one man, in his own proper person, afford stuff for a good joke to anybody, let him not be backward, but let him cheerfully allow himself to spend and be spent in that way. And the man that has anything bountifully laughable about him, be sure there is more in that man than you perhaps think for.

(v)

Later in the book Ishmael says: "that mortal man who hath more of joy than sorrow in him, that mortal man cannot be true—not true, or undeveloped. . . . The truest of all men was the Man of Sorrows" (XCVI). If despair is understood as the real ground of Ishmaelean humor, then the apparent contradiction between these two statements disappears: like Stubb, the consistent humorist "has his history" (CXIV), and that history is not entirely a happy one. The humorist is what he is in relation to what he knows of sorrow. And that Ishmael is aware of despair as the potential basis for his own humor, his description of humorous despair shows:

There are certain queer times and occasions in this strange mixed affair
we call life when a man takes this whole universe for a vast practical joke,
though the wit thereof he but dimly discerns, and more than suspects that
the joke is at nobody's expense but his own. However, nothing dispirits,
and nothing seems worthwhile disputing. He bolts down all events, all
creeds, and beliefs, and persuasions, all hard things visible and invisible,
never mind how knobby. . . . And as for small difficulties and worryings,
prospects of sudden disaster, peril of life and limb; all these, and death
itself, seem to him only sly, good-natured hits, and jolly punches in the
side bestowed by the unseen and unaccountable old joker. . . . There is
nothing like the perils of whaling to breed this free and easy sort of genial,
desperado [italics added] philosophy . . .

(XLIX)

If the universe in this hyena mood seems like an obscure practical
joke, the literary world Ishmael creates for us is often mined with hidden
banter. Often this is obscene. Sometimes it lurks as potential meaning
where it has no business to be: "Of erections, how few are domed like St.
Peters!" (LXVIII). Another instance seems to be when Pip, after equating
the doubloon with the ship's "navel," which all the lookers-at are "on fire
to unscrew" (XCIX), asks portentously: "But, unscrew your navel, and
what's the consequence?"—a question which only too readily brings to
mind the punch line of the old joke about the Hindu mystic. Sometimes
the nonpertinence of the potential ribaldry can be staggering. Lawrance
Thompson, for example, holds that the chapter "A Squeeze of the Hand,"
so important to critics who see the book's social-ethical admonitions as
final, is secretly obscene. Insisting upon a nonwhaling meaning for the
work "sperm," he naturally finds the whole passage full of the sort of
"accumulated off color word play" that, if indeed there, is positively Shakespearean in its trained bawdiness (even "country" makes it appearance):

Would that I could keep squeezing that sperm for ever! For now, since
by many prolonged, repeated experiences, I have perceived that in all
cases man must eventually lower, or at least shift, his conceit of attainable
felicity; not placing it anywhere in the intellect or the fancy; but in the
wife, the heart, the bed, the table, the saddle, the fire-side, the country;
now that I have perceived all this, I am ready to squeeze case eternally.
In thoughts of the visions of the night, I saw long rows of angels in
paradise, each with his hands in a jar of spermaceti.

In this passage, and throughout the four paragraphs preceding it, Thompson
finds Ishmael-Melville ridiculing by his obscenity the idea of Christian
brotherhood. While there is no doubt that Ishmael-Melville is capable of
this sort of word play—"archbishoprick" (XCV), about which there can

be no question, proves it—nevertheless, the hypothesized bawdry of "A Squeeze of the Hand" is so *very* strained, in addition to being violently out of congruence with the lyrical rhetoric of at least the crucial paragraph just quoted (the self-conscious sentimentality of the preceding paragraphs makes them more plausible game), that the hidden presence of obscenity here seems less certain than Thompson says it is. The real difficulty is that all such obscenity must finally be in the eye of the beholder, for the passage itself contains merely the grammatical possibility of obscenity. Yet is does contain that (and so do passages throughout the book); and because it does, once the sincerity of the expressed sentiments is doubted, the words themselves can make us uncomfortable without ever *necessarily* resolving themselves into either democratic pietism or scurrilous anti-Christianity.

Perhaps, in short, precisely that irresolution is one literary function of such passages. In the chapter in question, the democratic sentiments are undermined by the overt terms in which they are presented: it is explicitly "a strange sort of insanity" that comes over Ishmael to lead him to his "loving feeling," which is then dealt with in hyperbole appropriate to "insanity"; while the ideals of landed comfort are covertly undermined by Ishmael's continued bachelor-voyaging, for he has failed to choose the self and life he urges us to choose; and both *may* be further subverted by covert obscenity. What we have in such passages is a kind of willful destruction of specific meaning, meaning that is potential at several levels, but on no level is finally asserted.

Here humor has shaded into the problematics of Ishmaelean irony, wherein no firm standpoint is offered the reader, and his wishes tend to be projected into the material to provide one, the reader thereby being forced to become part of what he reads. Such irony reflects—just as the implicit rationale of lying does—the attitude of a man who knows he does not know. It is the attitude of negative intellectual freedom that allows all standpoints to be playfully adopted for the moment. Committed to nothing, the Ishmaelean ironist can mockingly play with everything, as a result of which everything he touches is eerily tinged with the color of mere possibility: his ironies, like his lies, are "white."

Because they are, they become part of the methods by which Ishmael constructs a literary universe in which many meanings cannot be certified, a universe that reflects his own experienced universe and makes the Ishmaelean self a type of the alienated mind of fluid contrarieties. Here, conventional theological despair that doubts God shows its links with Kierkegaardian despair which with every increase of consciousness is increasingly uncertain that there is such a thing as a true self; for with no positive beliefs to characterize him, Ishmael can hardly be a continuously unified character. And, as has been suggested, others in Ishmael's book parallel his mode of despair: Pip's despair reflects inner and outer void, Ahab's becomes an intensity of selfhood that conceals a blank, Stubb's jolly despair hides his history (presumably one involving infidelities by his "juicy little pear" of a wife who gives parties to the "last arrived harpooneers" while he is away, (XXXIX), Starbuck despairingly wills to be the self of his old land faith despite the kidnapping cannibal ways of the sea that would deny the fundamental bases of that self. In each instance, the Being of personal identity is related to inner and outer nonbeing, existing in intimate conjunction with it.

Indeed, when Ishmael survives at the end supported by an empty coffin, a thing significant of death has come to signify life by virtue of accident working together with man's forming intentions, and the survival can be read as in part a reflection of the book's ontology wherein Being is radically dependent on nonbeing. Taking this one step further, one might say that Ishmael survives also by virtue of the book itself recording his survival; he survives therefore as an artist, and as a rather desperado artist whose desperation reaches into his book's style. It is, as Constance Rourke noted, an oral style. As such it is a highly personal style that creates its own implicit dramatic situation which suggests, at first, that Ishmael has cornered one auditor in, say, a bar, and spins him a yarn full of arguments and asides of what happened one memorable voyage. As the book progresses, the implied situation of narrator and auditor quickly shifts to that of a practiced storyteller now writing a sometimes awkward book for anyone at all to read, but an anyone addressed personally from time to time to recall something of the original storytelling situation. Ishmael therefore remains an habitual raconteur convivially telling tales, like the Town-Ho's, in bars, like Lima's Golden Inn; and because his tale of a whale is obsessively told—the product of almost total recall, invention, and what can best be termed extensive scholarly research—it may be suggested that the narrator is *driven* to tell it, as if he were a younger version of the ancient mariner, and his book the end result of many compulsive rehearsals. Ishmael is compelled to report and create meaning in what happened to him both despite, and because of, his sense of the uncertainty of meanings available to temporal man. Once more, Kierkegaard's categories can help to place the situation: if Ahab's response to despair is in its special way religious, and Starbuck's finally ethical, Ishmael's, beginning with his tormenting drive to seek out "the interesting," is aesthetic.

And that Ishmael's response is aesthetic to the point of his writing a book is sufficient explanation for his survival. He does not survive because of some merit on his part; to argue this—that what Ishmael has learned is what allows him to be saved, that Ishmael lives right or sees things in reasonable perspective while Ahab does not—to argue this is to assume an ethical universe of some sort: a tragically lopsided one in which innocents, like Pip, and good men, like Starbuck, die horribly precisely because of Ahab's moral-perceptional errors even though Ishmael does not. But whether the universe has any ethical character at all, lopsidedly tragic or otherwise, is a major part of what is in question in the first place; the argument assumes what it must demonstrate. Ishmael's book is in this respect prior to tragedy, though Ahab's story may well not be. His survival is therefore prior to all ethics, and the existentially sufficient reason for his survival is that what transcends death in time is art: art is what in fact does survive, often accidentally, and about its survival and Ishmael's as artist storyteller there is very little ethical that can, it seems to me, be convincingly posited.

Insofar as Ishmael's book exists in order to record his manner of survival, it exists in order to exist its writer as a dialectical being. Negatively, the narrator becomes so involved with the not-self that he is often in danger of losing himself as a character in it—in events and in others, as if by virtue of his negative capability he experiences fully his own nonbeing as an analogue to the universal void. Positively, the narrator becomes most a "character" through his humor, which points out and reflects inner and outer limitations, but which also tends at times toward an optimism that can experience the naughting ambiguity of self and universe as the plenitude of intellectual freedom: as a nearly infinite number of things in the world and a multitude of potential meanings arising out of the interrelation of these things with men's minds which gives Ishmaelean man the real freedom to worship no unworthy gods, but instead to try all things, to explore, and by exploring to create his own world of meanings. One might summarize the self of the Ishmaelean narrator as that of an artist who has constructed, as Melville's contemporary Flaubert hoped to, a highly personal, stylized work: a something founded on nothing in the face of a nothing, a something which creates Ishmael's own ambivalent self for him and for us, and gives its peculiarly problematic existence to his world.

ROBERT PENN WARREN

Melville the Poet

F. O. Matthiessen has undertaken to give in twenty-two pages a cross section of the rather large body of the poetry of Herman Melville. If he had intended to give merely a little gathering of his poet's best blossoms, his task would have been relatively easy. But he has also undertaken, as he says in his brief but instructive preface [to *Selected Poems of Herman Melville*], to "take advantage of all the various interests attaching to any part of Melville's work." So some items appear because they present the basic symbols which are found in the prose or because they "serve to light up facets of Melville's mind as it developed in the years after his great creative period."

In one sense all one can do is to say that Mr. Matthiessen, with the space permitted by the series to which this book belongs ("The Poets of the Year"), has carried out his plan with the taste and discernment which could have been predicted by any reader of his discussion of Melville's poetry in the *American Renaissance*. But I shall take this occasion to offer a few remarks supplementary to the preface and to point out other poems and passages in Melville's work which I hope Mr. Matthiessen admires or finds interesting but which could have no place in his arbitrarily limited collection.

First, I wish to comment on Melville's style. It is ordinarily said that he did not master the craft of verse. Few of his poems are finished. Fine lines, exciting images, and bursts of eloquence often appear, but they appear side by side with limping lines, inexpressive images, and passages of bombast. In a way, he is a poet of shreds and patches. I do not wish to

From *Selected Essays of Robert Penn Warren*. Copyright © 1966 by Vintage Books.

deny the statement that he did not master his craft, but I do feel that it needs some special interpretation.

If, for example, we examine the poems under the title "Fruit of Travel Long Ago," in the *Timoleon* volume of 1891, we see that the verse here is fluent and competent. In his belated poetic apprenticeship, he was capable of writing verse which is respectable by the conventional standards of the time. But the effects which he could achieve within this verse did not satisfy him. Let us look at the poem called "In a Bye-Canal." The first section gives us verse that is conventionally competent:

> A swoon of noon, a trance of tide,
> The hushed siesta brooding wide
>   Like calms far off Peru;
> No floating wayfarer in sight,
> Dumb noon, and haunted like the night
>   When Jael the wiled one slew.
> A languid impulse from the car
> Plied by my indolent gondolier
> Tinkles against a palace hoar,
>   And hark, response I hear!
> A lattice clicks; and lo, I see
> Between the slats, mute summoning me,
> What loveliest eyes of scintillation,
> What basilisk glance of conjuration!

But the next eight lines are very different. The meterical pattern is sorely tried and wrenched.

> Fronted I have, part taken the span
> Of portent in nature and peril in man.
> I have swum—I have been
> 'Twixt the whale's black fluke and the white shark's fin;
> The enemy's desert have wandered in,
> And there have turned, have turned and scanned,
> Following me how noiselessly,
> Envy and Slander, lepers hand in hand.

Then the poem returns to its normal movement and tone:

> All this. But at the latticed eye—
> "Hey, Gondolier, you sleep, my man;
> Wake up!" And shooting by, we ran;
> The while I mused, This surely now,
> Confutes the Naturalists, allow!
> Sirens, true sirens verily be,
> Sirens, waylayers in the sea.

> Well, wooed by these same deadly misses,
> Is it shame to run?
> No! Flee them did divine Ulysses,
> Brave, wise, and Venus' son.

The poem breaks up. The central section simply does not go with the rest. It is as though we have here a statement of the poet's conviction that the verse which belonged to the world of respectability could not accommodate the rendering of the experience undergone " 'Twixt the whale's black fluke and the white shark's fin." Perhaps the violences, the distortions, the wrenchings in the versification of some of the poems are to be interpreted as the result not of mere ineptitude but of a conscious effort to develop a nervous, dramatic, masculine style. (In this connection, the effort at a familiar style in *John Marr and Other Sailors*, especially in "Jack Roy," is interesting.) That Melville was conscious of the relation of the mechanics of style to fundamental intentions is ably urgued by William Ellery Sedgwick in *Herman Melville: The Tragedy of Mind* in connection with the verse of *Clarel*. Mr. Sedgwick argues that the choice of short, four-beat lines, usually rhyming in couplets, a form the very opposite to what would have been expected, was dictated by a desire to confirm himself in his new perspective. "The form of *Clarel* was prop or support to his new state of consciousness, in which his spontaneous ego or self-consciousness no longer played an all-comanding role." I would merely extend the application of the principle beyond *Clarel*, without arguing, as Mr. Sedgwick argues in the case of *Clarel*, that Melville did develop a satisfactory solution for his problem.

If we return to "In a Bye-Canal," we may observe that the poem is broken no only by a shift in rhythm but also by a shift in tone. The temper of the poem is very mixed. For instance, the lines

> Dumb noon, and haunted like the night
> When Jael the wiled one slew

introduce a peculiarly weighted, serious reference into the casual first section which concludes with the playful *scintillation-conjuration* rhyme. Then we have the grand section of the whale and the shark. Then the realistic admonition to the gondolier. Then the conclusion, with its classical allusion, at the level of *vers de société*. Probably no one would argue that the disparate elements in this poem have beem assimilated, as they have, for example, in Marvell's "To His Coy Mistress." But I think that one may be well entitled to argue that the confusions of temper in this poem are not merely the result of ineptitude but are the result of an attempt to create a poetry of some vibrancy, range of reference, and richness of tone.

In another form we find the same effort much more successfully realized in "Jack Roy" in the difference between the two following stanzas:

> Sang Larry o' the Cannakin, smuggler o' the wine,
> At mess between guns, lad in jovial recline:
> "In Limbo our Jack he would chirrup up a cheer,
> The martinet there find a chaffing mutineer;
> From a thousand fathoms down under hatches o' your Hades
> He'd ascend in love-ditty, kissing fingers to your ladies!"

> Never relishing the knave, though allowing for the menial,
> Nor overmuch the king, Jack, nor prodigally genial.
> Ashore on liberty, he flashed in escapade,
> Vaulting over life in its levelness of grade,
> Like the dolphin off Africa in rainbow a-sweeping—
> Arch iridescent shot from seas languid sleeping.

Or we find the same fusion of disparate elements in "The March into Virginia," one of Melville's best poems:

> Did all the lets and bars appear
> To every just or larger end,
> Whence should come the trust and cheer?
> Youth must its ignorant impulse lend—
> Age finds place in the rear.
> All wars are boyish, and are fought by boys,
> The champions and enthusiasts of the state . . .

> No berrying party, pleasure-wooed,
> No picnic party in the May,
> Ever went less loath than they
> Into that leafy neighborhood.
> In Bacchic glee they file toward Fate,
> Moloch's uninitiate . . .

> But some who this blithe mood present,
> As on in lightsome files they fare,
> Shall die experienced ere three days are spent—
> Perish, enlightened by the volleyed glare;
> Or shame survive, and, like to adamant,
> The throe of Second Manassas share.

On a smaller scale, Melville's effort to get range and depth into his poetry is illustrated by the occasional boldness of his comparisons. For example, in "The Portent," the beard of John Brown protruding from the hangman's cap is like the trail of a comet or meteor presaging doom.

> Hidden in the cap
> Is the anguish none can draw;

> So your future veils its face,
> Shenandoah!
> But the streaming beard is shown
> (Weird John Brown),
> The meteor of the war.

Or in one of the early poems, "In a Church of Padua," we find the confessional compared to a diving-bell:

> Dread diving-bell! In thee inurned
> What hollows the priest must sound,
> Descending into consciences
> Where more is hid than found.

It must be admitted that Melville did not learn his craft. But the point is that the craft he did not learn was not the same craft which some of his more highly advertised contemporaries did learn with such glibness of tongue and complacency of spirit. Even behind some of Melville's failures we can catch the shadow of the poem which might have been. And if his poetry is, on the whole, a poetry of shreds and patches, many of the patches are of a massy and kingly fabric—no product of the local cotton mills.

But to turn to another line of thought: Both Mr. Matthiessen and Mr. Sedgwick have been aware of the importance of the short poems in relation to Melville's general development. Mr. Sedgwick does give a fairly detailed analysis of the relation of *Battle-Pieces* to *Clarel.* "Even in the *Battle-Pieces*," he says, "we feel the reservations of this (religious) consciousness set against the easy and partial affirmations of patriotism and partisan conflict." And he quotes, as Mr. Matthiessen has quoted in the preface to the present collection and in the *American Renaissance,* an extremely significant sentence from the prose essay which Melville appended to the *Battle-Pieces:* "Let us pray that the terrible historic tragedy of our time may not have been enacted without instructing our whole beloved country through pity and terror." And Mr. Sedgwick refers to one of the paradoxes of "The Conflict of Convictions," that the victory of the Civil War may betray the cause for which the North was fighting:

> Power unanointed may come—
> Dominion (unsought by the free)
> And the Iron Dome
> Stronger for stress and strain,
> Fling her huge shadow athwart the main;
> But the Founders' dream shall flee. . . .

But even in this poem there are other ideas which relate to Melville's concern with the fundamental ironical dualities of existence: will against necessity, action against ideas, youth against age, the changelessness of man's heart against the concept of moral progress, the bad doer against the good deed, the bad result against the good act, ignorance against fate, etc. These ideas appear again and again, as in "The March into Virginia":

> Did all the lets and bars appear
> To every just or larger end,
> Whence should come the trust and cheer?
> Youth must the ignorant impulse lend—
> Age finds place in the rear.
> All wars are boyish, and are fought by boys,
> The champions and enthusiasts of the state.

Or in "On the Slain Collegians":

> Youth is the time when hearts are large,
> And stirring wars
> Appeal to the spirit which appeals in turn
> To the blade it draws.
> If woman incite, and duty show
> (Though made the mask of Cain),
> Or whether it be Truth's sacred cause,
> Who can aloof remain
> That shares youth's ardour, uncooled by the snow
> Of wisdom or sordid gain?

Youth, action, will, ignorance—all appear in heroic and dynamic form as manifestations of what Mr. Sedgwick has called Melville's "radical Protestantism," the spirit which had informed *Moby Dick.* But in these poems the commitment is nicely balanced, and even as we find the praise of the dynamic and heroic we find them cast against the backdrop of age, idea, necessity, wisdom, fate. Duty may be made the "mask of Cain" and "lavish hearts" are but, as the poem on the Collegians puts it, "swept by the winds of their place and time." all bear their "fated" parts. All move toward death or toward the moment of wisdom when they will stand, as "The March into Virginia" puts it, "enlightened by the volleyed glare."

Man may wish to act for Truth and Right, but the problem of definitions is a difficult one and solution may be achieved only in terms of his own exercise of will and his appetite for action. That is, his "truth" and the Truth may be very different things in the end. "On the Slain Collegians" sums the matter up:

> What could they else—North or South?
> Each went forth with blessings given
> By priests and mothers in the name of Heaven;
> And honour in both was chief.

> Warred one for Right, and one for Wrong?
> So be it; but they both were young—
> Each grape to his cluster clung,
> All their elegies are sung.

Or there is "The College Colonel," the young officer who returns from the war, a crutch by his saddle, to receive the welcome of the crowd and especially, as "Boy," the salute of age. But to him comes "alloy."

> It is not that a leg is lost
> It is not that an arm is maimed.
> It is not that the fever has racked—
> Self he has long disclaimed.
> But all through the Seven Days' Fight,
> And deep in the Wilderness grim,
> And in the field-hospital tent,
> And Petersburg crater, and dim
> Lean brooding in Libby, there came—
> Ah heaven!—what *truth* to him.

The official truth and the official celebration are equally meaningless to him who has been "enlightened by the volleyed glare"—who has known pity and terror.

The event, the act, is never simple. Duty may be made the mask of Cain. In "The Conflict of Convictions," it is asked:

> Dashed aims, at which Christ's martyrs pale,
> Shall Mammon's slaves fulfill?

And in the same poem, in the passage which Mr. Sedgwick quotes, Melville conjectures that the Iron Dome, stronger for stress and strain, may fling its huge, imperial shadow across the main; but at the expense of the "Founders' dream." But other dire effects of the convulsion, even if it involves Right, may be possible. Hate on one side and Phariseeism on the other may breed a greater wrong than the one corrected by the conflict. The "gulfs" may bare "their slimed foundations," as it is phrased in the same poem in an image which is repeated in "America." The allegorical female figure, America, is shown sleeping:

> But in that sleep contortion showed
> The terror of the vision there—
> A silent vision unavowed,
> Revealing earth's foundations bare,
> And Gorgon in her hiding place.
> It was a thing of fear to see
> So foul a dream upon so fair a face,
> And the dreamer lying in that starry shroud.

Even if the victory is attained, there is no cause for innocent rejoicing. As, in "The College Colonel," the hero looks beyond the cheering crowd to his "truth," so in "Commemorative of a Naval Victory," the hero must look beyond his "festal fame":

> But seldom the laurel wreath is seen
> Unmixed with pensive pansies dark;
> There's a light and shadow on every man
> Who at last attains his lifted mark—
> Nursing through night the ethereal spark.
> Elate he never can be;
> He feels that spirits which glad had hailed his worth,
> Sleep in oblivion.—The shark
> Glides white through the phosphorous sea.

There is more involved here than the sadness over the loss of comrades. The shark comes as too violent and extravagant an image for that. The white shark belongs to the world of the "slimed foundations" which are exposed by the convulsion. It is between the whale's black fluke and the white shark's fin that wisdom is learned. He is the Maldive shark, which appears in the poem by that name, the "Gorgonian head" (the "Gorgon in her hiding place" appears too in the bared foundations of earth glimpsed in the dream of "America"), the "pale ravener of horrible meat," the Fate symbol.

We may ask what resolution of these dualities and dubieties may be found in Melville's work. For there is an effort at a resolution. The effort manifests itself in three different terms: nature, history, and religion.

In reference to the first term, we find the simple treatment of "Shiloh":

> Foemen at morn, but friends at eve—
> Fame or country least their care:
> (What like a bullet can undeceive!)
> But now they lie low,
> While over them the swallows skim
> And all is hushed at Shiloh.

Mortal passion and mortal definition dissolve in the natural process, as in "Malvern Hill":

> We elms of Malvern Hill
> Remember everything;
> But sap the twig will fill:
> Wag the world how it will,
> Leaves must be green in Spring.

The focal image at the end of "A Requiem for Soldiers Lost in Ocean Transports" repeats the same effect:

> Nor heed they now the lone bird's flight
> Round the lone spar where mid-sea surges pour.

There is, however, a step beyond this elegiac calm of the great natural process which absorbs the human effort and agony. There is also the historical process. It is possible, as Melville puts it in "The Conflict of Convictions," that the "throes of ages" may rear the "final empire and the happier world." The Negro woman in "Formerly a Slave" looks

> Far down the depth of thousand years,
> And marks the revel shine;
> Her dusky face is lit with sober light,
> Sibylline, yet benign.

In "America," the last poem of *Battle-Pieces*, the contorted expression on the face of the sleeping woman as she dreams the foul dream of earth's bared foundations is replaced, when she rises, by a "clear calm look."

> . . . It spake of pain,
> But such a purifier from stain—
> Sharp pangs that never come again—
> And triumph repressed by knowledge meet,
> And youth matured for age's seat—
> Law on her brow and empire in her eyes.
> So she, with graver air and lifted flag;
> While the shadow, chased by light,
> Fled along the far-drawn height,
> And left her on the crag.

"Secession, like Slavery, is against Destiny," Melville wrote in the prose supplement to *Battle-Pieces*. For to him, if history was fate (the "foulest crime" was inherited and was fixed by geographical accident upon its perpetrators), it might also prove to be redemption. In *Mardi*, in a passage which Mr. Sedgwick quotes in reference to the slaves of Vivenza, Melville exclaims: "Time—all-healing Time—Time, great philanthropist! Time must befriend these thralls." Melville, like Hardy, whom he resembles in so many respects and with whose war poems his own war poems share so much in tone and attitude, proclaimed that he was neither an optimist nor a pessimist, and in some of his own work we find a kind of guarded meliorism, like Hardy's, which manifests itself in the terms of destiny, fate, time, that is, in the historical process.

The historical process, however, does not appear always as this mechanism of meliorism. Sometimes the resolution it offers is of another sort, a sort similar to the elegiac calm of the natural process: the act is always poised on the verge of history, the passion, even at the moment of greatest intensity, is always about to become legend, the moral issue is always about to disappear into time and leave only the human figures, shadowy now, fixed in attitudes of the struggle. In "Battle of Stone River, Tennessee," we find the stanzas which best express this.

> With Tewksbury and Barnet heath,
> In days to come the field shall blend,
> The story dim and date obscure;
> In legend all shall end.
> Even now, involved in forest shade
> A Druid-dream the strife appears,
> The fray of yesterday assumes
> The haziness of years.
>   In North and South still beats the vein
>   Of Yorkist and Lancastrian. . . .
>
> But Rosecrans in the cedarn glade
> And, deep in denser cypress gloom,
> Dark Breckinridge, shall fade away
> Or thinly loom.
> The pale throngs who in forest cowed
> Before the spell of battle's pause,
> Forefelt the stillness that shall dwell
> On them and their wars.
>   North and South shall join the train
>   Of Yorkist and Lancastrian.

In "The March into Virginia" the young men laughing and chatting on the road to Manassas are "Moloch's uninitiate" who "file toward Fate."

> All they feel is this: 'tis glory,
> A rapture sharp, though transitory
> Yet lasting in belaurelled story.

The glory of the act ends in legend, in the perspective of history, which is fate. Human action enters the realm where it is, to take a line from "The Coming Storm,"

> Steeped in fable, steeped in fate.

Nature and history proved the chief terms of resolution in *Battle-Pieces*. Only rarely appears the third term, religion, and then in a conven-

tional form. For instance, there is "The Swamp-Angel," which deals with
the bombardment of Charleston:

> Who weeps for the woeful City
> Let him weep for our guilty kind;
> Who joys at her wild despairing—
> Christ, the Forgiver, convert his mind.

It is actually in the terms of nature and history that the attitude which
characterizes *Clarel* first begins to make itself felt. Mr. Sedgwick has defined
Melville's attitude as the result of a "religious conversion to life." In it he
renounced the quest for the "uncreated good," the individualistic idealism
of *Moby Dick,* the "radical Protestantism." Mr. Sedgwick continues: "Behind *Clarel* lies the recognition that for ripeness, there must be receptivity;
that from the point of view of the total consciousness it is not more blessed
to give than to receive. One receives in order to be received into life and
fulfilled by life. . . . Melville's act was toward humanity, not away from it.
He renounced all the prerogatives of individuality in order to enter into
the destiny which binds all human beings in one great spiritual and emotional organism. He abdicated his independence so as to be incorporated
into the mystical body of humanity." There is the affirmation at the end
of *Clarel:*

> But through such strange illusions have they passed
> Who in life's pilgrimage have baffled striven—
> Even death may prove unreal at the last,
> And stoics be astounded into heaven.
>
> Then keep thy heart, though yet but ill-resigned—
> Clarel, thy heart, the issues there but mind;
> That like the crocus budding through the snow—
> That like a swimmer rising from the deep—
> That like a burning secret which doth go
> Even from the bosom that would hoard and keep;
> Emerge thou mayst from the last whelming sea,
> And prove that death but routs life into victory.

Or we find the same attitude expressed by the comforting spirit which
appears at the end of "The Lake":

> She ceased and nearer slid, and hung
> In dewy guise; then softlier sung:
> "Since light and shade are equal set,
> And all revolves, nor more ye know;
> Ah, why should tears the pale cheek fret
> For aught that waneth here below.
> Let go, let go!"

With that, her warm lips thrilled me through,
She kissed me while her chaplet cold
Its rootlets brushed against my brow
With all their humid clinging mould.
She vanished, leaving fragrant breath
And warmth and chill of wedded life and death.

And when, in the light of these poems we look back upon "The Maldive Shark" we see its deeper significance. As the pilot fish may find a haven in the serrated teeth of the shark, so man, if he learns the last wisdom, may find an "asylum in the jaws of the Fates."

This end product of Melville's experience has, in the passage which I have already quoted from Mr. Sedgwick, been amply defined. What I wish to emphasize is the fact that there is an astonishing continuity between the early poems, especially *Battle-Pieces,* and *Clarel.* Under the terms of nature and history, the religious attitude of *Clarel* and "The Lake" is already being defined.

ELAINE BARRY

The Changing Face of Comedy

The most consistent, if not the most dominant, note in nineteenth-century criticism of Herman Melville was an acknowledgment of his comic sense. His early reputation rested quite as much on his "lively," "genial," and "amusing" style as on the authenticity of his sojourns in the South Seas (which was doubted) or the force of his social criticism (which was resented). In 1888, Robert Louis Stevenson, engaged in exploiting the same Pacific material, referred to his mentor Melville as "a howling cheese." In 1890, long after Melville had faded from the public limelight, and certainly long after the comedy had darkened, he was included in a survey-article for *Harper's Magazine* called "American Literary Comedians."

Yet, persistent though it was, the appreciation of Melville's comic sense remained fairly one-dimensional throughout the century. Even the critics who declared dismissively that *Pierre* was "mad" did not venture to explore the nature of its madness, or its progression from the early comedy. Twentieth-century critics have been more subtle in their analysis of this aspect of his work, but treatment of it has hardly been a major by-product of the Melville industry. One comprehensive book-length study, and a dozen or so excellent articles or chapters that offer something more than a passing note, scarcely make a critical summer. Given its range and its artistic complexity, Melville's use of comedy remains the most critically underrated aspect of his writing.

From *American Studies International* 4, vol. 16 (1978). Copyright ©1978 by *American Studies International*.

The comic spirit that invested Melville's early novels undoubtedly sprang from a personal bonhomie to which his own letters and those of his friends testify. The man who refused to believe in a temperance heaven, and who expressed such a Rabelaisian delight in food, pipe, and drink, to say nothing of more fleshly delights, had a promising temperament for a humorist; his image of himself as an Outsider figure—his persistent narrative stance—gave him the classic comic perspective. Melville complained of his own "infirmity of jocularity," but it is an essential part of the generosity of spirit and the largeness of sympathy of his creative imagination. When, even at the most intense period of their relationship, he sensed "something lacking" in Hawthorne ("He doesn't patronise the butcher—He needs roast-beef, done rare."), he is surely reacting to a certain bloodless overrefinement in the older writer, a lack of precisely that jocularity.

If the comic spirit of Melville's early work, then, was very largely the expression of his personal ebullience, it was also, for the young author anxious to make his writing pay, a good selling point. That it hit the right note with his public, both in England and America, the contemporary reviews testify. And Melville himself, trying to sell *Omoo* to the business-wise John Murray, shrewdly mentioned the comic aspects of the book: "I have another work now nearly completed which I am anxious to submit to you before presenting it to any other publishing house. It embraces adventures in the South Seas . . . and includes an eventful cruise in an English Colonial Whalesman . . . and a comical residence on the island of Tahiti."

But, beyond both these factors, Melville throughout his work exploited the resources and the stances of comedy for conscious literary purposes. If the changing face of comedy in his work is an index of the personality changes that carried Melville from the enthusiastic consciousness of natural delights to the state where he had "pretty much made up his mind to be annihilated," it is, more importantly, an index of the changing thematic preoccupations of his novels, and indeed of their changing form. From using comic motifs and camera angles to spice his adventure tales, Melville progresses steadily through a self-conscious examination of the psychological and philosophical value of a humorous perspective to a more abstract apprehension of the nature of comedy itself as a paradigm of the limitations of rationality in an irrational world. The implications of this final attitude bring Melville close to Joyce, to Camus, and to the speculations about the nature of language and literary reality that have dominated so much twentieth-century writing.

The sheer range of Melville's comedy is extraordinary. At its crudest and liveliest there is the element of slapstick, like the presentation of the "cancer specimen" to Cadwallader Cuticle in *White-Jacket*, or the open clowning of the young Ishmael in *Moby Dick*. At the other end of the tonal spectrum there is the refined whimsy of the belle-lettrist, as in the account in *Mardi* of "certain invisible spirits, ycleped the Plujii, arrant little knaves as ever gulped moonshine," or the Hawthornesque sentimental humor of *The Piazza Tales*. In between these extremes, Melville exploits a vast range of comic materials and styles: the sexual jokes throughout *Moby Dick*; the manipulation of the vernacular in Father Mapple's "four yarns" and of the Negro sermon tradition in Fleece's address to the sharks; the Yankee tall story, like the one in *White-Jacket* of the bullet that entered a man's Adam's Apple, ran a circuit round his neck, came out at the same hole and shot the next man in the ranks; the Vaudevillian overtones of Black Guinea's appearances in *The Confidence Man*; the traditional comedy of situation in most of *Omoo*, or of caricature in the genteel Aunt Charity or in Turkey, Nippers and Ginger Nut. Like Dickens, Melville has the humorist's eye for parody: Franklin and Emerson get the inevitable comeuppance of the over-serious in *Israel Potter* and *The Confidence Man*, and one suspects some particular contemporary barbs in the chapter on Oh Oh's Antiquarian Museum in *Mardi*. But, unlike Dickens, Melville is also capable of self-parody, as in the semi-deprecatory awareness of his own rhetoric in *Mardi* or, if we accept a measure of authorial identification with the narrator of *White-Jacket*, the humbling auction of the individualising jacket. On a broader scope, his satire ranges from the Swiftian generality of *Mardi*, through more particularised personal satire in a character like the Quaker Bildad, to the serious, cosmic satire of *The Confidence Man*. The changing ironic perspective from which we view the various narrator figures is a central dimension of their total meaning. Comedy spills over into the demonic in *Mardi*, and Melville follows through on that dimension in *Moby Dick* and *The Confidence Man*. Pervading all dimensions is the persistent rhetorical play that exults in its own inventiveness—in bursts of geniality, punning, literary allusions, and verbal wit.

A separate, more oblique category of comedy is the private joke that Melville plays on his publishers and public in the disguised sexual undertones of such pieces as "I and My Chimney" and "The Tartarus of Maids." It is a joke in which he had the last laugh. How he must have chuckled to himself when *Harper's* published "The Tartarus of Maids" without blinking an eyelid, after *Putnam's* had rejected the more orthodox satire of "The

Two Temples" on the grounds that it might offend contemporary sensibilities! Taken all in all, Melville's comic sense, though rarely as sharp or consistent as Mark Twain's, is far more multifaceted—a measure indicating that both his mind and his heart were larger.

Given the evidence of such an "infirmity of jocularity," the "perspectives for criticism"—if I can take a cue from the eminent Melville scholars—open out in several directions. Constance Rourke opened a door into the study of the origin of Melville's humor in the folk tradition—the tall story, the frontier spirit, the Yankee character and voice, etc.—and later critics have entered this area, though without adequately following up the promising lead that she gave in touching on the element of "terror" behind his comic masks. It is an important field, for it was presumably Melville's earliest comic influence, the local tradition he was most open to before those literature-charged months of his twenty-fifth year from which he dated his "growth." The "Old Zack" articles that he wrote for the *Yankee Doodle* magazine in 1847 are straight from this tradition. And, in the novels, so too is the character of Long Ghost, and Jack Chase's ranting bluster against whaling-men, and Fleece's sermon to the sharks. And so on. But establishing connections between Melville's comic devices and a native folk humor implies other, more challenging questions that barely have been explored at all.

What, for example, is the relation of such humor to the development of what Constance Rourke calls the "national character," and how does Melville reflect or contribute to that? Certainly much of the distinctiveness of nineteenth-century American humor represents the attempt of an expanding new society to locate its own identity. It's a flexing of the national muscles, as it were, in a comic stance poised between self-pride and self-doubt. In Melville this is subtly double-edged. There is, on the one hand, the standard figure of the naive American greenhorn—Redburn exploring Liverpool with an obsolete guidebook in his hand, Israel Potter on the road to London—meeting a world that is too wise or too wicked for him. The laugh is at him. In national terms he's the New World Innocent in the face of Old World Experience. In comic terms, he's not really very different from any eighteenth-century picaresque hero. But there is another side to this role—part of a more genuine national stance—in which the naiveté of such a figure is set off by some kind of national pride. When Israel Potter, for example, is democratically arguing with the servants of Sir John Millett about the appropriateness of a knighthood, or when he is defining American attitudes to George III (whose characterisation here is as comic as the Fanny Burney), we are no longer laughing at him but at the situation, in which he is holding his own. And Melville's humor here—as in Twain's later "innocent abroad"—is helping to define the national character and is not simply drawn from a stock confrontation.

Much scholarly detective work has gone into tracing the literary roots of Melville's humor to Irving, Rabelais, Swift, Shakespeare, Smollett, Sterne, and Cervantes. This is certainly a rich field to explore; Melville, unlike Twain, was consciously nonparochial in his attitudes. Besides, there is now a clear record of much of his reading, and what is known of his method of composition suggests that he relied heavily on other books. But what was his debt to the contemporary popular comedy that Miss Rourke mentions in passing? This might not have had the extensive influence it had on Dickens, for example, but the composition of certain scenes—like the bedroom scene with Queequeg and Ishmael—smacks of the stage.

Leaving behind the questions of the origins of Melville's comic sense, there are important questions of his literary attitude towards it, and its relation to artistic form. Firstly, in terms of characterisation, does Melville use comedy in any thematic way? Is a character's capacity for humor any kind of answer to, or weapon against, the agonising ambiguities of the Melvillian universe? What kind of self-awareness does it imply, and is this in any way redemptive? Certainly the nature of the humor embodied in Melville's characters changes radically over the span of his writing life; and the changes would seem to be related to his deepening psychological exploration rather than a matter simply of personal exuberance. Secondly, is there anything in Melville's whole concept of language in the later years that could be defined as "comic"? A large part of the early comic spirit found its expression, apart from character and situation, in rhetorical inventiveness, in punning, wit, and verbal sallies. From *Moby Dick* on, Melville's attitude toward the very possibilities of language becomes increasingly cynical, the puns more complex—less verbal gymnastics than a probing of the nature of reality. The interest in language as such becomes almost a theme in itself, and Melville's speculations on its nature and possibilities involve a concept of comedy that is close to the twentieth-century Absurdists'. The remainder of this essay will be concerned with these two questions.

Perhaps one reason for Melville's changing, in *Pierre*, to an omniscient narrator after six novels as a first-person narrator was that he had, by then, come to the end of a major thematic interest. In view of this, it can be no coincidence that, with the single exception of *Billy Budd*, *Pierre* is the least comic of all Melville's fictional works. He returned to the first-person narrator, of course, in many of the short stories; but the first six novels form a coherent unit that develops, as one of its themes, the human value, psychological and philosophical, of the comic perspective. In those novels he explores the strengths and the limitations of humor as a code of perception, an exploration centered in the most obvious "perceiver," the first-person narrator. Throughout, the nature of Melville's interest is basically humanistic. Although he runs the gamut of comic material and comic devices, including satire, his approach is more Shakespearean than Aristophanic, less intellectually argumentative than concerned with balance and reconciliation. In the constant vacillation of his central characters between annihilation and survival, a sense of humor is the most consistent index of their equilibrium.

In *Typee*, the narrative voice of Tommo is self-consciously humorous. But the humor is intermittent and heavy handed. When, for example, he contemplates the difficulties of deserting ship and eluding recapture, he notes:

> I knew that our worthy captain, who felt such a paternal solicitude for the welfare of his crew, would not willingly consent that one of his best hands should encounter the perils of a sojourn among the natives of a barbarous island; and I was certain that, in the event of my disappearance, his fatherly anxiety would prompt him to offer, by way of a reward, yard upon yard of gaily printed calico for my apprehension. He might even have appreciated my services at the value of a musket.

The irony is heavy and obvious. Like so much of frontier humor, it represents a way of coping with very real privations and fears. It sets up a distance between the narrator and the world he faces, and is a mode of controlling experience. Safe at that distance, Tommo can exploit all the potential comedy of the contrast between primitive and civilised societies. And the sheer observation of the book is certainly lively and often funny.

But the humor is not an integral part of Tommo's personality, and ultimately its very self-consciousness is a barrier to real perception, marking only his separation from the world of experience. Such self-consciousness misses opportunity after opportunity to enter his narrative material in a way that the later Ishmael would certainly not do (e.g., the unrealised symbolism of the thicket of canes, the precipitous descent, the "unmanning" wound, the birth-like final escape). It also prevents him from seeing his own contradictions. In his narrative standpoint, for example, he is continually falling between two incompatible clichés—on the one hand, the cliché of the Noble Savage, to whom civilised man has brought nothing but venereal disease (a subject on which he expatiates even while the Marquesan girls are swimming like mad to "take over" the ship and "make prisoners" of the crew); and, on the other hand, the cliché that natives are all treacherous devils and you can't trust one of 'em. Most of Tommo's humorous observations, in fact, are implicitly condescending.

While humor is by no means the dominant tone in *Typee*, it *is* an important element in Tommo's characterisation, and as such it is rather negative. It is one of the points of contrast between him and Toby, whom "no one ever saw laugh," whose shrewdness is less endearing than Tommo's impulsive naiveté, but who is nevertheless the first to come through the Typee experience. It may be extravagant to suggest a correlation between Tommo's childish, and largely humorous, perspective and the wound that he endures, but certainly his experience in the Typee valley is regressive, as he is nursed, carried, bathed, and fed like a baby. Tommo's sense of humor enlivens his narrative and allays his fears, but as a mode of apprehension, it opens no doors for him, offers no wisdom. It simply rests on the surface of the novel, as a kind of accretion on the narrative voice.

The picaresque structure of *Omoo* threw the burden of the comedy into incidents and character rather than narrative point of view, and it was not until *Redburn* that Melville again took up the theme of the limitations of the humorous perspective in quite the same way. Meanwhile, in *Mardi* he sounded other depths of the comic gambit. The geniality that pervaded the tone of *Omoo* and is the opening tone of *Mardi* (Annatoo is surely Melville's best comic character), is more ambivalent after the emergence of Taji. There is an evident, if somewhat too self-conscious, enjoyment of pipe and drink—the alcoholic consumption throughout *Mardi* is Hemingwayesque—but the spuriousness of such geniality is figured in Borobolla, and it brings little comfort to the questing Taji. On the whole the geniality is as hollow as in the later "Paradise of Bachelors." In the sustained satiric motifs of the second part of *Mardi*, Melville enters a new comic mode—part Rabelais, part Swift—and the comedy rests more in the material than in the narrative voice. But comedy, for the first time, now has an element of terror and ambiguity. The new dimension is hinted at in the grotesque figurehead of Media's boat as the party sets out on their voyage: "But what is this, in the head of the canoe, just under the shark's mouth? A grinning little imp of an image; a ring in its nose; cowrie bells jingling at its ears; with an abominable leer, like that of Silenus reeling on his ass. It was taking its ease; cosily smoking a pipe; its bowl a duodecimo edition of the face of the smoker. This image looked sternwards, everlastingly mocking us." The image draws together various motifs: the juxtaposition of masks of terror and laughter, the pipe-smoking, the sense of mockery endlessly attentuated as in a hall of mirrors. And indeed the laughter in much of *Mardi* is more demonic than mirthful. Babbalanja's alter-ego, Azzageddi, has a factitious gaiety that suggests only laughter is possible in the face of death and terror, and his nonsense-language mocks the very assumptions of rational discourse, as Pip's will do later. Significantly for *Moby Dick*, too, the hyena image is recurrent.

Mardi was the kind of book Melville felt "most moved to write," and toward which his philosophical preoccupations were pointing him. He retreated from its "madness," with reluctance and bitterness, to the saleable world of traditional fiction in *Redburn* and *White-Jacket*. Once again, the narrator assumes dominance; again he is naive. But his comic dimensions are subtler and more questioning, and Melville's control and use of humor in his narrator-figure is surer, than in *Typee* or *Omoo*. What makes the difference is that there is the beginning of a "split" in the narrative voice (a perspective that becomes crucial to *Moby Dick*), a sense that it is commenting on itself. The writer is naive (which is the source of most of the comedy), but he knows he is. And this is his saving grace. The self-detachment is evident, for example, in this passage involving the young Redburn, engaged in washing down the decks for the first time:

> . . . the water began to splash about all over the decks, and I began to think I should surely get my feet wet, and catch my death of cold. So I went to the chief mate and told him I thought I would just step below, till this miserable wetting was over; for I did not have any waterproof boots, and an aunt of mine had died of consumption. But he only roared out for me to get a broom and go to scrubbing, or he would prove a worse consumption to me than ever got hold of my poor aunt.

The humor in the narrative voice at this stage suggests a certain sanity, an ability to see himself in perspective; a real, and not simply a verbal, ability to cope with experience. It is the beginning of wisdom. The jackets of both Redburn and White-Jacket act as the traditional motley, a visual symbol of the wearer's consciousness of role-playing.

However, running contrapuntally to this in *Redburn* is another, more disturbing facet of comedy. The laughter of the captain who signs on the young Redburn is the first laughter in Melville's novels that is positively misleading—a mask not clarifying its role by belying it. Redburn is puzzled and disturbed by it. The ambiguity is darker in the sinister quality of Jackson's laugh—Jackson the cynical nihilist, the pre-figuration of Claggart. Comedy is starting to encompass a more ambiguous universe, to suggest elements of terror and deceit, giving a human embodiment to Babbalanja's claim that, "Mirth and Sorrow are kin; are published by identical nerves."

All these elements come together in *Moby Dick*. Here the narrative consciousness is far more decisively split than in *Redburn*. The older "saved"

Ishmael is recounting the story and recreating the consciousness of his younger self. There are thus two important modes of apprehension, two concentric points of view, two kinds of humorous perspectives. And one kind of humor is commenting on the other.

The young Ishmael, when we first meet him, has a rollicking sense of fun. He loves skylarking, plays practical jokes on Queequeg, exults in comic situations, has a healthy taste for the obscene, and, like the earlier narrators, enjoys puns and word-play. It is *this* consciousness that can say, in youthfully assertive rhetoric:

> However, a good laugh is a mighty good thing, and rather too scarce a good thing; the more's the pity. So if any one man, in his own proper person, afford stuff for a good joke to anybody, let him not be backward, but let him cheerfully allow himself to spend and be spent in that way. And the man that hath anything bountifully laughable about him, be sure there is more in that man than you perhaps think for.

Altogether, the young Ishmael seems unaffected by the bout of "hypos" he has just come through, and his humor at this stage reflects his lack of introspection.

But the humor *we* get from this boisterous character is not simply the one he gives us so consciously. The humor for us also comes from things that he is not conscious of, or that he takes seriously—like his planing of Peter Coffin's bench as a virtuous single bed, his portentous straining to find symbolic meanings in the whaling chapel, the superficially broad-minded judgments about Queequeg that are immediately undercut by his apprehensiveness. But this humor lies in the ironic distance with which the older Ishmael views his immature self. Within that total ironic perspective, the human value of a sense of humor becomes one of the novel's themes and a humorous irony emerges as a kind of moral resolution. Indeed, there is a conscious juxtaposition in the novel of various kinds of, and attitudes towards, humor: Stubb's "invulnerable jollity of indifference," Ahab's utter humorlessness, Pip's "fool" role, the frenetic gaiety of the Midnight Forecastle scene, and the growing, changing, humorous perspective of Ishmael. The humor that Ishmael grows into suggests, in a more fully developed way than in Redburn, a human wholeness, an ability to see oneself in perspective, that stands out in sharp contrast to the absolutist mentality of Ahab. If Ishmael is saved in any but a literal way, his salvation rests largely on this ability to hear himself talk.

But it is a muted salvation at best—one that defines the restrictions as much as the strengths of the humorous perspective. Ishmael is not Redburn at the end, confident in his world, secure in his engagement with it, made self-reliant by a sanity-inducing sense of humor. The older Ishmael, through the course of the adventures he describes, has come to realise the limitations, the essential youthfulness, the ultimate mindlessness of laughter. The voyage chastens him early. After the first lowering of the boats in a whale-chase, Ishmael begins to realise, in a chapter significantly called "The Hyena," that humor can control experience only in a very limited world (more specifically in the world of land and land values). Beyond its ken are realms of absurdity and despair. Ishmael describes his intimations of such realms in these terms:

> There are certain queer times and occasions in this strange mixed affair we call life when a man takes this whole universe for a vast practical joke, though the wit thereof he but dimly discerns, and more than suspects that the joke is at nobody's expense but his own. However nothing dispirits, and nothing seems worth while disputing. . . . And as for small difficulties and worryings, prospects of sudden disaster, peril of life and limb; all these, and death itself, seem to him only sly good-natured hits, and jolly punches in the side bestowed by the unseen and unaccountable old joker. That odd sort of wayward mood I am speaking of, comes over a man only in some time of extreme tribulation; it comes in the very midst of his earnestness, so that what just before might have seemed to him a thing most momentous, now seems but a part of the general joke. There is nothing like the perils of whaling to breed this free-and-easy sort of genial, desperate philosophy; and with it I now regarded this whole voyage of the *Pequod,* and the great White Whale its object.

With a similar view of just what this "genial desperado philosophy" is worth, Ahab frowns on Stubb's mindless jocularity, or that of the captain of the *Bachelor:* "Thou art too damned jolly," Ahab tells that Captain, who has never seen Moby Dick and doesn't believe in him. Just before the final chase, Ishmael records: "All humor, forced or natural, vanished."

Melville in *Moby Dick* has worked through the gamut of humor as a humanising and redemptive quality, and come out the other side, to show its limitations. Perhaps Robert Frost was thinking of the same kind of gamut when he made what seems at first an odd distinction between humor ("Humor is the most engaging cowardice"), and belief ("Belief is better than anything else, and it is best when rapt").

To allow for the possibility of growth from the youthful Ishmael to the Ishmael who is capable of telling the story, the exuberance of the early Ishmael passes over into the character of Stubb. Stubb's is the most constant and self-conscious laughter throughout the book, yet it is always "the invulnerable jollity of indifference." It has no moral dimension. Ahab's word for it is "mechanical"—the same word, incidentally, that D. H. Lawrence used to describe the transcendental spirit of Whitman. Ishmael, on the other hand, passes beyond this to a truly humanising self-awareness that combines the essential sanity of the humorous perspective, the ability to be "rapt" in the magnitude of Ahab's "belief," and an intuition of the nihilism that lies outside of all belief.

After *Moby Dick*, Melville never again explores the nature of humor and the humorous perspective in quite this thematic way. What laughter we get in *Pierre* or *The Confidence Man* is the ambiguous or frenetic laughter that is close to despair, in a world too complex and devious to allow a sense of humor to be any kind of saving grace.

When we turn from this thematic exploration of a comic sense to the nature of comedy in Melville's later writings, we turn not only to a different kind of literary preoccupation but also to a problem of definition. Melville is no longer concerned with examining the redemptive possibilities of humor in his narrators; he had worked through that to an all-too-negative answer. The interest has shifted to the implications of a certain kind of philosophy for the creative artist, and the nature of that philosophy is "comic" in the same way that the Theatre of the Absurd—or indeed the world of the Shakespearean fool—is "comic." In claiming that, except for "Bartleby," Melville's comic spirit dies out after *Moby Dick*, Rosenberry is surely operating on too narrow a definition of comedy. A complex, usually ironic impulse feeds most of the short stories; and if the nineteenth-century public could see *Pierre* and *The Confidence Man* only as "mad" and "clean daft," the twentieth century has caught up with their particular comic vision. Camus hailed *Moby Dick*, as one of the "truly absurd works," and the Beckett who sought a new art form that would be "the expression that there is nothing to express, nothing with which to express, nothing from which to express, no desire to express, together with the obligation to express," would have found in the post-*Moby Dick* Melville a fellow spirit.

For purposes of definition, the essential characteristics of Absurdist comedy may be summarised as a set of authorial assumptions in which the protagonist is alienated and out of harmony with the world around him (after all, every hero since the Romantics has been that), and in which there is a sense of irrationality and inconsequence in the world itself. Moreover, this world view shapes the form as well as the content of art: time is fluid, as the inner landscape is substituted for the outer world; setting has validity only as a visual metaphor for a spiritual condition; there is no clear division between fantasy and fact; and "truth," like a confidence-man, slips between the interstices of its verbal guises. Perhaps the central tenet of the Absurdist philosophy is a distrust of language itself, since language suggests some sort of coherence in experience where none in fact is acknowledged. This, for the writer, is the basic anomaly, expressed by Beckett in the above quotation, a paradigm of the central paradox of Absurdism: the disjunction between the mind's need for unity and the chaos of the world the mind actually experiences. Its logical, if hardly satisfactory, end is the "comedy of silence."

Melville's anticipation of such a philosophy is nowhere more evident than in his attitude to language throughout the course of his writing career. The prose of the early novels is rhetoric at its most ebullient. There is an evident delight in verbal gymnastics, in deliberate archaisms and comic names. Even the extravagances leave him unabashed. And its Whitman-esque flights (e.g., in *Mardi*) proclaim a language that is gloriously confident of its own reality.

Yet in *Mardi*, Melville's most rhetorically high-flying novel, there is also the final realisation that his wings are, after all, only wax. Taji, engaged in his hopeless, death-ending search, comes to acknowledge that "words are but algebraic signs conveying no meaning except what you please," while the endless disputations of Babbalanja, Zoomi, and Mohi demonstrate only the limitations of philosophy, poetry, and history, the traditional pathways to truth; and Azzageddi, Babbalanja's darker, madder self, finds his expression in nonsense language ("Fugli-Fi, fugle-fogle-orun . . .") that is halfway between nursery rhyme and the formal conjugations Pip will play on later.

Sheer economics forced Melville to abandon such suicidal specu-lations. He wrote *Redburn* and *White-Jacket* quickly, for the money. And perhaps he undervalued both, because they represented a setting-aside of a nagging self-doubt, and were written, as it were, under false assumptions. In *Moby Dick*, unable to restrain himself any longer from writing "the kind of book I would wish to," Melville returned to the same curious paradox: a novel that is a rhetorical *tour de force*, yet questions the fundamental relation between language and reality upon which such rhetoric is based.

His exploration of the question in *Moby Dick* is manifested on two levels. On the level of theme and characterisation, the dramatic contrast between Ahab and Ishmael is, in part at least, based on their differing responses to both reality and language. The error of believing that names and the things they signify are identical is Ahab's tragic flaw. Moby Dick simplistically represents for him "all his intellectual and spiritual exasper-ations . . . the general rage and hate felt by his whole race from Adam down." Hence Ahab is continually associated with images of fixing, nailing, charting, fastening down, and the final image of the *Pequod*—Tashtago's hand poised in hammering Ahab's flag to the mast as the waters engulf it and a sky-hawk interposing its wing between hammer and flag—is magnificently apt. Ishmael, in contrast, grows from a similar imaginative restrictiveness (e.g., his desire to impose a single metaphoric meaning on the whaling chapel and its pulpit, or on the mat-making), to a reluctance to analyse or to name. His "disappearance" during the major part of the book after such a rambunctious presence in the opening suggests his submergence into the world around him. There he develops the ability to accept ambiguities and symbolic resonances that, like Keats' negative capability, is his saving grace.

But on a second level, Melville's sense of the limitations of language manifests itself in a way that is much closer to Absurdist theatre: as content, it is beginning to help shape the form. The opening "Extracts" of the sub-sub-librarian are a lifeless (and often wrong) attempt to harpoon the whale in language; as such, they mock the whole process of language which the novel itself—ironically enough—so triumphantly affirms. The cetology chapters may be seen as the same sort of linguistic joke, scrupulously detailing—with that nineteenth-century American love of fact—what the whole dramatic thrust of the novel asserts is ultimately unknowable. Finally, there is the role of Pip. If Ishmael's experience of being turned around at the helm expresses a momentary dislocation from the world of logical predictability, a glimpse into the Absurdist world where both time and place are out of joint, Pip is a citizen of that world. As the one character on board who, in his near-drowning, has looked beyond the world of men, who has seen "God's foot upon the treadle of the loom," and has seen it as "indifferent," Pip is Melville's first fully developed absurd character. His separation from the world of ordinary rationality is reflected in his language. His first utterance after his return to the ship occurs in "The Doubloon" chapter and is simply a conjugation ("I look, you look, he looks . . ."), mocking not only the "looking" experience by which the complex symbol of the doubloon is variously interpreted, but also the traditional attempt to impose an order on experience with language. From this point on, Ahab's increasing affinity with Pip is a darker alliance than that of Lear and his Fool; the vacant pupils of Pip's eyes, in which Ahab is mesmerised, offer no possibility of either self-knowledge or redemption. Pip's language gives voice to that world beyond the "pasteboard masks" that Ahab recognised as a possible dimension of reality.

Bartleby gives voice to it in a more realistic way. The vacuity of walled-in world is the mirror image of the lawyer's "safe" liberalism ("Are we not both the sons of Adam?"), and in opposing an order of "preferences" to an order of "assumptions" Melville is questioning all the presuppositions of everyday reality. Bartleby would be perfectly at home in world of Camus, Beckett, or Ionesco.

In the totally absurd world of *The Confidence Man,* language is predominantly a disguise. Disguise, of course, is a traditional comic device, and Melville, fascinated by the question of human identity in an unknowable universe, exploited its resources often. In the earlier novels the disguises are visual; by *The Confidence Man* they have become verbal as well, and more subtly deceptive. *The Confidence Man* has outgrown the trickster figure of the frontier humorists. If the fools on this ship of fools are all victims, so too is the reader, for the style is continually undercutting not only normal values (as in the opening scene where the reader's sympathies have only hypocrisy or cruelty to chose between), but the very nature of reality. The only "truth" that is affirmed in the book turns out to be from the Book of Apocrypha, and the style, as R. W. B. Lewis has noted, is self-cancelling, like that of Beckett. The puns that echo through this book have moved from sheer rhetorical word play (e.g., "[Jarl] eschewed the chew"), through Dickensian satire (e.g., "snivelisation"), to a profound sense of the interpenetration of language and reality (e.g., "Dis poor old Darkie, and werry well wordy"). *The Confidence Man* is the darkest comedy in American literature until Vonnegut or Pynchon.

After this, it scarcely seems surprising that Melville, who drew so much emotional sustenance from his writing, felt that it and he were played out. There was nothing to say, and if there had been, there was no way of saying it—at least not in the fictional medium that had been his strength. It is tempting to regard Melville's "silence" after 1857 as simply a realistic recognition that he could not make a professional career out of writing. Certainly, this is a partial truth; Melville was undoubtedly hungry for both critical and financial success. Yet the faltering of such an intensely creative drive can hardly be seen in such cold-blooded terms. Melville's English admirer, Robert Buchanan, writing in 1889 of Melville's reported resolution "on account of the public neglect of his work, never to write another line," was at least more imaginatively in tune with the novelist's dilemma. He concludes with the comment: "Conceive this Titan silenced." Both internal and external evidence point to a deepening misanthropy in Melville from *Mardi* on. It is this, primarily, that Hawthorne commented on in his Liverpool journal. And, in the books Melville read during this period, the passages he chose to score invariably reflected a nihilism with which he identified. In Arnold's essay on Maurice de Guerin, for example, Melville scored and boxed the following quotation from Guerin: "The literary career seems to me unreal, both in its essence and in the rewards which one seeks from it, and therefore marred by a secret absurdity." In a marginal comment, he noted: "This is the finest verbal statement of a truth which everyone who thinks in these days must have felt." In the face of such misanthropy, Melville's literary impulse found the gulf between language and reality as wide as that between Babo's, or Benito Cereno's, secret knowledge (expressed only in silence) and the long-winded testamentary evidence of the court proceedings, or that between the succession of verbal masks in *The Confidence Man*. The fact that Melville's next expression was in poetry— a genre "eminently adapted for unpopularity"—suggests that financial motivations had ceased to matter at all. Whatever success he found in the new genre—and certainly both *Battle Pieces* and *Clarel* are major works— the writing was laborious, slow, and, for a thirty-year span, small; and, the sub-titles of his last privately-printed volumes (*Tiroleon* and *Other Ventures in Minor Verse* and *Weeds and Wildings Chiefly: With a Rose or Two*), reflect a certain self-deprecation. Significantly, though, Melville found his way back to fiction through poetry, beginning his painful five-year working of *Billy Budd* through the poem that remains such an odd finale to the novella.

In *Billy Budd* the fictional rhetoric is slow and tortuous, and it is a story very much about the failure of language. That preoccupation both determines the basic plot and frames the formal ordering of the narrative. Billy hits out at Claggart's unjust accusations and kills him simply because Billy has a stammer and cannot articulate the words to rebuff him in any other way. W. H. Auden, interpreting Billy as a symbol of the existence of Goodness, claimed that he "wore a stammer like a decoration." But Billy's stammer is only "a decoration" in the logically consistent world of his original ship—*The Rights of Man*—where he can act instinctively and constructively when he is threatened. When he punches the belligerent sailor on that ship, he wins respect and friendship for his action. The world of the *Bellipotent*, however, to which Billy is press-ganged into service, is a much more absurd world, where all natural logic and law are suspended, though their appearances are more scrupulously insisted on. Here the stammer becomes not so much a "decoration" as a pointed symbol of the failure of language to suggest any kind of conceptual truth.

This theme is a leitmotif throughout the story. Claggart uses clichés ("Handsome is as handsome does") to cloak his real, and ultimately inexplicable, antagonism. His language is not a revelation but a mask. The Old Dansker, bearing the visible scars of age and experience, is the only one on board who knows everything; but when Billy goes to him for advice, he communicates his knowledge only in cryptic riddles which Billy is unable to interpret. The most blatant dramatization of the failure of language is in Captain Vere's speech to the court. Here Vere's insistence on "forms, measured forms" is working in direct opposition to what his eyes and his instincts have shown him to be the truth. His claim that a different standard of justice operates in a war situation is a self-deception that is decried by the fact that he called a court at all, by the general opinion of the other members of the court, and by the surgeon beforehand. There was no need to hang Billy. Vere didn't want to. Billy is hoisted on the petard of purely rhetorical absurdities.

The leitmotif is continued through other examples of the incomprehensibility of language: Billy's enigmatic "God bless Captain Vere!"; the embryonic "wave of sound" from the crown witnessing the execution; the distortions of the newspaper account of the incident; and the poem at the end, by which Billy passes out of the world of realistic prose into the mythical world of poetry.

Thus, throughout Melville's work, as fictional sophistication increased so too did a conceptual awareness of language; and from using it as a vehicle to contain his comic spirit he moved to a gradual mocking of the very assumptions of language. The dark and peculiarly modern sense of comedy that arises from such mockery brings him close to Joyce as well as to Camus. One gets a hint of the change in the naming of characters. The sheer gusto of names like Yoomi and Babbalanja, or the Dickensian delight in names like Fleece, Ginger Nut, and Turkey, is simple enough. But the confusion of Queequeg and Quohog at the signing-on of the *Pequod's* crew hints, beyond the immediate burlesque comedy, at a deeper questioning of identity, while the slippery renamings of the Confidence Man suggest both conscious deceit and a denial of any identity. In *Billy Budd* there is a very real sense in which language has become for Melville the "vast practical joke" that the universe was for Ishmael. Though the character of Jarl in *Mardi* and the Old Dansker in *Billy Budd* apparently resemble each other, there is in fact a great conceptual jump from the "lock-jawed" Jarl, whose taciturnity is comically lamented by Taji on the ground of companionship, to the shrewd Dansker, who knows everything and chooses to tell it only in Delphic riddles.

Throughout Melville's long writing career, then, the devices, the perspectives, the deployment, the very concepts of comedy changed. As with most great artists, the changes were in the direction if increasing abstraction. What began as a set of inherited comic devices, exploited for their proven entertainment value, developed first into a psychological interest in the relation between a sense of humor and the mind that projects it. Later, as the concept of humor flowed into a sense of personal and cosmic absurdity, it developed into a philosophical interest in the relation between vision and expression, reality and language, "assumptions" and "preferences." The ultimate irony, of course, followed his death. Could the dispirited Melville, so conscious of having missed the laurel wreath in his own century, have foreseen the barrage of critical adulation he was to receive in the next, he would have died laughing.

RICHARD H. BRODHEAD

"Mardi":
Creating the Creative

'If this book be meant as a pleasantry, the mirth has been oddly left out—if as an allegory, the key of the casket is "buried in ocean deep"—if as a romance, it fails from tediousness—if as a prose-poem, it is chargeable with puerility.' This is what the reviewer of *The Athenaeum* had to say about Melville's *Mardi* and his comments no doubt express the views of many intelligent readers, both at the time of the book's appearance and since. Even readers who are enthusiastic about *Mardi* tend to hedge their praise with reservations—Melville's French admirer Philarète Chasles, who judged it 'un des plus singuliers livres qui aient paru depuis long-temps sur la face du globe', also called it 'oeuvre inouie, digne d'un Rabelais sans gaieté, d'un Cervantes sans grace, d'un Voltaire sans goût'; Hawthorne wrote: ' "Mardi" is a rich book, with depths here and there that compel a man to swim for his life. It is so good that one scarcely pardons the writer for not having brooded long over it, so as to make it a great deal better.'

Every unkind thing that has been said about *Mardi* is more or less true. It is the loosest and baggiest of prose monsters, a book that changes direction freely on its way it knows not where, its ramblings held together only by the flimsy framework of a quest for an insubstantial maiden that would itself be completely forgotten if a boatload of phantom damsels did not appear every eighty pages or so to pelt the quester with symbolic flowers.

From *New Perspectives on Meville*, edited by Faith Pullin. Copyright © 1978 by Edinburgh University Press.

The style of the book, with its addiction to bombast and the more mechanical sorts of poetic effects, is usually something to be endured, not enjoyed. Its metaphysical soarings, in which philosophical commonplaces are delivered as if they were newly discovered truths, are often enough to make a lover of Melville the deep diver blush. But the important thing is not that *Mardi* has flaws but that it has ones of such an order. The chaos of its narrative is not the petty fault of an author who has tried to make a work in a conventional form but failed for lack of skill, but the massive one of an author who has tried to construct a work in a radically new way. Similarly its more embarrassing passages of poetry and philosophy are products not of a simple stylistic or intellectual deficiency—the author of *Mardi* is obviously equipped to do many sorts of things well—but of the fact that Melville is straining after effects that are so grand in them, and so far beyond what he has the powers to achieve. What is remarkable about *Mardi* is not its specific virtues or defects but the boldness of its endeavour. Where did Melville find the confidence to depart so completely not just from his own earlier works but from any easily recognizable formal model? How could he have dared to go on working at a project that required him to live so far beyond his artistic means? Melville never was a cowardly author, but the writing of *Mardi* was little less than an exercise in sheer audacity.

As Merrell Davis has demonstrated, many of *Mardi*'s peculiarities are results of the peculiar way in which it was written. Melville's letters show that after finishing *Omoo* he planned a third work that would continue the story of his South Seas adventures where *Omoo* left off. But a report from his publisher on the sales of his books discouraged him from attempting another work in the same format. This coincided with an event of the first importance in Melville's inner life, an explosion of consciousness touched off by his discovery of great literary works of the past (in early 1848 he began reading Rabelais, Montaigne, Sir Thomas Browne, and Coleridge, among others) and by what he later called the 'burst[ing] out in himself' of a 'bottomless spring of original thought.' The combination of pressure from without and the activation of a powerful creative energy within him led to a series of changes in the plan of the book he was at work on. A letter to his English publisher, John Murray, on 1 January 1848, claims that 'the book now in hand, clothes the whole subject in new attractions & combines in one cluster all that is romantic, whimsical & poetic in Polynusia'. He is feeling his way toward a new mode of composition, one less tied to documentary fact and actual experience, but he has not yet made a complete break with his earlier works—'It is yet a continuous narrative', he hastens to add. But when he writes to Murray again, on 25 March, this break has been effected.

I believe that a letter I wrote you some time ago—I think my last but one—gave you to understand, or implied, that the work I then had in view was a bona-vide narrative of my adventures in the Pacific, continued from 'Omoo'—My object in now writing you—I should have done so ere this—is to inform you of a change in my determinations. To be blunt: the work I shall next publish will ⟨be⟩ in down-right earnest [be] a 'Romance of Polynisian Adventure'.

Melville goes on to explain here, as he does in the preface to *Mardi*, that his chief motive for writing such a work is to show readers who doubted the authenticity of *Typee* and *Omoo* that 'a *real* romance of mine . . . is made of different stuff altogether'. But another inducement to change his plans, he continues, is that Polynesia furnishes a rich poetic material

which to bring out suitably, required only that play of freedom & invention accorded only to the Romancer & poet.—However, I thought, that I would postpone trying my hand at any thing fanciful of this sort, till some future day: tho' at times when in the mood I threw off occasional sketches applicable to such a work.—Well: proceeding in my narrative of *facts* I began to feel an incurible distaste for the same; & a longing to plume my pinions for a flight, & felt irked, cramped & fettered by plodding along with dull common places,—So suddenly standing [abandoning?] the thing alltogether, I went to work heart & soul at a romance which is now in fair progress, since I had worked at it under an earnest ardor.—Shout not, nor exclaim 'Pshaw! Puh!'—My romance I assure you is no dish water nor its model borrowed from the Circulating Library. It is something new I assure you, & original if nothing more. But I can give you no adequate idea, of it. You must see it for yourself.—Only forbear to prejudge it.— It opens like a true narrative—like 'Omoo' for example, on ship board— & the romance & poetry of the thing thence grow continually, till it becomes a story wild enough I assure you & with a meaning too.

This letter, surely one of the most extraordinary ever sent by a young author to an established publisher, is a perfect expression of the audacity that brought *Mardi* into being. I got tired of what I was doing, Melville tells Murray, so I decided to do something else (without, of course, bothering to start the book over); and if you don't think that's a proper way to compose a book, you're wrong—'My *instinct* is to out with the Romance, & let me say that instincts are prophetic, & better than acquired wisdom—which alludes remotely to your experience in literature as an eminent publisher'. As Melville tells the story, having started writing a book like his earlier ones, he begins to feel the stirring of an urge that cannot find expression in that form. As he continues writing this urge becomes stronger and stronger until it begins to generate fragments of a second work, different in kind, alongside the first. Finally it becomes so imperious that he can no longer resist it or channel it off; at this point he discards his initial plans and allows this urge to take over the writing of his book. The letter that chronicles this usurpation marks a crucial turning point in Melville's career, the moment at which he starts conceiving of his works not as a record of preexisting experience—a narrative of *facts*—but as a creative imaginative activity. His letter suggests that in its change of design *Mardi* itself acts out this shift, that as one sort of book displaces another in it it bursts the fetters of conventional form ('true narrative') and a reportorial tie to reality ('dull common place'), freeing the imagination to soar into realms of beauty and strangeness.

Melville clearly feels that to be properly judged *Mardi* needs to be taken on its own terms, seen as making its own formal model rather than imitating an already available one, and that it needs to be read as a metamorphosis, a growth through radical changes of state. I am interested in trying to understand the strange thing that *Mardi* is, and also what it means for Melville to have undertaken such a work at this stage in his career; and it seems to me that Melville's directions to Murray point to the way in which the book should be approached. This is to pursue it through its changes—not to locate its chapters and sequences in relation to an externally established chronology, but to discover from within the book what sort of form it proposes for itself, and how this form evolves as the book unfolds.

As Melville's letters lead us to expect, the opening of *Mardi* does bear a direct resemblance to *Typee* and *Omoo*. Here again a sailor-narrator tells how he came to jump ship, with a companion, in search of adventure. He provides several reasons for his act, making sure that it seems plausibly motivated; he also provides a good deal of circumstantial information about nautical matters, taking care to locate his tale in a world that is solidly documented, if unfamiliar to us. But really *Mardi* is something quite different from *Typee* or *Omoo*, and it must be stressed that it is so from the first. While on watch in the masthead in the first chapter the narrator broods on the islands that lie westward in the Pacific, 'loosely laid down upon the charts, and invested with all the charms of dream-land', and that he will leave behind if he sails northward on the *Arcturion*.

> I cast my eyes downward to the brown planks of the dull, plodding ship, silent from stem to stern; then abroad.
>
> In the distance what visions were spread! The entire western horizon high piled with gold and crimson clouds; airy arches, domes, and minarets; as if the yellow, Moorish sun were setting behind some vast Alhambra. Vistas seemed leading to worlds beyond. To and fro, and all

over the towers of this Nineveh in the sky, flew troops of birds. Watching them long, one crossed my sight, flew through a low arch, and was lost to view. My spirit must have sailed in with it; for directly, as in a trance, came upon me the cadence of mild billows laving a beach of shells, the waving of boughs, and the voices of maidens, and the lulled beatings of my own dissolved heart, all blended together.

Shipboard life is a plodding affair, its very tedium heightening the lure for the narrator of what Ishmael calls the wonder world. Although he begins by thinking of this fascinating alternative in terms of actual Pacific islands, what attracts him quickly changes from an exotic location in the real geographical world to a vista in a world beyond, and from a place to be reached by physical travel to a state to be attained through the heightening of desire, ecstatic transformations of consciousness, and the flight of the visionary spirit. The narrator shares Melville's aversion to dull common-places; his adventure, like his creator's, defines itself as an imaginative flight into a romance world of expanded possibility.

What follows from this opening is a voyage not to strange lands but into strangeness itself. The narrative mode of *Mardi*'s opening phase has less in common with that of *Typee* than with that of Edgar Allan Poe's *Narrative of A. Gordon Pym*, which uses the format of the nautical adventure story to lead the reader on a magical mystery tour. The narrator's jumping ship, like Pym's running away from home, is presented not just as a rejection of a settled way of life but as a rejection of ordinary reality. His desertion is not just a lark but a knowing act of 'moral dereliction' that is also an act of suicide, leaving him feeling like 'his own ghost unlawfully tenanting a defunct carcass'; like Pym denying his identity to his grandfather and descending into the coffin-like enclosure in the ship's hold, this narrator's adventure begins with a conscious rejection of the moral obligations of ordinary life and a willed dying to his own ordinary self. The chapters that follow, describing life on the ocean in an open boat and the sense of immobility and unreality induced by the calm, do not function simply as accounts of actual experience; like Pym's minute dissection of his feelings in the wildly accelerating boat or in the dark confinement of the hold, these are records of an extreme dislocation in the experience of space and time, a dislocation that is itself one of these characters' means for breaking out of ordinary reality. Similarly the chapters on sharks, swordfish, and marine phosphorescence are not merely informative; like Pym's discussions of the Galapagos turtle or the nests of penguins, they evoke a vision of nature as full of strange and alien forms. As nature becomes more marvellous in these books, marvels become more natural—the ship *Parki* in *Mardi*, like the ship of death in *Pym*, is experienced as a phantom craft; Samoa, like Dirk Peters, looks like a hitherto unknown form of human life.

The same patterns govern the actions of these books on their progress into strangeness. One of these patterns is the repeated overthrow of figures of authority. The narrator of *Mardi* gains through desertion the freedom from his captain's control that Pym gains through a mutinous rising of the crew of the *Grampus*. The massacre of the officers of the *Parki* by savages who have cunningly concealed their diabolical malice exactly repeats the fate of the captain and crew of Poe's ship *Jane Guy*. Another is a pattern of violation of taboos and sacred interdicts. *Mardi* has nothing to match the cannibal episode in *Pym*, but its narrator's most pronounced trait is his urge to pry into what he has been warned away from. These two patterns come together in *Mardi* when, after the *Parki* episode, the narrator murders the priest and father Aleema, and, having been told 'that it would be profanation', pierces the tent to seize the sacred maiden Yillah. In both books the violation of taboos and the destruction of authorities are the means by which the adventurer breaks into forbidden territory. The massacre of the crew of the *Jane Guy* and his disregard of the natives' dread of its sacredness bring Pym closer to the unutterable experience enshrouded by the Pole's white veil. By the same logic the conjunction of murder, sexual penetration, and profanation committed by the narrator of *Mardi* has as its immediate consequence the opening up before him of Mardi, the world beyond for which he sought.

The list of similarities between *Mardi* and the *Narrative of A. Gordon Pym* could be greatly extended, but these few examples suggest how like the books are in their procedures. What is important about this is not so much that it reveals particular debts on Melville's part as that it demonstrates what kind of a book Melville is writing in *Mardi*'s first fifty chapters—like Poe, he is using the form of the adventure narrative to conduct an exploration into other modes of reality. But, interestingly, when his book comes upon the islands of Mardi this seems to be as much a moment of discovery for the author as it is for his hero. The archipelago spreads before him a whole world of fictional possibilities, and at first he does not seem certain what he is going to do with them. He keeps alluding to Jarl, Samoa, and Yillah as if he thinks that his story's way might lie in continuing his narrator's earlier adventures; meanwhile he begins staging episodes on the island of Oro, and as it were testing what he can make of it. All at once he seems to see how he can go about exploiting Mardi in his book, and at this point he modifies his narrative in a drastic way. Samoa and Jarl become effectively invisible; Yillah vanishes, leaving the narrator to pursue her just half-heartedly enough to provide a pretext for a voyage; King Media, the historian Mohi, the philosopher Babbalanja, and the poet Yoomy join him for a tour through Mardi; then the narrator himself recedes, leaving the book to carry on not as the record of his adventures and speech but as a freewheeling island-hopping symposium.

The section of *Mardi* that follows takes as its model the anatomy form that Melville would have been familiar with in Swift and Rabelais. As in the third book of *Gulliver's Travels* or the fourth book of *Pantagruel*, Melville's island voyaging permits him to people a world with shapes of his own invention. Some of these mirror features of the actual world more or less directly, as Pimminee reflects social affectation, or Maramma the collective blindness of institutional religion. Others seem completely unreal, wildly imaginative, until, as in a caricature, we recognize in their grotesque distortion a previously concealed feature of reality: the bloody war games through which the lords Hello and Piko maintain the population of Diranda in equilibrium thus bring into focus the nightmare of human destructiveness unleashed by a cynically calculated appeal to abstract values. But although the island voyage enables Melville to mirror actuality and to mock the lighter and graver follies of human behaviour, satire is only one ingredient of this part of the book, not the controlling intention. In the imagining of these islands the desire to expose specific abuses is subservient to the free play of fantastic invention. In any case the islands are surrounded by a sea of talk, insets in a never-adjourning colloquy that passes freely from poetic recitations to nonsense to philosophical speculations to celebrations of food and drink.

As Melville closes his Poe and opens his Rabelais the kind of book he is writing undergoes a radical shift. But it is also worth noting that the metaphysical adventure narrative in the manner of Poe and the Rabelaisian anatomy have similarities as narrative models. They are, thus, both episodic in structure. In the early parts of *Mardi* as in *Pym* ships appear out of nowhere and then vanish again, and the narrator goes through experiences which, although they are vividly real while they last, disappear without a trace when they are ended. The sequences of action simply succeed one another, without being caused by what came before them and without causing what comes after. The essence of organization of the anatomy, whether we see it in *Mardi* or in *Gargantua and Pantagruel* or in *The Tale of a Tub* or in *Tristram Shandy*, lies in the weakness of its narrative line, its failure to give the book's ramblings the coherence of motion directed to an end. Each island in Mardi is by definition a separate occasion for Melville, and each reopening of discussion offers him a chance to pursue a new topic. The result is that in both parts of his narrative Melville is remarkably free to project an imaginative possibility, toy with it, develop it further if he likes, and then drop it when he is tired of it, going on to project another without having to consult the requirements of an overall plan.

Not only do they emphasize the independence of parts over the coherence of a cumulative design; both of the forms Melville is working with also permit major structural modifications to be made while they go along. One of the most striking resemblances between *Mardi* and the *Narrative of A. Gordon Pym* is that in both of them characters and scenes that are distinctly defined at one moment undergo dreamlike metamorphoses at the next. In both books, for example, it is impossible to make the narrator compose into a consistent personality as, from chapter to chapter, he exhibits not only totally different amounts of knowledge and sensitivity but even totally different traits of character. This instability means that, while ostensibly pursuing the story of someone's adventures, the books actually keep revising the nature of their adventure—what is a dream voyage into mental darkness at one point becomes a white imperialist's voyage among primitive peoples at another, and so on. The anatomy form, in addition to encouraging frequent modulations of mode, also allows Melville to define and redefine the terms of his action while in the middle of it—it permits him thus to turn the visit to Mardi's islands into a tour of the contemporary social world, and then to continue it as such for twenty-five chapters, without violating the logic of the book. Both of the genres Melville employs in *Mardi* maximize the author's on-going freedom within his projected form. They require nothing of him but that he improvise, that he keep making his book up as it goes along.

After he has pursued his voyage through the countries of Europe and the regions of the United States Melville again seems uncertain what he is going to do next. At first he solves his dilemma simply by carrying on with his device, extending his tour through Asia, Africa, and the Middle East. But the tour is yielding rapidly diminishing returns, and it is clear from its accelerated pace that Melville has little interest in its continuation. Then he sees another way to solve his problem. He simply puts his device aside and steps forward from behind his book's action, addressing us now in his own voice:

> Oh, reader, list! I've chartless voyaged. With compass and the lead, we had not found these Mardian Isles. Those who boldly launch, cast off all cables. . . . Hug the shore, naught new is seen; and 'Land ho!' at last was sung, when a new world was sought.

What appears to happen here is that the breakdown of his narrative device precipitates a moment of genuine self-recognition for Melville. He begins with what sounds like an explanation specifically of his present predicament —I don't know where I'm going, I've been writing without a plan; his blustering invocations of New World explorers sound like pieces of bravado, attempts to present his directionlessness as a sign of courage. But having opened the subject, he now goes on to define more and more precisely how his book came to be written, and what it might mean to have written a book in this way.

> And though essaying but a sportive sail, I was driven from my course, by a blast resistless; and ill-provided, young, and bowed to the brunt of things before my prime, still fly before the gale;—hard have I striven to keep stout heart.
>
> And if it harder be, than e'er before, to find new climes, when now our seas have oft been circled by ten thousand prows,—much more the glory!
>
> But this new world here sought, is stranger far then his, who stretched his vans from Palos. It is the world of mind; wherein the wanderer may gaze round, with more of wonder than Balboa's band roving through the golden Aztec glades.
>
> But fiery yearnings their own phantom-future make, and deem it present. So, if after all these fearful, fainting trances, the verdict be, the golden haven was not gained;—yet, in bold quest thereof, better to sink in boundless deeps, than float on vulgar shoals; and give me, ye gods, an utter wreck, if wreck I do.

Here Melville brings to consciousness what he has been doing in writing *Mardi*, and as he does so he redefines his book from within one more time. He comes to see that its true action is not his characters' adventures but his own creative process: that its real voyage is the imaginative one he has undertaken in conceiving *Mardi*, that the real object of its quest is nothing his characters seek but the mental world he himself discloses through the act of creating his book. His metaphors of exploration lose their initial defensiveness and develop into a fully formed aesthetic of adventure, an aesthetic that validates his audacity in writing *Mardi* as the boldness necessary for new discovery, and that enables him to recognize the possibility of the book's failure and to accept it as proof that its attempt was bold enough.

After 'Sailing On' Melville continues with his symposium-cruise, and at the end of the book he even reaches back to pick up the thread of the narrator's progress through profanation into strange new worlds. But it is hard not to feel that *Mardi* reaches its real culmination in this chapter and the meditations that follow from it. Subsequent discussions are increasingly preoccupied with what Media calls 'the metaphysics of genius', and in Babbalanja's discourse on the poet Lombardo in chapter 180 *Mardi* renews its consideration of itself as its author's creation. The author who alluded to a blast resistless that led him prematurely to attempt such a work becomes even more candidly confessional here, taking us behind the curtain to reveal the financial and family pressures that are driving him to finish his book, and sharing what he has learned about the genesis of works of art and the experience of inspiration in composing it. He also formulates more clearly what the writing of *Mardi* signifies. Babbalanja tells King Abrazza:

> When Lombardo set about his work, he knew not what it would become. He did not build himself in with plans; he wrote right on; and so doing, got deeper and deeper into himself; and like a resolute traveler, plunging through baffling woods, at last was rewarded for his toils. 'In good time,' saith he, in his autobiography, 'I came out into a serene, sunny, ravishing region; full of sweet scents, singing birds, wild plaints, roguish laughs, prophetic voices. Here we are at last, then,' he cried; 'I have created the creative'.

Where in 'Sailing On' he implied that there is some connection between chartless voyaging and coming upon new worlds of mind, Melville sees much more clearly here how writing and discovery are linked, and he is able to specify much more precisely what the 'world of mind' consists of. Writing spontaneously and with out plan is the means by which Lombardo blazes a trail into the wilderness of his mind until, at its centre, he finds a paradise within. This paradise is not so much a place as a deep source of generative mental energy; and it is not something already existing yet concealed but something that needs to be brought into being. Through the act of writing, thus, Lombardo creates the creative.

In this chapter the novel unfolded without direction and without a governing intention finds out where it was headed and why it followed the course it did. The novel that revelled in improvisation for five hundred pages discovers what improvisation is for—discovers that it is through the exercise of its freedom and invention, its unconstrained play of conception and articulation, that the creative imagination brings itself into being. Having, by means of it, created the creative, Lombardo can discard his first writing and begin a work of greatness. In the images of the chapter it is the trash that needed to be removed from the mine for the ore of genius to be reached, the callow form that the eagle had to pass through on its way to attaining maturity and power. Melville is similarly detached from his own writing in *Mardi*. Having lavished his inventive energy on them he shows no further interest in the book's individual episodes. He is the first to admit that it has deep flaws—Hawthorne's assessment of *Mardi*, for instance, echoes Melville's own, made in the book itself; ' "It has faults—all mine; its merits all its own;—but I can toil no longer. . . . My canvas was small," said [Lombardo]; "crowded out were hosts of things that came last. But Fate is in it" '. What sustains his equanimity in the face of its faults is the fact that the aim implicit in the book is not the production of the perfect work Hawthorne has in mind. What he intends to achieve in writing it is not really to be understood at the level of the work itself at all. If Lombardo expresses Melville's thoughts, as there is every reason to assume he does, the value of *Mardi* for its author lies not in what it is but in what his composition of it could bring into being—his own mature creative self.

Melville consistently thinks of *Mardi* in terms of a future attainment that it points toward. Shortly after finishing it he writes to Evert Duyckinck:

> Would that a man could do something & then say—It is finished.—not that tone thing only, but all others—that he has reached his uttermost, & can never exceed it. But live & push—tho' we put one leg forward ten miles—its no reason the other must lag behind—no, *that* must again distance the other . . . .

The writing of *Mardi* is a step; even though he longs for it to be a final achievement he recognizes that it is truly only a stage in the ongoing process of realizing his creative potential. In a letter to *Mardi*'s English publisher, Richard Bentley, Melville speaks of the book in terms of germination and maturing: 'you know perhaps that there are goodly harvests which ripen late, especially when the grain is remarkably strong'. In another letter to Duyckinck he speaks of it in terms of education: 'I admit that I learn by experience & not by divine intuitions. Had I not written & published 'Mardi', in all likelihood, I would not be as wise as I am now, or may be.' We know, as Melville at this point could not, what the author of *Mardi* would go on to achieve. Since he himself conceives of it as pointing forward we might now look back at *Mardi* from Melville's later works, and try to discern what relation it actually has to what comes after it.

In terms of his career as a whole perhaps the most striking thing about *Mardi* is the emergence in it of the Melville who compulsively engages in ontological heroics. In *Mardi* Melville meets metaphysics and succumbs to its charms. The symposium format enables him to stage his first comedy of thought, to play with intellectual puzzles and explore the paradoxes of intellectual positions. The figure of Babbalanja embodies for the first time in Melville's fiction an obsession with cosmic riddles and a resolution to uncover 'that which is beneath the seeming'. Certainly one of the main functions of the anatomy form that he adopts midway through the book is that it permits him to speculate, with varying degrees of seriousness, on questions like what man is, what truth is, and what happens after death.

What Melville has to say about the problem of the universe in *Mardi* is often trite and naive. He is so excited by his discoveries for instance of how classical ethics prefigure Christian ones or of Hartley's distinction between the Necessitarian and the Fatalist that he presents them as unexampled profundities. Their sophomoric quality is not lessened by the style in which he carries out his investigations, a style that can sink to such lows as 'Are we angels, or dogs?' or 'It hinges upon this: Have we angelic spirits?' Above all there is a certain glibness about *Mardi*'s philosophizings. Its demonstration that the omnipresence of a good God is incompatible with the existence of evil comes across more as a clever logical trick than anything else. Statements like Babbalanja's 'truth is in things, and not in words' or Media's 'final, last thoughts you mortals have none; nor can have' are almost purely throwaway lines. The problem of evil, of the relation of knowledge to reality, of the impossibility of attaining final truth—Melville addresses them all in *Mardi*, but without yet being tasked and heaped by them. The result is that throughout the book ideas are simply tossed off by an author who does not suspect that what he says may be truer than he knows.

But even at their feeblest *Mardi*'s philosophical excursions are not without importance. In them Melville is appropriating a kingdom of thought. If he repeats ideas without having assimilated them, nevertheless *by* repeating them he begins to possess them, to make them his own. Thus as his writing proceeds his thought grows in depth. He keeps returning to subjects like the relation of belief to truth, considering it once in terms of religious belief, another time in terms of storytelling, another time in terms of our knowledge of the physical world—he never stops to treat it systematically, but with each return to it he extends the range of its implications. As he goes along ideas seem to be pressing up into his mind, making themselves felt in a number of places until finally, by grasping and articulating them, he brings them fully to the surface. Thus he discusses at one point how the alternating domination of his psyche by 'contrary impulses, over which he had not the faintest control' makes King Peepi incapable of 'moral obligation to virtue'; at another Babbalanja broaches a psychological theory based on demonic possession; at another the narrator, rapt in an ecstasy of inspiration, describes his mastery by 'this Dionysius that rides me'. All of these are partial versions of a notion that finally gets fully explored in chapter 143, where, discoursing on 'the incomprehensible stranger in me', Babbalanja develops the idea that an instinctive, involuntary energy lies beneath the conscious rational self, governing and impelling it.

This notion is familiar from the works that follow *Mardi*. Babbalanja's 'one dark chamber in me is retained by the old mystery' recalls Ishmael's allusion to an old State-secret kept at the bottom of the self, and his '[men] do not govern themselves, but are governed by their very natures' is echoed by Ahab's discovery of his identity as a mysterious fatality in 'The Symphony'. His explanation of the priority of instinctive passions to the moral sense looks forward to Melville's study of the play of unconscious sexual impulses on the ethical consciousness in *Pierre*. *Mardi's* treatment of belief and truth is similarly familiar: not only does it explore the involuted relations of truth, fiction, falsehood, trust, and doubt that will be pursued again in *The Confidence-Man*, but it also begins to establish the convertibility of frames of reference that makes that book possible—that it is with fiction as with religion is an idea already implicit in *Mardi*. Any reader of *Mardi* could extend the list of its thematic similarities to the books that follow it. This is the work in which Melville begins brooding on what will concern him in his major novels. But it is not just that his essential preoccupations are all present in *Mardi*. It is in this book that he generates his own themes, discovers and brings them to initial formulation. Finally the fact that *Mardi* lacks the sophistication or profundity of Melville's mature work seems less significant than the fact that it originates what they continue.

There is the same teasing likeness between the images of *Mardi* and those of Melville's later books as there is between their themes. This is Melville's description of Aleema:

> The old priest, like a scroll of old parchment, covered all over with hieroglyphical devices, harder to interpret, I'll warrant, than any old Sanscrit manuscript. And upon his broad brow, deep-graven in wrinkles, were characters still more mysterious, which no Champollion nor gipsy could have deciphered.

It is impossible to read this without thinking of Queequeg's tattooing, those 'hieroglyphical marks' in which a departed seer 'had written out on his body a complete theory of the heavens and the earth, and a mystical treatise on the art of attaining truth . . . but whose mysteries not even himself could read, though his own live heart beat against them'. It is echoed even more precisely by the end of the chapter 'The Prairie' in *Moby-Dick*:

Champollion deciphered the wrinkled granite hieroglyphics. But there is no Champollion to decipher the Egypt of every man's and every being's face. Physiognomy, like every other human science, is but a passing fable. If the, Sir William Jones, who read in thirty languages, could not read the simplest peasant's face in its profounder and more subtle meanings, how may unlettered Ishmael hope to read the awful Chaldee of the Sperm Whale's brow? I but put that brow before you. Read it if you can.

To put it alongside these passages from Moby-Dick is to see how undeveloped Melville's image is in Mardi. He has got so far as to link Polynesian tattooing, wrinkles, hieroglyphics, and the deciphering achievements of Champollion and Sir William Jones, but he appears unaware of the symbolic content the resultant image could carry—the undecipherable hieroglyph has yet to become his preferred figure for a cosmic mystery that invites but perpetually thwarts the human effort to solve it. Describing a calm at sea in chapter 16 of Mardi Melville images a process by which the totality of elements fuse with one another to produce a nothingness, a 'blank', a 'vacuum', 'colorless', 'gray chaos in conception'. We are on the verge, here, of Moby-Dick's 'colorless, all-color of atheism from which we shrink'; all that is missing is a perception of the metaphysical condition such a fusion could symbolize. With these images as with his philosophical throwaways Melville produces out of nowhere something that will be saturated with significance in his future work, but that has yet to acquire that significance.

How is it that 'The Prairie' manages so to intensify and extend the implications of the figure through which Aleema's brow is described in Mardi? Certainly part of the answer lies in Ishmael's (and the Melville of Moby-Dick's) universalizing habit of mind. While Mardi keeps focussing on Aleema's face Ishmael moves from the Whale's brow to 'every being's face', and from the face physically understood to the face 'in its profounder and more subtle meanings'. But this difference is itself a function of the different ways in which they handle figurative language. Melville's prose in Mardi keeps the image and the reality it describes rigidly separate. It isolates the precise points (like, harder, more) at which comparisons between the face and a scroll of mysterious writing are being established. Further, it establishes comparisons only between features the two already share—the face's lines already are hieroglyphical devices; it is not the analogy of the scroll that makes them so. In the passage from Moby-Dick, by contrast, analogy becomes a dynamic process, and a process of genuine transfiguration. Features associated with faces and features associated with writing continue to interfuse with one another. The result of this fusion is that each of these normally separate areas of experience provides a new idiom in which the other may be expressed (wrinkled granite hieroglyphics, the Egypt of the face, the awful Chaldee of the brow) and a new set of terms in which the other may be understood—here legibility or illegibility is not a property already possessed by the face but one it acquires by virtue of being conceived of in terms of language. The essential difference between the two passages is that in the one from *Moby-Dick* Melville commits himself to metaphor, allowing the play of figuration to generate meaning as it evolves.

Mardi is full of restricted images, images that have not undergone such a genuinely metaphorical development. King Uhia, a moody aspirer who lunges through the present toward future achievements and who feels intolerably confined by the limits reality imposes on his will, clearly prefigures Captain Ahab, as his perception of the human cost of his aspiration—'Here am I vexed and tormented by ambition; no peace night nor day; my temples chafed sore by this cursed crown that I wear'—looks forward to Ahab's in 'Sunset' and 'The Symphony'. But only when the crown and the experience of wearing it are imagined in an expanding series of particularized details, details that are allowed to stand for ambition's self-inflicted pain, will Uhia's lament open out into Ahab's 'Is, then, the crown too heavy that I wear? . . . 'Tis iron—that I know—not gold.'Tis split, too—that I feel; the jagged edge galls me so, my brain seems to beat against the solid metal'. The ending of 'Sailing On'—'yet, in bold quest thereof, better to sink in boundless deeps, than float on vulgar shoals'—links pressing off into the ocean with heroic intellectual questing as Melville will again in 'The Lee Shore', and it even establishes the rhythms of 'The Lee Shore's' prose—'so, better is it to perish in that howling infinite, than be ingloriously dashed upon the lee, even if that were safety!' The difference is not that 'The Lee Shore' celebrates such questing more ardently than 'Sailing On' but that, by allowing the opposition of sea and shore to develop itself ('the port is pitiful; in the port is safety, comfort, hearthstone . . . ') and by allowing the figures thus generated to define the opposition between independence and spiritual timidity, it gives such questing an increasingly rich and precise content.

Many more examples could be added of images that are introduced in *Mardi* but only fully realized in Melville's later books—indeed almost every image central to his major work is present here in embryonic form. Really what is surprising is not that his later versions of these are richer but that so many of them are so exactly prefigured in this earlier book. And again, it is not just that Melville's personal symbolism is present in *Mardi*; what needs to be stressed is that in writing the book he is generating this symbolism, conceiving its figures, bringing them into focus, and beginning to explore what they might mean. Although he may not yet be fully aware of what they could signify, he is fashioning what has the capacity to carry significance. Although he has not yet connected his images with his metaphysical preoccupations, he is forging the means for their mature expression—what makes his later versions of *Mardi*'s philosophical insights original and profound is not an increase in their content as intellectual propositions but the dazzling metaphorical formulation Melville gives them, his expression of them through the very images we see him creating here. As he writes Melville is articulating his own mental world. In the process of composing *Mardi* he is conceiving ideas and images and partially unfolding their content; and what he does this with here is what he then possesses as the means for creating more fully developed work later.

We might look at one final example of how Melville works in *Mardi* and how what he writes here relates to his later writing. In chapter 180 Babbalanja explains that the opening of the artist's creative consciousness requires that he suffer:

> Woe it is, that reveals these things. He knows himself, and all that's in him, who knows adversity. To scale great heights, we must come out of lowermost depths. The way to heaven is through hell. We need fiery baptisms in the fiercest flames of our own bosoms. We must feel our hearts hot—hissing in us. And ere their fire is revealed, it must burn its way out of us; though it consume us and itself. Oh, sleek-cheeked Plenty! smiling at thine own dimples;—vain for thee to reach out after greatness. Turn! turn! from all your tiers of cushions of eider-down—turn! and be broken on the wheels of many woes. At white-heat, brand thyself; and count the scars, like old war-worn veterans, over campfires. Soft poet! brushing tears from lilies—this way! and howl in sackcloth and in ashes! Know, thou, that the lines that live are turned out of a furrowed brow. Oh! there is a fierce, a cannibal delight, in the grief that shrieks to multiply itself. That grief is miserly of its own; it pities all the happy.

The relation of suffering to greatness is a new idea to Melville here, and this paragraph is not so much a statement of it as an attempt to grasp it. Melville thus keeps talking and talking, trying to express his conception one way, then another, then another. And by saying it over and over, he comes to find out more fully what it means. Certainly the ideas of the first three or four sentences are commonplace enough, but by repeating these commonplaces he begins to be able to go beyond them. Similarly the images in the opening sentences are the merest clichés, but having practised on them he begins to generate more daring and original ones; and it is by becoming more vitally metaphoric that the passage comes to give its conception a distinctive and memorable formulation. We can see here in little the process by which, through the act of writing, Melville acquires augmented powers of thought and expression. We may not feel that the passage is perfectly successful. It is repetitious, it is excessively rhetorical, its images are uneven in quality. But it contains the germ of what Melville does successfully elsewhere. In its weaving of an association between greatness, woe, a ravaging flame, and a fiery scar it prefigures the introduction of the scarred and branded Ahab in *Moby-Dick*, looking 'like a man cut away from the stake, when the fire has overrunningly wasted all the limbs without consuming them'. Its explication of a wisdom that is woe prefigures Ishmael's meditations in 'The Try-Works', the conclusion of which, by reconceiving it in terms of the Catskill eagle, even manages to purge this passage's third sentence of its banality. And if Melville is able to develop these images and ideas more successfully elsewhere, it is in part because he has already attempted them for the first time here.

So many passages in the later books resemble *Mardi* in some way as to suggest that Melville is rewriting rather than writing. As he comes to realize in it, the true significance of *Mardi* is that it is the first draft of all his subsequent works. Not a draft in the sense that it consciously undertakes to produce a rough version of a work whose subject or form is defined, however vaguely, in advance—as we have seen, Melville refuses to build himself in with plans, asserting his right to improvise without constraint. Rather, it is a draft in the sense that, without attempting to foresee what it is a preparation for, it nevertheless gives initial formulation to the work that comes after it—without being directed toward any end, Melville's improvisational act generates themes, thoughts, characters, images, narrative forms, and stylistic features out of which other creations can then be made. In giving him the particular materials and skills that their composition required, and more generally in making him capable of conceiving and expressing them, the writing of *Mardi* made Melville the author who could then go on to write *Moby-Dick, Pierre,* and *The Confidence-Man.* To use Keats's words *Mardi* is the form in which the Genius of Poetry in Melville worked out its own salvation. Its spirited performance is the necessary prelude to the mature career of an author who always gained in power by exercising his power—who grew imaginative by exerting his invention, who grew profound by diving after deep thoughts, and who grew creative by engaging in the act of creation.

We have been considering how images and ideas that germinate in *Mardi* reappear in more fully developed forms in Melville's later novels. By way of an epilogue we might note that *Mardi*'s vision of the nature of its own creative act undergoes the same process of maturation. 'Sailing On' and Babbalanja's discourse on the Poet Lombardo are the first drafts of the concluding sections of *Pierre*, the sections treating Pierre's experience as an immature author attempting a mature work. Melville's earlier descriptions of how he was blown off course by a blast resistless and how Lombardo was 'churned into consciousness' are expanded into a full-scale analysis of how through 'a varied scope of reading' and the welling up of 'that bottomless spring of original thought which the occasion and time had caused to burst out in himself' Pierre is 'swayed to universality of thought'. The peculiar impulse of artistic confession, Melville's compulsion to push aside his narrative and share with us directly his personal experience as an author, reasserts itself here: *Pierre's* comments on authors composing 'paltry and despicable' works, 'born of unwillingness and the bill of the baker', repeat and elaborate on Babbalanja's description of Lombardo's anguished consciousness of his work's imperfections, a work undertaken through 'the necessity of bestirring himself to procure his yams'. Melville also returns to the notion of writing as an act of self-discovery and self-creation, expanding the story of Lombardo's creation of the creative into an even more detailed account of the symbiotic relation between verbal articulation and the generation of creative consciousness:

> that which now absorbs the time and the life of Pierre, is not the book, but the primitive elementalizing of the strange stuff, which in the act of attempting that book, has upheaved and upgushed in his soul. Two books are being writ; of which the world shall only see one, and that the bungled one. The larger book, and the infinitely better, is for Pierre's own private shelf. That it is, whose unfathomable cravings drink his blood; the other only demands his ink. But circumstances have so decreed, that the one can not be composed on the paper, but only as the other is writ down in his soul.

The amazing thing about *Mardi*'s concluding chapters is how well Melville's creative self comes to understand its doings and its needs in them. The wonder of these sections of *Pierre* is that, over the space of only three years, that self has come to know itself so much better—in terms of Melville's letter to Duyckinck they are the twenty-mile step through which his other leg catches up with and outdistances his first's ten-mile step. Thus the Melville who so enthusiastically goes about furnishing *Mardi* with what he is finding in books of literature and philosophy has recognized, by the time he writes *Pierre*, that 'all mere reading is apt to prove but an obstacle hard to overcome', that others' works can only obstruct the author's imagination unless he uses them 'simply [as] an exhilarative and provocative' to his own 'spontaneous creative thought'. Thus too the Melville who rejects all controls on the artist's work except that of the 'one autocrat within—his crowned and sceptered instinct' has discovered, by the time of *Pierre*, the artist's need to learn the discipline of a formal craft: however fine the marble in his mental quarry, Melville writes there, if he is to make a lasting work the young author 'must wholly quit . . . the quarry, for awhile; and not only go forth, and get tools to use in the quarry, but must go and thoroughly study architecture'. Above all he recognizes in *Pierre* that the mental stride he took in writing *Mardi* was not a completed movement but 'one of the stages of the transition' of his evolution, that in it he had only initiated the process of discovering a world of mind.

If they reveal a growth of self-knowledge, Melville's rewritings of *Mardi* in *Pierre* also reveal a radical reversal of vision. Thus, developing *Mardi*'s conceit that 'genius is full of trash', Melville writes in *Pierre*:

> it is often to be observed, that as in digging for precious metals in the mines, much earthy rubbish has first to be troublesomely handled and thrown out; so, in digging in one's soul for the fine gold of genius, much dullness and common-place is first brought to light. Happy would it be, if the man possessed in himself some receptacle for his own rubbish of this sort; but he is like the occupant of a dwelling, whose refuse can not be clapped into his own cellar, but must be deposited in the street before his own door, for the public functionaries to take care of. No common-place is ever effectually got rid of, except by essentially emptying one's self of it into a book; for once trapped in a book, then the book can be put into the fire, and all will be well. But they are not always put into the fire; and this accounts for the vast majority of miserable books over those of positive merit.

Here again the production of inferior work is seen as a stage through which an author must pass on his way to producing superior work, but here this process has costs as well as gains. The trash through the writing of which genius evolves persists as an encumbrance to the emerging artist; by writing it he becomes implicated in producing the mediocre literature in which works of merit are smothered. The image of Lombardo going deeper and deeper into himself is revised even more drastically.

> Yet now, forsooth, because Pierre began to see through the first superficiality of the world, he fondly weens he has come to the unlayered substance. But, far as any geologist has yet gone down into the world, it is found to consist of nothing but surface stratified on surface. To its axis, the world being nothing but superinduced superficies. By vast pains we mine into the pyramid; by horrible gropings we come to the central room; with joy we espy the sarcophagus; but we lift the lid—and no body is there!—appallingly vacant as vast is the soul of a man!

Here the act of probing discloses not a paradise of creative fullness but the nightmare of a central emptiness.

In these passages we see Melville remaking *Mardi* into the vision of *Pierre*, the vision of the world as an imposture that every effort to escape only deepens one's involvement in. But the difference between these books is less a matter of their metaphysical stances than of their moods. *Pierre* is a book in which the creative impulse has lost faith in its own creativeness. Where *Mardi* images itself as a strong grain ripening into a rich harvest, *Pierre* is haunted by the spectacle of failed maturation—'Oh God, that man should spoil and rust on the stalk, and be wilted and threshed ere the harvest hath come!' It is sobering to turn from *Mardi* to *Pierre*, and to see how quickly Melville's sense of artistic promise turns into despair. But to think of the two books together is also to see more clearly the spirit in which *Mardi* is made. Of all his works *Mardi* is the one in which Melville's genius rejoices most unabashedly and unreservedly in its own powers. As no other novel in the world quite does, *Mardi* embodies the spectacle of a great author advancing, with perfect confidence and good cheer, to greet his own mature creative self.

EDGAR A. DRYDEN

The Entangled Text: "Pierre" and the Problem of Reading

Pierre is a book about reading and writing, about the consumption and production of literary texts—a double problem that fascinates Melville from the beginning to the end of his writing career. For unlike some of his romantic contemporaries he does not regard reading as a passive and parasitical activity that is the pale complement of the original and glamourous act of creation itself. Melville is free of the Hawthornian nostalgia for a "Gentle," "Indulgent," appreciative reader who graciously accepts unquestioningly the beautiful tapestry "woven with the best of the artist's skill, and cunningly arranged with a view to the harmonious exhibiton of its colours." For Melville the writer is himself originally a reader: indeed his creative powers depend on the depth and breadth of his reading, "spontaneous creative thought" being a process whereby "all existing great works must be federated in the fancy; and so regarded as a miscellaneous and Pantheistic whole." [*Pierre; or, the Ambiguities.* Evanston: Northwestern Univ. Press, 1971, p. 284. All subsequent references to *Pierre* will be from this edition.] The fabric of *Moby-Dick,* for example, is woven more from the threads of the texts that fill Ishmael's library than it is from the lines and ropes of the whaling world. Indeed Ishmael's relation to that world he seeks to represent is that of a reader to a text, and he tries to organize and arrange it as he previously has done his library by establishing a bibliographical system. Productive reading, however, is not an easy or casual activity; "no ordinary letter sorter . . .

From *Boundary 2*, 3, vol. 7 (1979). Copyright © 1979 by *Boundary 2*.

is equal to it." In "Hawthrone and His Mosses," Melville distinguishes between that reader who sees Shakespeare as a "mere man of Richard-the-Third humps, and Macbeth daggers," who responds only to the "popularizing noise and the show of broad farce, and blood-besmeared tragedy," and the more discriminating reader who seeks out the "still rich utterances of a great intellect in repose." In the place of "blind, unbridled" reading Melville proposes a deeply committed one that is capable of discerning those truths that the writer "craftily says," or "insinuates" in his text. As Ishmael demonstrates when he tells the "Town Ho's Story" by "interweaving in its proper place the darker thread [the secret part of the tale] with the story as publicly narrated on the ship," story-telling is a process of representing a dark truth that will only be available to the readers whose response is in the form of deep and probing examination.

At first glance, then, the Hawthorne essay seems equally to celebrate reading and writing, to regard both as distinguished and difficult but non-problematic activities. Composed during the period when Melville was hard at work on *Moby-Dick*, the essay implies a direct and unambiguous link between Shakespeare and Hawthorne and more importantly, records the positive effects of both writers on Melville. These effects are clearly discernible in the novel he was about to dedicate to Hawthorne. However, important if unacknowledged problems exist in the essay. At the same time that Melville records the way in which the "soft ravishments of [Hawthorne] spin [him] round about in a web of dreams" and celebrates Shakespeare's "great Art of Telling the Truth," he also "boldly condemn[s] all imitation, though it comes to us graceful and fragrant as the morning; and foster[s] all originality, though, at first, it be crabbed and ugly as our own pine knots." The essay, in other words, raises and then ignores the problems of derivation: authority and priority, tradition and the individual talent, literary fathers and sons. But his consideration of these issues is postponed only until *Moby-Dick* is completed, for in *Pierre* Melville focuses on them with an almost desperate insistence.

I

Dearest Lucy!—well, well;—'twill be a pretty time we'll have this evening; there's the book of Flemish prints—that first we must look over; then, second, is Flaxman's Homer—clear-cut outlines, yet full of unadorned barbaric nobleness. Then Flaxman's Dante;—Dante! Night's and Hell's poet he. No, we will not open Dante. Methinks now the face—the face—minds me a little of pensive, sweet Francesca's face—or, rather, as it had been Francesca's daughter's face—wafted on the sad dark wind, toward observant Virgil and the blistered Florentine. No, we will not open

Flaxman's Dante. Francesca's mournful face is now ideal to me. Flaxman
might evoke it wholly,—make it present in lines of misery—bewitching
power. No! I will not open Flaxman's Dante! Damned be the hour I read
in Dante! more damned than that wherein Paolo and Francesca read in
fatal Launcelot!

(P, 42)

Woven and entangled in this passage are most of the thematic strands of
Pierre: the problem of reading; the question of relatedness, of genealogical
continuity and intertextuality (family structures and narrative forms); and
linking them all the larger issues of repetition and representation. The
generative energy of the passage (and the novel) is a story, the "story of
the face," a story that Pierre can narrate but cannot read because it exists
for him in the form of a "riddle" (P, 37) or "mournful mystery" whose
meaning is "veiled" behind a "concealing screen" (P, 41). Nevertheless,
he is determined to understand it fully, to confront its meaning, as he says,
"face to face" (P, 41). But as the labyrinthine quality of the passage suggests,
the meaning of the story is difficult to decipher, and Pierre's attempt to
read it will generate a second and even more entangled and problematic
narrative, that of the novel itself.

Many of these complexities must be put aside to be gathered up
later, but we can at least notice at this point that although the face "was
not of enchanged air" but had been "visibly beheld by Pierre" (P, 43), it
nevertheless exists for him in an ambiguous representational mode. The
"wretched vagueness" (P, 41) that haunts his memory stands not in the
place of its "mortal lineaments" (P, 43) but in the place of something else:
in this instance Dante's description of Francesca's face, or, perhaps, in the
place of Flaxman's graphic representation of Dante's description, or, more
problematically, in the place of Pierre's imaginary conception of Francesca's
daughter's face. Pierre's initial encounter with Isabel, the—an encounter
he is later to see as the central and authenticiating one of his life—is cast
in terms of signs rather than substances. It is derived, not immediate. Any
sense of the face as a living reality dissolves before the "long line of dependencies" (P, 67) implied in the passage. The focus here is on purely
textual entities, on questions of the relations between literary works (the
chivalric tale, Dante's poem, Melville's novel), between graphic and linguistic signs (Flaxman's illustrations, Dante's poem) and on the bewitching
power these entities possess to produce others that displace and represent
them. In this sense the story of the face, and by extension Pierre's own
story, is necessarily written and read from the perspective of the "already
written." The Paolo and Francesca episode implies that not even passion
itself is natural in the sense of being an underived and spontaneous emotion

(it comes from books) and hence suggests an entangled relation between one's natural genealogy and the inherited texts of one's culture.

This problem of relatedness raised by Pierre's imaginative creation of literary parents for the mysterious face is the first one to appear in the novel. It begins with the celebration of the apparent differences between the "great genealogical and real-estate dignity of some families in America" (P, 12) and the "winding and manufactured nobility" of the "grafted families" (P, 10) of the old world. Unlike the English Peerage, which is kept alive by "restorations and creations" (P, 10), Pierre's pedigree seems straight and unflawed. We meet the young hero "issuing from the high gabled old home" of his father and entering a world where the "very horizon [is] to him as a memorial ring," where all the "hills and swales seemed as sanctified through their very long uninterrupted possession by his race" (P, 8). Unlike the orphaned Ishmael, he seems to find himself in a world where he truly belongs, a world where his identity, place and destiny are confirmed by the self-reflecting environment of a "powerful and populous family" (P, 7). Moreover, his position as the only "surnamed Glendinning extant" and the "solitary head of his family" seems to assure him that his only "duplicate" is the "one reflected to him in the mirror" (P, 8). Pierre, in other words, seems to enjoy the security of a family circle within which he can define and fix himself and at the same time remain free of the fear of any challenge to his originality or authority. He can possess at once the feeling of belonging enjoyed by the son and the procreative power of the father as well, hence his dream of achieving a "monopoly of glory in capping the fame-column, whose tall shaft had been erected by his noble sires" (P, 8).

However, this is a dream based on the assumption of an absolute correspondence between the natural and the human, on the notion that institutions and language possess the characteristics of the biological structure of generation. Families, however, are not trees, even though they may seem to "stand as the oak" (P, 9) for they do not originate and develop in the same way. The permanence, stability, and order implied by a genealogical chart or by the metaphor of the family tree conceals a host of discontinuities, disjunctions, entanglements, and desires that mark human relationships. The seemingly unentangled lines of the Glendinning genealogy are actually twisted and interwoven by the young heir's problematic relation to his family. Pierre's relation to his mother, for example, equivocates the orderly process whereby the father and mother produce a son who marries and continues the line: "In the playfulness of their unclouded love, and with that strange licence which a perfect confidence and mutual understanding at all points had long bred between them, they were wont to call each other brother and sister" (P, 5). The entangling and confusing of relationships implied by this behavior is further complicated by their domestic practice that anticipates the "sweet dreams of those religious enthusiasts who paint to us a Paradise to come, where etherialized from the drosses and stains, the holiest passion of man shall unite all kindred and climes in one circle of pure and unimpairable delight" (P, 16). Pierre's relation to his mother, in short, is an only partially disguised expression of a set of inhibited desires generated by a genealogical system that condemns the son to a derived and secondary existence. These desires, partially displaced here by the religious language in which they are manifested, are more concretely expressed in Pierre's "strange yearning . . . for a sister" as well as by the narrator's smug observation, "He who is sisterless, is as a bachelor before his time. For much that goes to make up the deliciousness of a wife, already lies in the sister" (P, 7). This barely concealed expression of brother-sister incestuous desire, like the more deeply displaced mother-son relationship, suggests the extent to which Pierre unconsciously resists the defining authority of the father as well as the sense that he is no more than his father "transformed into youth once again" (P, 73). Both his relation to his mother and the nature of his longing for a sister constitute a challenge to the paternal role: they subtly entangle the genealogical line by disrupting its temporal development. The "striking personal resemblance" between Pierre and his mother—she sees "her own graces strangely translated into the opposite sex"—makes it seem as if the mother has "long stood still in her beauty, heedless of the passing years" and Pierre seems to "meet her half-way," to have "almost advanced himself to that mature stand-point in Time, where his pedestaled mother so long had stood" (P, 5).

But it is Pierre's response to the phantom face haunting him and enchanting him with its suggestions of dark foreignness that is the most obvious expression of his suppressed desire to free himself from a family prison. Its magnetic quality derives in part from the fact that it is at once "wholly unknown to him" (P, 49) and yet somehow familiar, thus making him aware of a "certain condition of his being, which was most painful, and every way uncongenial to his natural, wonted self" (P, 53). The nature and speed of Pierre's response to Isabel's disruptive note, of course, makes explicit the status of these hidden desires. In Pierre's mind the note completely undermines the dignity and authority of the father and forces him to abandon all the "hereditary beliefs" (P, 87) he has been unconsciously resisting all along. "I will have no more father," he says, as he rejects all "earthly kith and kin" and "orphan-like stagger[s] back upon himself and find[s] support in himself" (P, 89). "Henceforth, cast-out Pierre has no paternity and no past . . . twice disinherited Pierre stands . . . free to do his own self-will and present fancy to whatever end" (P, 199). Because he feels himself "divinely dedicated" he decides that he can abandon all "common conventional regardings," including his "hereditary duty to this mother" and his "pledged worldly faith and honor to the hand and seal of his affiancement" (P, 140). Personal faith will replace hereditary beliefs and the result will be a more orderly as well as more authentic life; for the genealogical tradition that seems to promise continuity and unity is actually intertwined in the "infinite entanglements of all social things" (P, 191). From the "long line of dependencies" that constitute it come the "thousand proprieties and polished finenesses" (P, 83) that characterize the social. Like Christ, Pierre believes that he can free himself from these "myriad alliances and crisscrossings (P, 191) and disentangle himself from "all fleshly alliances" (P, 164) by substituting for the genealogical imperative a new and celebate enterprise.

> Not that at present all these things did thus present themselves to Pierre; but these things were foetally forming in him. Impregnations from high enthusiasms he had received; and the now incipient offspring which so stirred, with such painful, vague vibrations in his soul; this, in its mature development, when it should at last come forth in living deeds, would scorn all personal relationship with Pierre, and hold his heart's dearest interests for naught.
>
> Thus, in the Enthusiast to Duty, the heaven-begotten Christ is born; and will not own a mortal parent, and spurns and rends all mortal bonds.
>
> (P, 106)

In the place of inherited values and relations Pierre places an orphaned, self-begotten identity and that in turn generates a miraculous conception. In effect a spiritual genealogy supplants the physical one, apparently making possible a new family structure. For both Isabel and Lucy, Pierre seems capable of fulfilling all the traditional familial roles. " 'I want none in the world but thee' " (P, 312), Isabel tells him, and Lucy insists that he is " 'my mother and my brother, and all the world, and all heaven, and all the universe to me—thou art my Pierre' " (P, 311). Moreover, the new relationships, as Pierre sees them, are free from the ambiguities of the more traditional ones: he and Isabel are " 'wide brother and sister in common humanity' " (P, 273) and he and Lucy spiritual cousins with " 'no declaration; no bridal' " (P, 310) who " 'love as angels do' " (P, 309).

Pierre, then, seems to have made himself his "own Alpha and Omega," to have reached a point where he can "feel himself in himself, and not by reflection in others" (P, 261). Moreover, having freed himself from the defining relationships of the paternal tradition, he has also made himself independent of its economic imperatives. When he abandons his "fine social position" and "noble patrimony" he boldly asserts that he will "live on himself" (P, 261); that is to say, he will become an author and support himself by putting his "soul to labor . . . and pay his body her wages" (P, 261). In the place of fathering a natural son who will be his unwilling copy even as he was his father's, he will give the world a book, "a child born solely from one parent" (P, 259), that through its radical originality will "gospelize the world anew" (P, 273).

Pierre assumes that as an author he will wield an authority that is not subject to confining and restricing definitions from the past. However, behind the differences that seem to separate the act of authoring from that of physical engenderment is a notion common to both, that what one makes is one's offspring, legacy, and representative. This element of sameness puts into question Pierre's claims of absolute authority and originality. As the Paolo-Francesca passage implies, the process of representation involves questions of inherited tendencies as well as originating intentions. These issues appear in their most obvious form in the novel's focus on painted images of the father, an especially likely association, for, as Paul de Man has shown, it is in painting (and especially in eighteenth-century theories of painting) that the process of representation appears in its most unambiguous aspects. Conceived of as imitation, painting (as de Man points out) has the effect of seeming to restore the represented object to view as if it were present, miraculously bringing back into existence a presence that existed in another time and in another place. This duplication of the objects of perception, however, does not exhaust the power of the painted image. Even more impressive is its apparent ability to transform inward and ideal experiences into objects of perception and, by making them visible, confer upon them the ontological stability of objective existence. The military portrait of Pierre's grandfather, for example, at once captures the image of the original so completely that the young Pierre feels a "mournful longing to meet his living aspect in real life," and it possesses the "heavenly persuasiveness of angelic speech; a glorious gospel framed and hung upon the wall, and declaring to all people, as from the Mount, that man is a noble, god-like being, full of choicest juices; made up of strength and beauty" (P, 30). This description, of course, equivocates Pierre's decision to "gospelize the world anew" by associating it with a related and prior originating act, but it also undermines the assumption that imitation duplicates presence. The "mournful longing" which the painting generates in Pierre is a reminder of one problematic aspect of representation since it points to the absence of the represented entity, and the disquieting effects of that absence are strengthened by the irony implicit in the fact that a military portrait seems to the young man to be a concrete expression of the ideals of Christ's Sermon on the Mount.

The painted image of the old Pierre Glendinning points to an absence rather than a presence, to "once living but now impossible ancestries in the past" (P, 32), and raises the problem of genealogy as representation by illustrating what the narrator calls the "endless descendedness of names" (P, 9). Not only is Pierre his father's "namesake" (P, 73) but his grandfather's as well, hence from one point of view doubly derived, the copy of a copy and as such a diminution, a smaller, weaker version of the authoritative original:

> The grandfather of Pierre measured six feet four inches in height; during a fire in the old manorial mansion, with one dash of his foot, he had smitten down an oaken door, to admit the buckets of his negro slaves; Pierre had often tried on his military vest, which still remained an heirloom at Saddle Meadows, and found the pockets below his knees. . . .
>
> (P, 29)

Pierre in his "most extended length measures not the proud six feet four of his John of Gaunt Sire," and as the "stature of the warrior is cut down" so is the "glory of the fight" (P, 271).

Pierre's assumption, however, is that his position in the genealogical chain is a matter of "empty nominalness," not "vital realness" (P, 192); for if his name on the one hand seems to bind him to his paternal precursors, on the other it suggests a means of escape. The French origins of his Christian name allow him, through a series of substitutions, to link himself to another tradition that counters the democratic, revolutionary one represented by his ancestors. This is the one suggested by the mysterious "foreigner" of "noblest birth" and "allied to the royal family" (P, 76) of France who enchants Pierre's father and perhaps becomes the mother of Isabel. Although the signs of this "foreign feminineness" (P, 76) are less objective, less concrete, than the portrait of Pierre's grandfather—they consist of a "subtle expression of the portrait of [Pierre's] then youthful father" (P, 112), the word "Isabel" written in the interior of a guitar, and a "touch of foreignness in the accent" (P, 113) of the mysterious Isabel—Pierre is so convinced of her reality and her spiritual link to him through Isabel that he willingly breaks the lines linking him to his forefathers and, by a process of substitution based on the French meaning of his Christian name, becomes Peter, the rock on which Christ builds his church rather than the grandson of the old warrior.

At first glance his progress seems significant. Replacing the authority of the grandfather and the father is that of Christ as expressed in "those first, wise words, wherewith [he] first spoke in his first speech to men" (P, 91), the Sermon on the Mount. Although Christ's words come to Pierre in the secondary form of the Biblical text, he at least no longer has to receive them indirectly and ambiguously by way of the military portrait of his grandfather. And just as he seems to have replaced a physical genealogy by a spiritual one and an interpreted, metaphoric "gospel" by the actual one, so he seems to have turned from the socially and conventionally determined aspects of his name toward its literal meaning. A detailed analysis of this remarkable process of substitution must await a discussion of a set of similar acts, but one can note at this point that Pierre's career is developing in the context of a series of conflicting but related representations.

This is a process that is at once complicated and illuminated by the narrator's discussion of Pierre's attitudes toward several other portraits that represent the father and associate his authority and power with Biblical models. The most interesting of these, of course, are the two paintings of his dead father: the one, the drawing room portrait, commissioned by Pierre's mother, painted by a "celebrated artist," protraying the father "during the last and rosiest days of their wedded union" (P, 82–83); the other, the chair portrait, non-commissioned, the product of an amateur, portraying an "unentangled, young bachelor, gayly ranging up and down in the world" (P, 73). The dissimilarity of these "precious memorials" (P, 73) of his father, who is "now dead and irrevocably gone," presents young Pierre with a set of teasing interpretive problems, problems that call for a "careful, candid estimation" (P, 73) and "cunning analysis (P, 82). Unlike his mother, who simply asserts that the chair portrait is not her husband because it does not "correctly . . . convey his features in detail" (P, 72), Pierre is unwilling to reject either portrait and wonders if in some mysterious way the "two paintings might not make only one." Neither painting is "all of [his] father" (P, 83) but if regarded intertextually, if the "family legend" (P, 73) of the smaller painting is read in the context of the "latter tales and legends of . . . devoted wedded love" "rehearsed" (P, 83) by the other portrait, then the father may be restored to view as if he were actually present. Hence the chair portrait seems to Pierre to contain a strange mystery that he can fancifully solve:

> Thus sometimes in the mystical, outer quietude of the long country nights; either when the hushed mansion was banked round by the thick-fallen December snows, or banked round by the immoveable white August moon-

light; in the haunted repose of a wide story, tenanted only by himself; and sentineling his own little closet; and standing guard, as it were, before the mystical tent of the picture; and ever watching the strangely concealed lights of the meanings that so mysteriously moved to and fro within; thus sometimes stood Pierre before the portrait of his father, unconsciously throwing himself open to all those ineffable hints and ambiguities, and undefined half-suggestions, which now and then people the soul's atmosphere, as thickly as in a soft, steady snow-storm, the snow-flakes people the air.

(P, 84)

In this passage the "precious memorial" (P, 73) combines with Pierre's "revered memory of [his] father" (P, 81) to confirm, perhaps to bring back, the plenitude of the dead father. Pierre's ancestral home is figured as a carefully enclosed monument that sustains history and embalms memory by preserving deep inside itself the sign of an authoritative presence even as the Tabernacle of the Hebrews held within a central tent the veiled Ark of the Lord, the Tables of Stone, God's testimony to man (Exod. 25: 10–16). While the meanings of the painting remain hidden, the mode of concealment seems, paradoxically, a form of revelation, in the same manner that God remains hidden in the Cloud of Glory that is the sign of his immediate presence and that at times surrounds and protects the sacred Ark. Nor are these impressions simply mystifications, the result of "reveries and trances" that give to the painting the qualities of "legendary romance" (P, 85). The arrival of Isabel's letter seems to confirm the portrait's power and to "rip . . . open as with a keen sword" all the "preceding mysteries." "Now his remotest infantile reminiscences—the wandering mind of his father—the empty hand, and the ashen—the strange story of Aunt Dorothea—the mystical midnight suggestions of the portrait itself; and, above all, his mother's intuitive aversion, all, all overwhelmed him with reciprocal testimonies" (P, 85). The problem, then, is not that the letter undermines the power and authority of the painted image but rather that it confirms it in a particularly disturbing way, validating the "story of the picture" (P, 74) as narrated by his aunt. For that story had implied that the artist in "stealing" the portrait had "detected" the subject's "innermost secrets" and "published them in a portrait" (P, 79), thereby conferring upon mental experience the stability of a perceived object. It is precisely because the portrait presents an image of the father in such a palpable and immediate way that Pierre first reverses it on the wall and then removes it entirely, hoping in that way to "banish the least trace of his altered father" (P, 87). However, "in a square space of slightly discolored wall, the picture still left its shadowy, but vacant and desolate trace" (P, 87), apparently maintaining its vitality and influence even while locked away in Pierre's trunk:

In the strange relativeness, reciprocalness, and transmittedness, between the long-dead father's portrait, and the living daughter's face, Pierre might have seemed to see reflected to him, by visible and uncontradictable symbols, the tyranny of Time and Fate. Painted before the daughter was conceived or born, like a dumb seer, the portrait still seemed leveling its prophetic finger at that empty air, from which Isabel did finally emerge. There seemed to lurk some mystical intelligence and vitality in the picture; because, since in his own memory of his father, Pierre could not recall any distinct lineament transmitted to Isabel, but vaguely saw such in the portrait; therefore, not Pierre's parent, as anyway rememberable by him, but the portrait's painted *self* seemed the real father of Isabel; for, so far as all sense went, Isabel had inherited one peculiar trait no-whither traceable but to it.

And as his father was now sought to be banished from his mind, as a most bitter presence there, but Isabel was become a thing of intense and fearful love for him; therefore, it was loathsome to him, that in the smiling and ambiguous portrait, her sweet mournful image should be so sinisterly becrooked, bemixed, and mutilated to him.

(P, 197)

Here as in the Paolo-Francesca passage, the usual view of human life as a linear, natural, biological process of generation and procreation is replaced by one that portrays it as a confusing play of images. Although an "unsolid duplicate" of a "vanished solidity" (P, 198), the portrait seems to preserve the power of the dead father; but the procreative authority manifests itself in the form of a "strange transfer" of its own represented "lineaments" to the "countenance of Isabel" (P, 196). The result is that she seems to exist not as a "thing of life . . . but a thing of breath, evoked by the wanton magic of a creative hand" (P, 169) that is itself a representation. The portrait functions, then, to undermine the substantiality of both Pierre's own and Isabel's existences, and for that reason he decides to destroy it along with all other external signs of the paternal past.

Since it is the portrait that carries the disturbing trace of his father's presence, Pierre assumes that his problems will vanish when he burns it and " 'urn[s] [it] in the great vase of air,' " this being the second and final time that he will see his father's "obsequies performed" (P, 198). To escape from the burden of the past and from ordinary historical and genealogical principles, he believes, one has only to destroy their signs and refuse any longer "to reverse the decree of death, by essaying the poor perpetuating image of the original" (P, 197–198). This plan of action, however, is based on the assumption that the individual exists independently of and has control over the "momentoes and monuments of the past" (P, 197), and assumption that ignores the "myriad alliances and criss-crossing among mankind, the infinite entanglements of all social things, which forbid that one thread should fly the general fabric, on some new line of duty, without tearing itself and tearing others" (P, 191). It is not surprising, then, that the act of burning the portrait and the other contents of his trunk—"packages of family letters and all sorts of miscellaneous memorials in paper" (P, 198)—does not free Pierre from the influence of the past. The entangled aspects of his predicament are implied in the contradictory language he uses to express it: "Thus, and thus, and thus! on thy manes I fling fresh spoils! pour out all my memory in one libation!—so, so, so, lower, lower, lower; now all is done and all is ashes" (P, 198–99). Needless to say, Pierre's metaphors are hopelessly mixed and entangled, implying that he at once feeds the fire and extinguishes it, rejects his father and celebrates him. And adding to the ambiguity is the fact that in Melville's day it was generally assumed that the word pyramid derived from *pyr*, fire: since fire ascends in the figure of a cone, it was accepted that a pyramid imitates the shape of a flame. So in a certain sense to burn the portrait is but to "mummy it in a visible memorial for every passing beggar's dust to gather on" (P, 197), or, as Pierre says to " 'urn [it] in the great vase of air.' "

Subsequent events mark the ambiguity present here. Late in the novel Pierre discovers, in a "gallery of paintings recently imported from Europe" (P, 349), a portrait that undermines his assumption that he can free himself from the mediation of all signs and relics. Belonging to another heritage, painted by an "Unknown Hand" (P, 351), portraying a stranger, hence tied to the Glendinning family neither by legend nor by personal reminiscence, the portrait nevertheless represents the father to both Isabel and Pierre. Because Isabel "knew nothing of the painting Pierre had destroyed," she sees the foreign portrait as signifying the "living being who—under the designation of her father—had visited her at the cheerful house" (P, 352). It also seems to contain "certain shadowy traces of her own unmistakable likeness" (P, 351). To Pierre, however, it seems a "resurrection of the one he had burnt at the inn" (P, 351). But no matter how the painting is regarded—whether it is seen as the sign of a sign or the sign of once living being—it signals the non-presence of an origin, the ambiguity of any inscription of an origin in the present: "Then the original of this second portrait was as much the father of Isabel as the original of the chair portrait. But perhaps there was no original at all to this second portrait; it might have been a pure fancy piece . . ." (P, 353). This insight destroys once and for all Pierre's belief that the presence of his father can ever be located in or constituted by a sign that can then be either worshipped or destroyed. The "resurrection" of the chair portrait in the form of The Stranger's Head, in other words, is a repetition that places the entangled issues of genealogy and representation within the content of loss and absence and thereby substitutes a notion of meaning as presence and plenitude with one of meaning as void.

II

The themes of loss and absence, of course, are woven thickly into the text of *Pierre*. The language of the novel is heavy with images of devasting earthquakes, flowing rivers of lava, piles of drifting sands, ruined cities, abandoned excavation sites, and empty and desecrated burial places, all of which associate culture with man's vain attempts to resist the ravages of time and death and situate Pierre's career in a context that robs it of its uniqueness by making it no more than a minor repetition of a process as old as civilization itself. His early naive view of the world is expressed partially by his idealization of his dead father, a process represented by a figurative "shrine of marble" in which stands the perfect marble form of his departed father, a shrine as imposing as that of "Prince Mausolus," one that manages to take things "evanescent" and make them "unchangeable" and "eternal" (P, 68) and one that remains "spotless and still new as the marble tomb of his of Arimathea" (P, 69). These references to the ruins of Helecarnassus and to Joseph, the rich man of Arimathea who claims Christ's body and buries it in his own tomb, subversively link pagan and Christian burial practices and indirectly introduce the theme of ruined and empty tombs, a theme that becomes explicit with the arrival of Isabel's letter, which has the destructive force of a volcanic eruption rolling "down on [Pierre's] soul like melted lava, and [leaving] so deep a deposit of desolation, that all his subsequent endeavors never restored the original temples to the soil, nor all his culture completely revived its buried bloom" (P, 67–68). That "one little bit of paper scratched over with a few small characters by a sharpened feather "obliterates the meaning of characters inscribed in marble, for it strips Pierre's "holiest shrine of all overlaid bloom" and "desecrates" that "casket, wherein he had placed [his] holiest and most final joy" (P, 69). At issue here is the complicated relation between the acts of interment and inscription, both of which seem to mark the point separating man from nature by expressing his humanity. It is significant, for example, that Pierre's first response to the mysterious Isabel, who comes from a world without tombs or inscriptions—"No name; no scrawled or written thing; no book . . . no one memorial . . . no gravestone or mound on any hillock around the house, betrayed any past burials of man or child"

(P, 115)—is to seek out a "remarkable stone, or rather, smoothed mass of rock" (P, 131) bearing the mysterious inscription S ye W. The first of two such objects to occupy his attention, the Memnon Stone or Terror Stone marks the first stage of Pierre's career, as the rock of Enceladus does the final one. From one point of view the stone is no more than a "natural curiosity" (P, 133) but the mysterious writing on it gives it a privileged position (one both scriptural and natural), associating it with a remote but human past and investing it with a mystery that seems to justify Pierre's poetical interpretation of its significance.

> When in his imaginative ruminating moods of early youth, Pierre had christened the wonderful stone by the old resounding name of Memnon, he had done so merely from certain associative remembrances of that Egyptian marvel, of which all Eastern travelers speak. And when the fugitive thought had long ago entered him of desiring that same stone for his head-stone, when he should be no more; then he had only yielded to one of those innumerable fanciful notions, tinged with dreamy painless melancholy, which are frequently suggested to the mind of a poetic boy. But in aftertimes, when placed in far different circumstances, from those surrounding him at the Meadows, Pierre pondered on the stone, and his young thoughts concerning it, and, later, his desperate act in crawling under it; then an immense significance came to him, and the long-passed unconscious movements of his then youthful heart, seemed now prophetic to him, and allegorically verified by the subsequent events.
>
> For, not to speak of the other and subtler meanings which lie crouching behind the colossal haunches of this stone, regarded as the menacingly impending Terror Stone . . . consider its aspects as the Memnon Stone. . . .
>
> Herein lies an unsummed world of grief. For in this plaintive fable we find embodied the Hamletism of the antique world; the Hamletism of three thousand years ago: "The flower of virtue cropped by a too rare mischance." And the English Tragedy is but Egyptian Memnon, Montaignized and modernized; for being but a mortal man Shakespeare had his fathers too.
>
> (P, 135)

This suggestive passage focuses directly on two important and related themes: the problematic aspect of funerary monuments and the nature of interpretation. When Pierre first contemplates the "ponderous inscrutableness" (P, 134), he reads its meaning in terms of "associative remembrances" of his Occidental culture's fascination with the Orient, in particular with the myth of the singing monument said to produce a dirge-like sound at sunrise in the memory of the young boy it commemorates; and then he personalizes his poetic reverie by associating that "sweet boy long since departed in antediluvian times" (P, 134) with himself and imagines that the "imposing pile" will provide him with a fitting headstone. This is a process of thought that derives directly from the tradition of romantic nature inscriptions, a tradition expressed by Wordsworth in his *Essays on Epitaphs,* where he argues that inscribed monuments imply a faith that man is an immortal being by expressing on the one hand the desire of the individual "to survive in the remembrance of his fellows" and on the other a "wish to preserve for future times vestiges of the departed." This double desire is present in man's attempt "to give to the language of senseless stone" (P, 125) a voice that assures "that some part of our nature is imperishable" (P, 122). However, as Geoffrey Hartman has noticed, inscribing and naming are secondary and elegiac acts that can produce the death feeling they try to deny. Pierre's poetic "melancholy" is "painless" precisely because it ignores the elegiac aspects of the stone and imbues it with the force of a living presence.

Nevertheless, the stone has a darker side even for the dreamy youth, and that aspect is acknowledged by the other name with which Pierre designates it, the Terror Stone. This is an aspect that emphasizes its anonymous, natural side, for if at times there seems to "lurk" about the stone "some mournful and lamenting plaint," at other times it seems simply a "Mute Massiveness" (P, 134), a "ponderous mass" balanced in such a way as to create beneath itself a "vacancy" (P, 132), a "horrible interspace" (P, 134). Considered from this point of view its "music . . . is lost among . . . drifting sands" (P, 136) and it becomes the "monument of a lost significance."

The juxtaposition of the apparently opposing designations—Memnon Stone and Terror Stone—has the effect of suggesting other "subtler meanings which lie crouching behind the collosal haunches" (P, 135) of the sphinx-like stone. Read from the perspective of his future recollections, Pierre's "young thoughts concerning [the stone]" seem to him at once prophetic and allegorical; and to say that recollection is prophecy, that one's life is an allegory, is to say that every individual act derives it meaning or significance from an earlier one that it displaces and repeats (often unconsciously) in much the same way that the son displaces and repeats the father in the genealogical chain. Hence in the "plaintive fable" of Memnon "we find embodied the Hamletism of the antique world," the English tragedy being nothing but the "Egyptian Memnon, Montaignized and modernized; for being but a mortal man Shakespeare had his fathers too"; and Pierre's story by extension is yet another repetition of that "melancholy type" (P, 136).

The implications of this repetition are spelled out in the second of the two symbolic stones that mark the stages of Pierre's career. The "sphinx-like shape" (P, 345) of Enceladus appears in the text first in the form of a "remarkable dream or vision" that Pierre experiences during a "state of semi-unconsciousness" (P, 342), but that dream represents the unwilled return of earlier experiences and reconstitutes them as a form of repetition. The dream returns him once again to the "blue hills encircling his ancestral manor" and surrounds him with still another confining and defining relationship. Since "nature is not so much her own ever-sweet interpreter, as the mere supplier of that cunning alphabet, whereby selecting and combining as he pleases, each man reads his own particular lesson according to his own particular mind or mood" (P, 342), Pierre now sees the "familiar features" of the landscape in a new and different way. In the same way that the Christian name (The Delectable Mountain) of the Mount of the Titans is displaced by the apparently more appropriate pagan one, so the "hills and swales" of Saddle Meadows that had once seemed to Pierre to be "sanctified through their very long uninterrupted possession by his race" (P, 8), are now read in the context of an older genealogy, that of "Coelus and Terra . . . incestuous Heaven and Earth" (P, 347).

From the perspective of Pierre's vision, the landscape of the New World duplicates that of the Old: "curtained by [a] cunning purpleness," there is "stark desolation; ruin, merciless and ceaseless; chills and gloom,— all here lived a hidden life" (P, 344):

> And, as among the rolling sea-like sands of Egypt, disordered rows of broken Sphinxes lead to the Cheopian pyramid itself; so this long acclivity was thickly strewn with enormous rocky masses, grotesque in shape, and with wonderful features on them, which seemed to express that slumbering intelligence visible in some recumbent beasts—beasts whose intelligence seems struck dumb in them by some sorrowful and inexplicable spell.
>
> (P, 343)

Among these "sphinx-like shapes" (P, 345) is a rock wrought by the "vigorous hand of nature's self" (P, 346), a natural rather than an intentional object, that is partially uncovered and designated Enceladus by a "strolling company of young collegian pedestrians" (P, 345). As Pierre recalls the "Titan's armless trunk," he suddenly sees "his own duplicate face and features" gleaming "upon him with prophetic discomfiture and woe" (P, 346).

This dream vision is the final manifestation of a pattern of doubling that has tormented Pierre from the beginning of the novel. He has resisted being merely the "likeness" (P, 73) and the namesake of his father, the "glass" (P, 90) in which his mother sees her own reflected beauty, and the "personal duplicate" (P, 289) of his hated cousin. But in resisting these familial doublings he is led at last to see his life as a fated repetition of certain tragic types, first Christ, then the Memnon-Hamlet type, and finally the Enceladus one. This development, moreover, is one that moves from a sense of repetition as a willed reappropriation of the past (as in the cases of Pierre's associating himself with Christ, Memnon, and Hamlet) toward a sense of repetition as an inevitable and unwilled nonhuman movement (as in the case of the dream of Enceladus). And this shift from one mode of repetition to another mirrors a movement at the level of language from the lyricism of the gospels to the silence of senseless stone.

Both of these developments are marked in the novel by the shifting meanings of Pierre's name, which like his face would seem to contain and express his uniqueness but which instead suggests to him the extent to which he is contained and defined by others. As we have seen, he attempts to resist being no more than Pierre Glendinning the Third by dedicating himself to what he perceives as a Christ-like duty and associating himself with Peter, the rock on which Christ builds his church. However, this act as well as his assertion that " 'I am Pierre' " (P, 373) calls attention to the literal meaning of his name, and it becomes his fate to live out that meaning, to become at the end a rock "arbored . . . in ebon vines" (P, 362).

The implications of this movement from name to thing, from the signifier to the signified, are important concerns of *Pierre*, and they are symbolized most clearly in the related figures of the mountain and the pyramid, a natural object and an intentional representation of it. As I have noted elsewhere, the mountain is a recurring image in *Pierre*. The novel is dedicated to the "magestic mountain, Greylock," the "sovereign lord and king" of the "amphitheatre over which his central majesty presides," and important roles are given to Mount Sinai, meeting place of God and Moses; the "divine mount," site of Christ's famous sermon; Bunyan's Delectable Mountains, from which the Celestial City may be seen; and Pelion and Ossa, mountains of Thessaly used by the Titans in the war against the gods' stronghold on Mount Olympus. These "crude forms of the natural earth" are the "cunning alphabet, whereby selecting and combining as he pleases, each man reads his own peculiar lesson according to his own peculiar mind or mood" (P, 342). Hence divine speech is associated with mountain tops as first Moses and then Christ, following their pagan predecessors, interpret that "profound Silence," that "divine thing without a name."

This process is emblematized in the figure of the pyramid, regarded by Melville as the source of the idea of Jehovah as well as the first work of art. Metaphysically the pyramid seems to suggest permanence, to proclaim a tenacious resistance to the pillages of time, and yet inside it contains decayed human ruins, or, more frighteningly, absolutely nothing: "By vast pains we mine into the pyramid; by horrible gropings we come to the central room; with joy we espy the sarcophagus; but we lift the lid—and no body is there . . ." (P, 285). Like Hegel, Melville is fascinated by the pyramid because it offers him an external man-made form that represents the "forms of the natural earth." It has the appearance of a natural product and yet conceals as its meaning a hollow void, the sign perhaps of the "horrible interspace" (P, 134) of the Memnon stone and the "Hollow" (P, 139) of God's hand. For as Hegel points out, this is the "realm of death and the invisible." The pyramid, in other words, aptly symbolizes the process of representation itself, for it points to the absence that all signs carry within them. Contained within language is a "Silence" that "permeates all things" (P, 204) and within all man-made objects and inscriptions a hollow void. Hence that "all-controlling and all-permeating wonderfulness, which, when imperfectly and isolatedly recognized by the generality, is so significantly denominated The Finger of God" is not "merely the Finger, it is the whole outspread Hand of God; for doth not Scripture intimate, that He holdeth all of us in the hollow of His Hand?—a Hollow, truly!" (P, 139).

It is the Finger of God, of course, that inscribes the Tablets of Stone given to Moses on Mount Sinai (Exod. 31:18) and that furnishes Christ with the power to give speech to the dumb (Luke 11:14–20). Inscribed within all cultural constructs, then, and within language itself is a radical absence suggesting an original loss. It is the pyramid situated in the cradle of civilization and the birthplace of the gods that marks the point beyond which it is impossible to go and that at the same time indicates that the moment of origin is not one of plenitude and presence but the sign of a loss. At the beginning for Melville there is already an unrecoverable past signified by the empty sarcophagus, and it is the burden of present and future architects that no matter how hard they may seek to establish an original relation to the forms of the natural earth, they must inscribe that empty tomb within all their monuments. Implied in the voice of culture is the silence of the tomb.

III

What then of the acts of reading and writing? How does the reader in the silence of his solitude define his relation to the verbose narrator of *Pierre* and to his "book of sacred truth" (P, 107)? This is a problem that is inscribed in the text of *Pierre*. The life of its hero is the story of a reader who attempts to become a writer. His growth is rendered in terms of the development of his interpretive faculties and his maturity is defined by his decision to "give the world a book" (P, 283). As a youth Pierre is a naive, unquestioning reader of novels, impatient with the "sublime . . . Dante" because his "dark ravings . . . are in eternal opposition to [his] own free-spun shallow dreams" (P, 54) and incapable of understanding even the "superficial and purely incidental lessons" of *Hamlet*, much less of glimpsing the "hopeless gloom of its interior meaning" (P, 169).

The extent to which the content and mode of Pierre's reading constitute his world is suggested by the fact that the act of reading provides the grid through which all aspects of his early life are seen. His life is an "illuminated scroll" (P, 7); love is a "volume bound in rose leaves, clasped with violets, and by the beaks of humming birds printed with peach juice on the leaves of lilies" (P, 34); grief is "still a ghost story" (P, 4); and human relations are intertextual: " 'Read me through and through,' " says Lucy to Pierre, " 'I am entirely thine' " (P, 40). The arrival of Isabel's letter, "the fit scroll of a torn as well as a bleeding heart" (P, 65), of course, reveals to Pierre the artificial and conventional structure of this world and produces a new understanding of reading and interpretation: " 'Oh, hitherto I have but piled up words: bought books, and bought some small experiences and built me in libraries; now I sit down and read' " (P, 91).

One result of Pierre's new view of things is that he is able to re-cuperate a number of memories that to this point in his life have existed as unreadable and meaningless details of his inner world. His dying father's delirious ravings, his mother's ambiguous reaction to the chair portrait, and other "imaginings of dimness" that "seemed to survive to no real life" (P, 71) are suddenly rendered intelligible by Isabel's letter, the pre-text that "puts the chemic key of the cipher into his hands; then how swiftly and how wonderfully, he reads all the obscurest and most obliterate in-scriptions he finds in his memory; yea, and rummages himself all over, for still hidden writings to read" (P, 70). Nor is the effect limited to the inscriptions of memory. The letter also allows Pierre to read Dante and Shakespeare in a deeper, more profound way, and this re-reading leads him to see that "after all he had been finely juggling with himself, and postponing with himself, and in meditative sentimentalities wasting the moments con-secrated to instant action" (P, 170).

Isabel's letter, then seems to provide a context or model that renders intelligible textual details which to this point have been unreadable or misread. The full implications of this complicated process, however, are not immediately obvious. But a number of them are illuminated by the narrator's account of Pierre's reading of two apparently contradictory texts: the gospel of Matthew and the pamphlet "Chronometricals and Horologicals." Matthew, of course, is an important text for Pierre since in his enthusiasm he has decided to model his life in Christ's, to be directed by "those first wise words, wherewith our Savior Christ first spoke in his first speech to man" (P, 91), the Sermon on the Mount. His "acts" then will be a "gospel" (P, 156) perfectly intelligible and natural if read in the context of his scriptural model. However, in the darkness and silence of the coach that carries him and his "mournful party" (P, 104) away from his ancestral home, Pierre begins to question his conduct, and to escape from the "evil mood" that becomes "well nigh insupportable," he "plunge[s] himself" (P, 207) into a mysterious pamphlet that he has found:

> There is a singular infatuation in most men, which leads them in odd moments, intermitting between their regular occupations, and when they find themselves all alone in some quiet corner or nook, to fasten with unaccountable fondness upon the merest rag of old printed paper—some shred of a long-exploded advertisement perhaps—and read it, and study it, and re-read it, and pore over it, and fairly agonize themselves over this miserable, sleazy paper-rag, which at any other time, or in any other place, they would hardly touch with St. Dunstan's long tongs. So now, in a degree, with Pierre. But notwithstanding that he, with most other human beings, shared in the strange hallucination above mentioned, yet the first glimpse of the title of the dried-fish-like, pamphlet-shaped rag, did almost tempt him to pitch it out of the window . . .
>
> Nevertheless, the silence still continued; the road ran through an almost unplowed and uninhabited region; the slumberers still slumbered before him; the evil mood was becoming well nigh insupportable to him; so, more to force his mind away from the dark realities of things than from any other motive, Pierre finally tried his best to plunge himself into the pamphlet.
>
> (P, 206–07)

Here reading appears as a form of "infatuation" or "hallucination" the nature of which is "strange" and "unaccountable." Nevertheless, its function is to fill the voids of doubt, silence, and loneliness; for it is either that which we do to escape the "dark realities of things" or that which we do in the face of nothing to do. Pierre, as he slowly unfingers, unbolts, unrolls, and smooths out the piece of "waste paper" "accidentally left there by some previous traveller" (P, 206), resembles the person alone at breakfast intensely studying the back of an empty cereal box or the one absorbed in a year-old magazine in a doctor's office, for that which fascinates him is a discarded fragment of the past that now exists independently of both its original intent and content. Here then is a situation that seems to promise a totally naive and innocent reading: on the one hand a displaced reader seeking only relief from the loneliness and boredom of everyday life; on the other an orphaned and abandoned text picked up unconsciously and accidentally: a situation, in other words, that seems removed from the vicious cycle of the return of repressed and inhibited desire that previously has marked Pierre's reading.

Once Pierre becomes absorbed in the pamphlet, however, he discovers that he cannot "master [its] pivot idea" (P, 292). Indeed, the "more he read and re-read, the more [his] interest deepened, but still the more likewise did his failure to comprehend the writer increase. He seemed somehow to derive some general vague inkling concerning it, but the central conceit refused to become clear to him" (P, 209). Moreover, not only is the pamphlet unreadable but the reason for its being so is itself undecidable.

> If a man be in any vague latent doubt about the intrinsic correctness and excellence of his general life-theory and practical course of life; then, if that man chance to light on any other man, or any little treatise, or sermon, which unintendingly, as it were, yet very palpably illustrates to him the intrinsic incorrectness and non-excellence of both the theory and the practice of his life; then that man will—more or less unconsciously—try hard to hold himself back from the self-admitted comprehension of a matter which thus condemns him. . . . Again. If a man be told a thing wholly new, then—during the time of its first announcement to him—it is entirely impossible for him to comprehend it. For—absurd as it may seem—men are only made to comprehend things which they comprehended before (though but in embryo, as it were). Things new it is impossible to make them comprehend, by merely talking to them about it . . . Possibly, they may afterward come, of themselves, to inhale this new idea from the circumambient air, and so come to comprehend it; but not otherwise at all. It will be observed, that neither points of the above speculations do we, in set terms, attribute to Pierre in connection with the rag pamphlet. Possibly both may be applicable; possibly neither.
>
> (P, 209)

Two possible explanations are offered here for Pierre's inability to comprehend the pamphlet, but neither is presented as absolutely applicable. Worth noticing, however, is that both have the effect of seriously limiting the dimensions of reading as an activity. We can read only the old and the familiar, the narrator seems to suggest, that which confirms and supports our normal assumptions and expectations. This is an insight that is confirmed later in the novel when Pierre meets Plotinus Plinlimmon, the "ostensible author" of the pamphlet, and seeks to re-read and understand it by the "commentary of [his] mystic-mild face" (P, 239). For now, having found the "author," he has "lost" (P, 293) the text:

> Pierre must have ignorantly thrust it into his pocket, in the stage, and it had worked through a rent there, and worked its way clean down into the skirt, and there helped pad the padding. So that all the time he was hunting for this pamphlet, he himself was wearing the pamphlet. . . .
>
> Possibly this curious circumstance may in some sort illustrate his self-supposed non-understanding of the pamphlet, as first read by him in the stage. Could he likewise have carried about with him in his mind the thorough understanding of the book, and yet not be aware that he so understood it?
>
> (P, 294)

To say that Pierre wears the pamphlet even as he searches for it and that his understanding is an unconscious one is to imply that the act of reading is not so much one of recovery or discovery of an original meaning as it is one of becoming aware of relationships between texts. This is an insight confirmed by the fact that the narrator interrupts and delays his account of the fascinating pamphlet in order to discuss what appears to be another kind of reading and a completely different sort of text:

> the earnest reperusal of the Gospels: the intense self-absorbtion into the greatest real miracle of all religions, the Sermon on the Mount. From that divine mount, to all earnest-loving youths, flows an inexhaustible soul-melting stream of tenderness and loving-kindness; and they leap exulting to their feet, to think that the founder of their holy religion gave utterance to sentences so infinitely sweet and soothing as these; sentences which embody all the love of the Past, and all the love which can be imagined in any conceivable Future. Such emotions as that Sermon raises in the enthusiastic heart; such emotions all youthful hearts refuse to ascribe to humanity as their origin. This is of God! cries the heart, and in that cry ceases all inquisition.
>
> (P, 207–08)

Here of course the focus is on a sacred text rather than a "sleazy pamphlet"; here reading seems an activity directed toward action in the world rather than a mystified escape from the "dark realities of things" (P, 207). The particular text in question is the gospel of St. Matthew, and within it, the account of Christ's "first wise words . . . in his first speech to men" (P, 91), words that Christ speaks "as one having authority, and not as the scribes" (Matt. 7:29) and that are transcribed by the author with unusual instructions: "whoso readeth, let him understand" (Matt. 24:15). The written text is presented, in short, as the authoritative and unambiguous record of speech, thereby restoring for the reader the full presence of Christ's words. Christ, however, presents himself as Son, as the re-presentative of God the Father, who speaks through him. In that sense his words have a secondary quality and this aspect of his message is underlined when it is given printed form. As Melville is well aware, Matthew, like the other gospels, was written years after the death of Christ; our knowledge of its author is skimpy at best; and there is some question as to whether the Greek text is the original or a translation from an earlier Hebrew text. All of these aspects signal non-presence and remind us that Christ, like Moses, his Old Testament precursor, insists that he can get a voice out of silence and hence resembles certain philosophers who pretend to have found the "Talismanic Secret" that will reconcile man's desire for full presence with the fact of his orphaned existence:

> That profound Silence, that only Voice of our God, which I before spoke of; from that divine thing without a name, those impostor philosophers pretend somehow to have got an answer; which is as absurd, as though they should say they have got water out of stone; for how can a man get a Voice out of Silence?
>
> (P, 208)

The sacred text, then, has inscribed within it the very silence and absence that motivates Pierre to plunge himself into the sleazy pamphlet he finds in the coach, a text that seems to offer a model for human action directly contradicting that of the Sermon on the Mount since it emphasizes the incompatibility of Christian ideals and the practical demands of life in this world. However, as the narrator points out, the pamphlet is more of a "restatement of a problem, than the solution to the problem itself" (P, 210). And, indeed, the apparent differences between the two texts are equivocated by a set of ironic similarities that exist between them. The pamphlet's parabolic structure—based on a "strange conceit . . . apparently one of the plainest in the world; so natural a child might almost have originated it" and yet "again so profound, that scarce Juggalarius himself could be the author" (P, 210)—and the fact that it exists not as the product of the author who appears to have signed it but is rather his "verbal things, taken down at random, and bunglingly methodized by his young disciples" (P, 210), tie it to its Biblical pretext. This knotted relationship, moreover, appears to be inevitable rather than accidental since it is the product of a law as basic as that of gravity itself:

> thus over the most vigorous and soaring conceits, doth the cloud of Truth come stealing; thus doth the shot, even a sixty-two pounder pointed upward, light at last on the earth; for strive we how we may, we cannot

overshoot the earth's orbit, to receive the attractions of other planets; Earth's law of gravitation extends far beyond her own atmosphere.

(P, 261)

All words and conceits are subject to an "insensible sliding process" (P, 7) that mixes and entangles their paths and destines them to return at last to their silent source.

Reading consequently is an activity controlled by conceits that promise both wonder and enlightment but produce disenchantment and confusion by entangling man in such a complex web of relationships that the "three dextrous maids themselves could hardly disentangle him" (P, 175). Such is Isabel's experience when she reads a "talismanic word" (P, 147) inscribed in the center of a book-like handkerchief. Before she can decipher the mysterious inscription, she must teach herself to read, and that process radically changes her relation to the world. To this point in her life her relation to the man who calls himself her father has been a special and unconventional one:

> The word father only seemed a word of general love and endearment to me—little or nothing more; it did not seem to involve any claims of any sort, one way or the other. I did not ask the name of my father; for I could have had no motive to hear him named, except to individualize the person who was so peculiarly kind to me; and individualized in that way he already was, since he was generally called by us *the gentleman,* and sometimes *my father.*

(P, 145)

For Isabel at this point "father" is simply the "word of kindness and kisses" (P, 124), a word that raises neither the problem of origins nor of authority, for it implies only the "tenderness and beautifulness of humaness" (P, 122). Although when she looks in the pool of water behind the house she sees the "likeness—something strangely like, and yet unlike, the like-ness of his face" (P, 124), the play of images does not generate sinister ambiguities but simply confirms her sense of the value of the human "in a world of snakes and lightenings, in a world of horrible and inscrutable inhumanities" (P, 122). Her father, however, on the last visit to her before his death, leaves behind a handkerchief bearing in its middle a "small line of fine faded yellowish writing" that becomes for her a "precious memorial":

> But when the impression of his death became a fixed thing to me, then again I washed and dried and ironed the precious memorial of him, and put it away where none should find it but myself . . . and I folded it in such a manner, that the name was invisibly buried in the heart of it, and it was like opening a book and turning over many blank leaves before I

came to the mysterious writing, which I knew should be one day read by me, without direct help from any one. Now I resolved to learn my letters, and learn to read, in order that of myself I might learn the meaning of those faded characters. . . . I soon mastered the alphabet, and went on to spelling, and by-and-by to reading, and at last to the complete deciphering of the talismanic word—Glendinning. I was yet very ignorant. *Glendinning,* thought I, what is that? It sounds something like *gentleman;*— Glen-din-ing;—just as many syllables as gentleman; and—G—it begins with the same letter; yes, it must mean *my father.* I will think of him by that word now:—I will not think of the *gentleman,* but of *Glendinning.* . . . as I still grew up and thought more to myself, that word was ever humming in my head; I saw it would only prove the key to more.

(P, 146–47)

The inscribed handkerchief that is abandoned by "chance" and found "lying on the uncarpeted floor" (P, 146) is an object totally separated from its originating source, cut loose from the authority who could testify to the meaning of the "faded yellowish writing" on it. (Is its author the gentleman's wife, his sister who initials his neckcloths, or some anonymous seamstress like those who sew "in concert" at the Miss Pennies' house?) Consequently, the meaning of the word does not lie behind or within it but in its relation to other words and social conventions. For Isabel the word "Glendinning" does not stand first in the place of a person but in the place of another word, "gentleman," which it echoes, supplements, and particularizes. Ironically, it is this orphaned sign that leads Isabel to the second and even more problematic key to her origins, the word "Isabel" "gilded" in the "heart of [her] guitar" (P, 148). Even more than the handkerchief the guitar, having been purchased by Isabel from a peddlar who had "got it in barter from the servants" (P, 152) at the Glendinning estate, is a free-floating object, and the origins and meaning of the word in its interior are more mysterious than that of the one written on the handkerchief. Does it refer to the guitar's maker, to its owner, or to neither? As a given name rather than a patronym it is more clearly an object in its own right, its signification determined completely by the circumstances in which it functions, a truth that is confirmed by the fact that Isabel claims the name as her own only after she has read it in the guitar, having to that point "always gone by the name of Bell" (P, 148).

These two words, then, concealed in the interiors of the handkerchief and the guitar and associated by Isabel with her absent parents, function for her as keys that unlock and reveal a previously hidden set of relationships. These keys, however, are ambiguously inside the objects whose meanings they are supposed to unlock and their significance derives from a set of purely arbitrary associations. In this sense Isabel as a reader may be said to be the author of her own parentage; she has arrested the motion of two free-floating words and placed them within a genealogical order that is partially discovered, partially invented. And Pierre, through his reading and interpretation of the note that proclaims Isabel's relation to this order, entangles himself in a "fictitious alliance" (P, 175) that will lead him at last to his decision to become a writer and to "gospelize the world anew" (P, 273).

This process is the one the narrator refers to when he insists that "to a mind bent on producing some thoughtful thing of absolute truth, all mere reading is apt to prove an obstacle hard to overcome" (P, 283). Since the only non-textual reality is the silence of the crude forms of the natural earth, any act of speaking and writing is bound to be a repetition, a displacement or a representation of a purely textual entity, and necessarily derived, secondary and inessential. This is the perception that marks the text of *Pierre*, a text that is written against the "countless tribes of common novels and countless tribes of common dramas" as well as against those "profounder emanations of the human mind" (P, 141); yet it is doomed to contain and repeat them. Empty conventions from the domestic sentimental novel—the country-city setting, the incest theme, the dark and light ladies, the romantic symbols of guitar and portrait—combine with references to Dante, Spenser, Shakespeare, Milton, and others to produce a text that undermines the notion of writing as original creation and reading as an authentic act of discovery. "Had Milton's been the lot of Casper Hauser," the narrator insists, "Milton would have been as vacant as he" (P, 259). Hence the writer is portrayed as a whore who sells herself for money—"careless of life herself, and reckless of the germ life she contains"; as an actor in an empty melodrama performing a part not written by him— "only hired to appear on the stage, not voluntarily claiming the public attention" (P, 258); and as an improvisator, echoing the music of others and creating off hand, on the spur of the moment, variations on any proposed subject—"it is pleasant to chat ere we go to our beds; and speech is further incited, when like strolling improvisators of Italy, we are paid for our breath" (P, 259). Correspondingly, the reader is portrayed as the victim of this "lurking insincerity . . . of written thoughts," the enchanted dupe of books whose leaves "like knavish cards" are "covertly packed" (P, 339). For that "wonderful" and mysterious "story" of the illegitimate and orphaned child may have been "by some strange arts . . . forged for her, in her childhood, and craftily impressed upon her youthful mind; which so—like a mark in a young tree—had enlargingly grown with her growth, till it had become the immense staring marvel" (P, 354). Her story like all stories is inevitably genealogical; it resembles a family tree that "annually puts forth new branches" (P, 9), but it also bears a "mark" that at once implies the activity of an originating intention and signifies our distance from it. For it points not to the authoritative source but to the tangle of other such inscriptions scattered throughout the text of *Pierre*, inscriptions that seem at first to embody a presence but that actually condemn us to absence.

BRYAN C. SHORT

Form as Vision in "Clarel"

In his foreward to Vincent Kenny's book on *Clarel*, Gay Wilson Allen recommends three "routes" for approaching the poem. The first relates *Clarel* to Melville's "spiritual quest for the meaning of existence." The second reaches *Clarel* by way of Melville's actual trip to Palestine. The third explores Melville's anticipation of the pessimism so important to later thought. Efforts by such recent critics as Kenny and William H. Shurr . . . have moved us far enough along these routes that another can be glimpsed. *Clarel* demands a reading in the light of relationships between Melville's poetic technique and modifications which the practice of verse wrought in his view of literature. A reverence for organic unity pervaded Romantic poetics in America; Melville's changing interpretation of this doctrine determines the adapting of versification to the narrative purpose which gives *Clarel* its unique shape. Such a study promises a better understanding of how Melville's later verse grew out of the impatient questing of the novels, an explanation of his curious abandonment of tetrameter in the *Clarel* epilogue, and a more flattering image of his state of mind than has been current. The protean nature of Melville's poetry suggests that the promise of artistic rather than philosophical accomplishment motivated the varied forms of his mature works. Although his themes reflect the depression which adorns his family correspondence, his incessant technical experiments bespeak an undying vitality. Our view of Melville should include the literary interests, both practical and theoretical, which kept him active at his desk in spite of obscurity, money problems, family tragedy, poor health, and civil service. *Clarel*, with its

From *American Literature* 4, vol. 50 (January 1979). Copyright © 1979 by Duke University Press.

profound dedication to organic poetics, reveals these springs and motives as well as any other work in the canon.

Battle-Pieces lays the groundwork for organic form in *Clarel* by achieving a well-tested strategy for facing the terrors of experience, a style which both suits and embodies that strategy, and a new confidence, noted by critics, *vis à vis* the spiritual quest whose enticements survived the foundering of Melville's fiction. Without this foundation, *Clarel* is unthinkable, for *Clarel* presents a world as blasted and a plot as depressing as any met previously in Melville's works. A study of organicism in the epic begins with *Battle-Pieces,* upon whose successes rests Melville's decision, in the teeth of his woes, to grapple with old and crushing obsessions in the medium of eighteen thousand tetrameter lines.

The main strategy carried from *Battle-Pieces* into *Clarel* is the abrogation of "deep diving" after "chronometrical" truths in favor of a disciplined objectivity. Melville signals this strategy in a prefatory note:

> The aspects which the strife as a memory assumes are as manifold as are the moods of involuntary meditation. . . . Yielding instinctively, one after another, to feelings not inspired from any once source exclusively, and unmindful, without purposing to be, of consistency, I seem, in most of these verses, to have but placed a harp in a window, and noted the contrasted airs which wayward winds have played upon the strings.

Poetry responds to the winds of war without forcing an artificial consistency on them. *Battle-Pieces* wagers that clearly "noted" historical movements may reveal the meaning of existence more effectively than the single-minded vision of a Taji, and that a valuable organic bond can unite fact and verse. This is not to say that Melville eschews fictionalization but that fictionalization plays a more limited and descriptive role than in his novels.

Objectivity suits Melville's main *persona,* an aging observer remote from the action. However, during the course of *Battle-Pieces,* Melville discovers important correspondences between poetic and battlefield deeds; the Civil War gives birth to modern man, brave, self-controlled, and fatalistic, and Melville adopts this new hero as a model for his own literary goals. Courageous warriors display the same discipline as the poet, and both stand in the mainstream of history. Praising the pilot of a suicide-launch, Melville writes:

> In Cushing's eager deed was shown
> A spirit which brave poets own—
> That scorn of life which earns life's crown.
> ("At the Cannon's Mouth")

Poetry can strive for an organic encompassing of heroic action because it embodies a parallel heroism.

However brave, neither poet nor soldier, art nor experience, can claim knowledge beyond death; in this objective limitation all share equally. The living must be satisfied with mere hints at the meaning of existence without hoping that some heroic act or literary "deep dive" will yield more:

> Obscure as the wood, the entangled rhyme
> But hints at the maze of war—
> Vivid glimpses or livid through peopled gloom,
> And fires which creep and char—
> A riddle of death, of which the slain
> Sole solvers are.
> ("The Armies of the Wilderness")

The equality of art and action only partly explains Melville's confidence in an objective, unified poetry. Art goes a step further by so revealing the human heart that it anticipates experience. In " 'The Coming Storm' " Melville takes the example of Shakespeare:

> No utter surprises can come to him
> Who reaches Shakespeare's core;
> That which we seek and shun is there—
> Man's final lore.

The truths of the heart cannot transcend mortality, but, as illuminated by art, they predict whatever shocks may come—a function which in *Clarel* takes the place of attempts to penetrate the pasteboard mask of reality. If one picks a great experience—the Civil War, a pilgrimage to the Holy Land—a poetry which reflects its varied aspects organically and without preconception can capture whatever lessons the experience teaches. Imposing transcendental hopes on the experience will only destroy both its heroic discipline and its validity.

In seeking to respond objectively to the winds of history, Melville evolves a style in line with Emerson's organicist dictum that "it is not metres but a metre-making argument which makes a poem." He describes the style in "A Utilitarian View of the Monitor's Fight":

> Plain be the phrase, yet apt the verse,
> More ponderous than nimble;
> For since grimed War here laid aside
> His painted pomp, 'twould ill befit
> Overmuch to ply
> The rhyme's barbaric cymbal.

The plain, apt verse of *Battle-Pieces* matures in "Lee in the Capitol," the penultimate poem in the volume, into the full-blown *Clarel* form; loose iambic tetrameter, a prominent line throughout the collection, falls into unequal verse paragraphs; flexible rhyme patterns intrude on the predominant couplets. The poem presents a dramatic yet essentially verbal scene much like those of *Clarel* and reflects a similar relationship between narrator and character. "Lee in the Capitol" presents the final hero of *Battle-Pieces* abandoning his avowed silence to speak before a hostile public. Both the circumstances of Lee's act and the repetition of his views in a prose supplement suggest Melville's identification with him. Hero and poet come together to climax the hope for both art and experience, a hope which rests on the bravery, aptness, and objectivity of Lee's words, compellingly turned into verse. Out of the narrowed horizons and clouded dreams of war comes a vision of honest courage and unified art. Lee's act, like Melville's bow to history, reveals an ability to anticipate if not transcend experience, for his plea catches "the light in the future's skies." Discipline and self-control sustain most of the *Clarel* pilgrims. The belief that a verse like that of "Lee in the Capitol" can contain metaphysical anxieties within an objective framework and thereby anticipate their ravages is the heaviest weapon carried by Melville from *Battle-Pieces* into the epic. Melville's willingness to fictionalize Lee's speech demonstrates his willingness to sum up the lesson of the war as he sees it; the abandonment of preconceived transcendental goals does not stop art from reaching conclusions. *Clarel* begins on the hope that new, if circumscribed, insights into the "meaning of existence" are possible.

In line with principles of organic unity, Melville's substitution of disciplined objectivity for deep diving dramatically modifies the "diagram" of his characteristic quest. In *Clarel,* the search leads away from rather than toward the symbol which promises resolution. Whereas Taji incessantly follows Yillah, Clarel's pilgrimage leads him from Ruth. This change in direction, to some a structural disharmony, reflects Melville's wish to distinguish spiritual knowledge from emotional satisfaction and to keep the transcendent questing of his earlier works from dominating experience. The lesson of Civil War fatalism permits Melville to build into *Clarel* his misgivings about the nobility of both pilgrims and pilgrimage; vivid adventure gives way to desultory wandering and endless talk; systems of belief no longer command attention on the basis of logical force. Robert Penn Warren comments that "Melville is trying to show ideals not as abstractions but as a function of the life process." This impulse, both objective and organic, leads Melville to conclude that grand ideas have little positive impact on human happiness; they do Clarel no more good than they do the wounded veterans of the war.

Just as the search for knowledge in Clarel separates from the promise of satisfaction, the views of the characters have little to do with their importance. The sociability of Derwent, whose meliorism subjects him to derision, keeps him at the center of the group. Vine says so little that his influence on Clarel partakes of the irrational. Rolfe's heartiness outweighs his contradictions. Walter Bezanson concludes that Clarel "goes increasingly from asking whose beliefs are right to asking who is the right kind of man." A concomitant question which Melville asks is not what truth is deepest but what kind of art is both unified and honest, a question which finally undercuts all abstractions. Melville's objectivity challenges even Lee's resigned wisdom. Removed from the realm of historical greatness, experience offers less comfort than blind faith; the wise soldiers of Battle-Pieces condense into Ungar, whose heroism is irrelevant to his needs. Versification follows suit by seeking effects of plainness and tension rather than ease or dramatic brilliance. The tetrameters borrowed from "Lee in the Captial" come to embody, and finally to symbolize, the hard realities of a wasted world.

Clarel is not, however, without a hint of redemption, but redemption, operating within the sphere of satisfaction rather than knowledge, finally contradicts both the experience of its characters and the outcome of its plot, creating a disintegration which threatens to ruin the organic unity at the heart of the work. Redemption comes secondhand in Melville's curiously bouyant epilogue. It is here that Melville redefines organic form in order to escape the objective decorum of his narrative. Like the palinode of a Medieval allegory or the epilogue of an Elizabethan play, the Clarel epilogue removes Melville's conclusion from the context of the tale. Clarel is left alone shouldering a greater burden than ever; none of his friends can comfort him; but Melville blithely tells us that things are not so bad. In reevaluating the search for truth, Melville denies the final value of brave and disciplined objectivity, the archetypal virtues of Battle-Pieces; art, in the epilogue, is left alone to find its own satisfactions. Melville salvages the principal of organic unity by shifting to a new and fitting form. He abandons the tetrameters which have stood for "apt" art since their emergence and takes on a pentameter line. Once Clarel has conveyed it charge of depressing truth it flees into emotional and stylistic exuberance. If, as the epilogue says, "death but routs life into victory," hard facts seem to rout an art of truth into an art of pleasure in which style answers organically not to experience but to the immediate delights of literature. The Clarel epilogue trades tension, plainness, discipline, and objective seriousness for wit, exaggeration, delicate stylistic artifice, and casual sophistication.

In the *Clarel* epilogue, Melville moves away from the typically Romantic organicism of Emerson's "metre-making argument" to a perspective in which poetry, by creating its own decorum, becomes an argument-making meter equally unified but liberated from objectivity. How this happens, and what it implies for Melville's poetics, reflect in the ways by which Melville prepares for the epilogue. Given Melville's doubts, it is hardly surprising objectivity and organic unity result in the bleak finale of *Clarel*, but the ability of art to anticipate this bleakness enables Melville to detach and distance his poetic voice from experience and finally to elevate it, like "the spirit about the dust" over the predetermined ruins surrounding it. Melville knows what is coming and has time to prepare an escape. The heroism of poetry, discovered in *Battle-Pieces*, has given the created world, the world of literature, an immediacy and a power previously reserved for bold adventure and half-glimpsed spiritual forces; when the potential emotional attractiveness of art rather than either mysterious meanings or observed facts determines the style and form of a work, that work can achieve an expressiveness and beauty denied to an art of objective observation. It is in the context of Melville's shift in focus from truth to beauty that the symbolic value of his versification comes into focus.

In *Moby-Dick*, Ishmael's consciousness is a territory in which opposing views conflict; in *Clarel*, verse itself plays a similar role. Poetry transforms Melville's narrative voice from that of a first-person participant or an objective observer into a less well-defined authorial presence. The constraints of meter, rhyme, and third-person detachment make it difficult for the narrator to submerge himself in the events of *Clarel* as Ishmael does when the *Pequod* sets sail; his voice, identified with versification, is less malleable. How Melville defines this voice and makes it embody the conflict between experience and freedom, truth and beauty, is best illuminated by Northrop Frye's apt description of musical rhythm in English epic verse:

> When we find sharp barking accents, crabbed and obscure language, mouthfuls of consonants, and long lumbering polysyllables, we are probably dealing with *melos,* or poetry which shows an analogy to music, if not an actual influence from it.
>
> The musical diction . . . is congenial to a gnarled intellectualism of the so-called "metaphysical" type. It is irregular in metre (because of the syncopation against stress), leans heavily on enjambement, and employs a long cumulative rhythm sweeping the lines up into larger rhythmical units such as the paragraph.

Combined with his assertion that English epic verse naturally tends to a four-beat line, Frye's description suits *Clarel* in all but one respect; the longer line of the English epic tradition—from alliterative to blank verse—permits four accentual stresses to appear in a line less frequently than every other syllable, thus providing a hedge against strict metrics. A pentameter line, for example, can easily show four major accents, without either contradicting or abandoning its meters, simply by deemphasizing one metrical stress. If the octosyllabic line of *Clarel* is to escape from tetrameters into accentual rhythm, it must resort to extra syllables, feminine endings, violent substitutions, and continual enjambement. Although these occur with frequency, they lack the sustained force necessary to efface the movement of Melville's tetrameters, whose effect of disciplined plainness gave few problems in the shorter compass of "Lee in the Capitol." Consequently, the rudiments of accentual rhythm, *melos,* continually struggle against metrics, producing a tension which Melville finds valuable enough to his theme to reinforce through rhyme and indentation.

Melville generally indents or breaks a line whenever his focus shifts from one character to another or to the narrator, and whenever the narrative changes mode (conversation, song, thought, commentary, description). However, indentation also varies the texture of the verse, occurring more frequently in passages of agitation such as that in which Clarel learns of Ruth's death. Indentation speeds the flow of verse by introducing new rhyme sounds and patterns. Melville lends stability to calmer passages by utilizing couplets and quatrains, as in "Clarel and Ruth"; elsewhere, as in "Celio," rhymes change and rhyme patterns mutate so rapidly as to prevent the easy division of the poem into units smaller than the paragraph. Taken together, indentations, breaks, rapid rhyme mutations, and metrical irregularities call attention to the jagged and cumulative effects defined by Frye, and the absence of these devices returns the poem to the unchallenged metrics of "Lee in the Capitol." Regular metrics predominate in many places expressing hope for consolation within the world of objective experience; accentual freedom struggles more violently against meter where the discipline of established doctrines threatens to collapse. When the climax of the tale brings utter despair, Melville escapes to a pentameter in which ease and rhythmic freedom prevail, thus tolling the death of his organic combination of objectivity with stylistic plainness and metrical tension. Melville makes sure that collapses in established order result from events within the sphere of human anticipation, and thus that they pinpoint the poverty of vision which now goes hand-in-hand with both heroic discipline and the commitment of poetry to an organic "noting" of factual trends.

The promise of escape which Melville consummates in the epilogue informs the lyrics of *Clarel*. Although sometimes frivolous, as a group they celebrate freedom from discipline, beauty, and related values which receive little reinforcement from the pilgrims—hedonism as opposed to self-denial, satisfaction as opposed to knowledge, faith as opposed to reason, feeling as opposed to thought. Twenty-two of them, nearly half, are sung by four characters—Glaucon, the Cypriote, the Lesbian, and the Lyonese—who question the asceticism of the pilgrimage; thirteen express a more comforting faith than that of Clarel. The lyrics also give certain characters the opportunity to speak more personally than they can elsewhere. Vine's depth receives a major witness in his two songs; Ungar reveals his hidden wishes in verse. From the beginning, the lyrics undercut the constraint which weighs upon the pilgrimage; they presage Melville's leap into the epilogue by exemplifying the qualities which make art satisfying even in the face of blankness and by employing poetic forms less restrained than that of the narrative.

The first lyric peeps out at Clarel from under the peeling whitewash of his hotel room in Jerusalem. In the only sustained pentameters outside the epilogue, it tells of an answer to doubt found by an earlier tenant who sees the decayed remains of the Biblical world as symbols of a personal emotional faith:

> So much the more in pathos I adore
> The low lamps flickering in Syria's Tomb.

The lyric embodies the ability to make subjective feelings and alluring symbols into the bases for a satisfying faith—an ability which Clarel lacks. Melville's sophisticated use of alliteration in such lines as "Triumph and taunt that shame the winning side," and "My unweaned thoughts in steadfast trade-wind stream" produces an accentual rhythm which does not jar against metrics. Shortly thereafter, Clarel's actual pilgrimage begins and the message of satisfaction and the pleasing style of the lyric are forgotten.

The start of the journey introduces Glaucon, Melville's first hedonist, who abandons the group after singing four lyrics warning against the deliberate rejection of beauty for a life of trial. Glaucon's final song suggests that the psychological effect of a blasted landscape is dangerous for those who traverse it:

> Tarry never there
> Where the air
> Lends a lone Hadean spell—
> Where the ruin and the wreck
> Vine and ivy never deck

> And wizard wan and sibyl dwell:
> There, oh, beware!

However, the pilgrims continue in their belief that the search for knowledge supercedes all sensations, a view which prevails until the final section of the poem.

Following Glaucon's departure, a Dominican friar sings a song of praise for the Church which is mocked by Margoth in an important negative example of the lyric promise:

> Patcher of the rotten cloth,
> Pickler of the wing o' the moth,
> Toaster of bread stale in date,
> Tinker of the rusty plate,
> Botcher of a crumbling tomb,
> Pounder with the holy hammer,
> Gaffer-gammer, gaffer-gammer-
> Rome!

Margoth criticizes the Church in a poem whose metrical pounding and short, parallel, end-stopped phrases produce a mechanical effect more rigid than any other in the volume. The oppressive meter of Margoth's poem relates to its meaning in three ways; it symbolizes his view of church activities, it exemplifies his own rigidly dogmatic beliefs, and it embodies the danger that repeated formal patterns can degenerate into empty, deadening convention. Melville satirizes both the Church and Margoth for the programmed nature of their responses to life, and his metrics demonstrate the need for freedom in art, personal attitude, and doctrine. For all his scientific sanctimony, Margoth is as unsatisfied as the others; his trochaic tetrameter merely offers an exaggerated mirror image of the iambic tetrameter of the narrative. Margoth's song makes it clear that an organic fitting of form to theme cannot alone produce a verse of comforting emotional power.

The Dead Sea cantos of *Clarel* contain important lyrics by Nehemiah and Mortmain, both of which reaffirm the significance of a faith like that in the first lyric. Mortmain laments the death of the now "unadored" Southern Cross as a Christian symbol, and Nehemiah's psalm paraphrase finds comfort in a candle shining in the "valley of shade." Both seek a religion supported by simple affective symbols comparable to the "low lamps flickering in Syria's Tomb" rather than intellectual abstractions—a religion of satisfactions rather than truths. Mortmain's song conveys an impression of the attractiveness of the dead symbol:

> How far removed, thou Tree divine,
> Whose tender fruit did reach so low—

> Love apples of New-Paradise!
> About the wide Australian sea.

Ultimately, Nehemiah's narrow fundamentalism and Mortmain's bitterness prevent them from accepting the emotional and imaginative freedom which is Melville's key to escape from eternal pilgrimage; neither can create his own symbols of faith; both sing in the iambic tetrameter of the narrative, and both die on the journey. The presence of such delicate yet tragic songs in iambic tetrameter implies that the lyric and narrative sensibilities can merge, that experience can lay the groundwork for freedom if one can achieve the proper combination of sensitivity and aesthetic distance—gifts which begin to replace discipline and objectivity at the center of Melville's art.

"Mar Saba" introduces the Cypriote and the Lesbian, whose songs of love and pleasure contrast with the asceticism of the monastery. Their sensuality awakens Clarel to the attractions of a return to Ruth, thus contributing to the erotic theme discussed by Nina Baym. The Cypriote's first song is particularly symbolic; after two stanzas describing the lasting delights enjoyed by the gods, he finishes with an imperative:

> Ever blandly adore them;
> But spare to implore them:
> They rest, they discharge them from time;
>   Yet believe, light believe
>   They would succor, reprieve—
>   Nay, retrieve—
> Might but revelers pause in the prime!

For the Cypriote, earthly and heavenly revelry provoke comparison, and revelry expresses faith; no gaping dichotomy separates flesh and spirit, satisfaction and knowledge, beauty and truth. The proper approach to the gods combines adoration, affirmed in the first lyric and lamented by Mortmain, with respect for the senses. The Cypriote's anapests and widely varied line lengths again suggest an alternative to tetrameters. Hearing his song, the central group of pilgrims are deeply touched.

"Mar Saba" climaxes when Melville brings Vine, Mortmain, and Rolfe face to face with the famous palm tree of the monastery, while Clarel looks on. Each of the three undergoes a moment of inspiration, a hint at the unity of dream and experience available to the liberated mind, and then each reverts to doubt and questioning. In each, the choice of experience and objective reason over sensuality and emotion prevents the acceptance of a vision woven out of momentary ecstasy. In the face of the most eloquent symbol and the deepest feelings in the poem, they relapse. Mortmain, an Ahab stripped of his command by Melville's objectivity, dies

in anguish. Moved, Clarel begins to reflect on his love for Ruth; he acknowledges the importance of erotic symbols to Christianity and the beauty
which they possess, but his belief in his own impurity keeps him from
rejecting a discipline which, unlike the Cypriote, he identifies with religion.
He continues to think of Ruth in abstract terms, as if she too were an item
of knowledge. As the pilgrimage leaves Mar Saba, the stage is set for Ungar
and the Lyonese, who restate the conflict between order and freedom.

Ungar sings the swansong of Melville's identification with Civil War
heroism. His two fragments, both metrically rigid, express a philosophy of
resignation and a secret hope for revenge. Ungar senses the vanity of his
wish and the split between his knowledge of life and his dream of vindi-
cation. Rather than finding a way of uniting himself, he controls his dis-
integrated personality through relentless mental discipline. He presides over
the now stale pilgrimage which, with the coming of the Lyonese, begins
to give way to the end of Clarel's quest for knowledge and his concomitant
acceptance of satisfaction as a goal.

After arguing with a monk on the importance of sexuality, Clarel
dreams of the choice before him:

> And Clarel dreamed, and seemed to stand
> Betwixt a Shushan and a sand;
> The Lyonese was lord of one,
> The desert did the Tuscan own,
> The pale pure monk. A zephyr fanned;
> It vanished, and he felt the strain
> Of clasping arms which would detain
> His heart from each ascetic range.

Just a movement from end-stopped to run-on lines gives the passage a sense
of emerging freedom, Clarel awakens to feel an "organic change" working
within him; the arms of love which draw him from Mar Saba promise a
unity of spirit unknown to him before; he experiences a sudden impatience
with his journey. The Lyonese then sings the folly of a discipline which
contradicts nature:

> Rules, who rules?
> Fools the wise, makes wise the fools—
> Every ruling overrules?
> Who the dame that keeps the house,
> Provides the diet, and oh, so quiet,
> Brings all to pass, the slyest mouse?
> Tell, tell it me:
> Signora Nature, who but she!

The four songs of the Lyonese accentuate his freedom from dogma. They employ such rapidly shifting feet and strong alliteration that they often attain an accentual rhythm which obliterates metrics, anticipating Melville's experiments in *John Marr and Other Sailors:*

> Over the river
> In gloaming, ah, still do ye plain?
> Dove—dove in the mangroves,
> How dear is thy pain!

Clarel hears the Lyonese without heeding the elegiac tone central to his lyrics. Dame nature both brings all to pass and makes all pass away. The Lyonese, wise compared to the other hedonists, has bought his freedom by a deliberate distancing of himself from the religion which draws him to the Holy Land. His poems acknowledge and integrate his sense of loss, creating out of pain a promise of consoling beauty. Clarel also ignores the power of time sung by the Cypriote, Ungar, and the Lyonese; he attaches his hopes not to freedom, imagination, beauty, and emotion but to Ruth herself. Fellowship and love may well be experiences in which Melville takes unambiguous pleasure, but his works tell us that only the very lucky gather their fruit; we are unprepared for life unless we prepare for loneliness. When Ruth dies, Clarel, like Mortmain, relapses into anguish.

Melville's final lyric, a dirge on the death of Ruth, firmly establishes the value of an art of expressive beauty; in it, Melville's narrative voice takes its new direction. The dirge sings in tetrameters, hinting that disciplined objectivity can coexist with imaginative freedom for those who are not blind. In order to avoid confusing this possibility with the vain hope that experience will reward the resolute, Melville ends his story on an objective note, leaving Clarel to the fate which has been anticipated.

Melville's dirge places Ruth in a sensually pleasing realm of "honey" and "mosses sweet" where her lover may hope to rejoin her. It creates a mental image of death as gentle and feeling, an imaginative leap which it justifies through literary symbolism rather than experiential data. The final image sums up its main affirmation:

> And if, ere yet the lover's free.
> Some added dusk they rule decree—
> That shadow only let it be
> Thrown in the moon-glade by the palm.

The palm recalls that of Mar Saba, which cast a shadow over the pilgrims by confronting them with the ephemeral nature of their dreams. And yet, that shadow, the despair of Mortmain, the resignation of Vine and Rolfe, proves the imaginative force of those dreams. The dirge, a sophisticated intrusion of art on ritual, affirms the emotional appropriateness of such dreams even in a context which also proves them insubstantial. Only in the world of personal emotion and aesthetic sensitivity do they persist, yet life inhabits this world as well as the objective realm of physical experience. The dirge shows poetry capable of creating an alluring vision in response to the most pressing tragedy, of establishing an organic symbol of hope comparable to the adored symbols of Christianity. The true artist, lover, or worshipper is he who sustains his faith creatively by keeping the Southern Cross, the low lamps, Ruth, imaginatively alive or by replacing them with equally compelling phenomena.

After the dirge, Melville dissociates his viewpoint from that of his less imaginative protagonist; he describes Clarel's Easter Week activities with reserve and artistic distance in order to fulfill his tale of experience before retreating into the epilogue. However, during the Passion Week canto, Melville imbues Christian ritual with the same imaginative grace and delicate sensuality seen in the lyrics and the dirge:

> With the blest anthem, censers sway,
> Whose opal vapor, spiral borne,
> Blends with the heavens' own azure Morn
> Of Palms; for 'twas Palm Sunday bright,
> Though thereof he, oblivious quite,
> Knew nothing.

Clarel, in his depression, ignores the procession—another of the sources of inspiration which experience offers to those who are sensitive to beauty and uncommitted to doubt. Remaining blind, Clarel vanishes into the "obscurer town" a final victim of Melville's molding of heroism, discipline, and objectivity into an organic art.

The epilogue reaffirms the satisfactions of the *Clarel* lyrics. Not only does Melville abandon his jagged tetrameters for an easier, freer-flowing rhythm, but he displays a wit rare in both *Clarel* and his earlier verse:

> But through such strange illusions have they passed
> Who in life's pilgrimage have baffled striven—
> Even death may prove unreal at the last,
> And stoics be astounded into heaven.

Melville playfully mocks the blinding egoism of the intellect; the urbanity of the verse prevents our reading it as either a true confession of newfound religious faith or as an ironic joke. He offers, above all, an elegant and clever literary antidote to the gloom of the narrative. The determinism of "Darwin's year" can be read into "Luther's day" if one wishes, but for the poet history is the raw material of poetry, which stands on imagination, sensual pleasure, and beauty. Life is a victory if celebrated rather than merely endured. Like Glaucon, Melville abandons the pilgrimage with a warning for those who deem it "life's pilgrimage," the only path to walk.

The *Clarel* epilogue in all its conscious artificiality fits form to theme as carefully as any of Melville's verses. Frequent couplets and quatrains reinforce the witty comparisons which give it an Augustan quality. Images and symbols are tossed off or piled on one another with a breezy casualness which challenges intellectual rigor. Vast generalizations explode into aphorism without warning, and disappear as rapidly, hinting at their own insignificance. The verse coolly recommends to Clarel, wracked by anguish,

> Then keep thy heart, though yet but ill-resigned—
> Clarel, thy heart, the issues there but mind.

Lightness of tone gives the caution a hollow ring which even an image from *The Scarlet Letter* ("like a burning secret which doth go / Even from the bosom that would hoard and keep") cannot counteract. Without the amusing stylistic artifice and exaggeration which frames it, Melville's conclusion would demand a deep evaluation. What the style of the epilogue warns us is that such a conclusion, always objectively problematical, is absurd in an art whose job should be to create attractive, emotionally accessible, organic manifestations of whatever it affirms, and not to give sententious speeches. The lesson of Melville's changing art in *Clarel* is that truth-seeking, whether transcendental or objective, too easily produces a truth which is useless while ignoring opportunity after opportunity for beauty and satisfaction. The *Clarel* epilogue, in its marvelously complex self-consciousness, gives the best proof of Melville's faith in literature and playful delight in creative freedom since the early pages of *Moby-Dick*.

Battle-Pieces and *Clarel* tell the tale of Melville's interest in a serious, disciplined, realistic, and organically unified verse; as such, *Clarel* can be called America's greatest Victorian poem. Melville found in *Battle-Pieces* a new approach to the doubts and ambiguities hovering over his later fiction. As reservations about this approach arose, he built them organically into the structure, the versification, and the lyrics of *Clarel*, evolving an alternative vision at the fringes of his epic. By the end, the alternative—faith in the satisfactions of beauty, imaginative freedom, and art—moves from the fringe to the center, and the epilogue gives it the last word. Here, Melville prefigures the witty and technically sophisticated verse of his later years. *Clarel* proves Melville's tenacity and clear-sightedness in bringing to completion a staggeringly difficult work, his alertness to sources of new inspiration, and his willingness to risk stylistic audacity when his vision warrants.

MICHAEL PAUL ROGIN

The "Somers" Mutiny and "Billy Budd": Melville in the Penal Colony

On December 1, 1842, on board the USS *Somers*, the son of the secretary of war and two common sailors were hanged at sea for mutiny. No actual mutiny had occurred on the *Somers*. But the eighteen-year-old midshipman, Philip Spencer, had approached another member of the crew with a plot to seize the ship, murder the captain, and sail the *Somers* as a pirate. Young Spencer had written, in Greek, a list of other sailors who he thought would join the conspiracy. He had been seen talking mysteriously to two companions, petty officer Samuel Cromwell and captain of the maintop, Elisha Small. Captain Alexander Mackenzie feared that the plot had spread beyond these three, and that his ship was in danger. He convened an informal officers' court. Guert Gansevoort, who had carried the tale of mutiny to his captain, presided over that court. Under Mackenzie's prodding, it sentenced the sailors to hang. When the *Somers* docked in New York harbor two weeks later, she brought home twelve seamen in irons; Spencer, Small and Cromwell had been buried at sea.

The *Somers* affair caused a national scandal. It was front-page news for months in New York City newspapers, and in the Albany *Argus* as well. The papers carried prominently the testimony, including Guert

From *Subversive Genealogy: The Politics and Art of Herman Melville*. Copyright © 1979, 1980, 1983 by Michael Paul Rogin. University of California Press.

Gansevoort's, concerning the events on the *Somers*. These dramatic and disputed events had political ramifications. Secretary of War John Spencer, Philip's father, was a close political ally of President Tyler. Mackenzie's family connections reached high in New York Democratic politics, and to the top of the naval hierarchy as well. His standing and the fear of anarchy proved more powerful than John Spencer. A naval court of inquiry exonerated the captain. Then to head off a civil prosecution for murder instigated by the secretary of war, Mackenzie was tried in a naval court-martial. He was acquitted there, too. Nevertheless, while Mackenzie was becoming a national hero, the remaining imprisoned sailors were quietly released. . . .

II

At the end of his life Melville wrote not only elegies to his family ashore, but also reveries of his life at sea. *Billy Budd* began as the poem of a middle-aged mutineer, on the eve of his execution. As the Jack Gentian sketches recalled a lost revolutionary world, so such a poem would have bid farewell to the natural authority in which Melville had sought an alternative to his familial inheritance, and which he had associated with Jacksonian democracy. It would have paid tribute to Jack Chase, "Captain of the Maintop" on the USS *Neversink*, and [*White-Jacket's*] "liege lord . . . sea tutor and sire." Billy Budd remained, in his final conception, a descendant of Jack Chase, and Melville dedicated Billy's story to him. Billy Budd and Jack Chase were natural children, disinherited of their patrimony. Their authority derived not from the aristocrats who illegitimately fathered them, but from their natural regality. Both were identified with "the rights of man." Both replaced the failed legal family on ship with "the happy family" of fraternal love. But Jack Chase was a mature alternative to figures of legal and inherited authority. Billy, "a flower scarcely yet fully released from the bud," was killed before he bloomed. As Melville reconceived *Billy Budd*, he split his adult mutineer into three: innocent youth, depraved accuser, and figure of naval authority. *Billy Budd*, responded to the emergence of the social question in antebellum America when middle-class fears of servile insurrection focused on workers instead of slaves. But as the tale developed, it shifted away from presenting mutiny either as consummated fact or as imminent danger. The version of the story that Melville left at his death did not simply participate in patrician anxieties over anarchy; it also analyzed the anxieties it shared. Just as Ahab had forced himself into *Moby-*

Dick and transformed a sea adventure into a "wicked book," so the more Melville worked over *Billy Budd*, the more Captain Vere gained in complexity and dominated the action. The splitting of Vere from Billy deprived Melville of his safe havens of nostalgia, with Jack Gentian ashore and Jack Chase at sea. It reawakened the conflicts that had characterized his family history and been sources of his art. It reawakened them, however, in a new context that made reconciliation possible. "I am the Fate's lieutenant. I act under orders," said Ahab. "We fight at command," agreed Vere. (*Billy Budd*) But Ahab was fate's lieutenant as expansionist Jacksonian. Vere acted under orders to the king. *Billy Budd* reunited instinct with authority not in Ahab's demonic destructiveness but in Vere's loving surrender to the state.

No single memory can account for the reworking of *Billy Budd*. Yet, after Melville wrote his first sketch of the mutineer, the national press revived the *Somers* mutiny affair, which had caused a national scandal half a century earlier. Like a nation, wrote Melville in *Billy Budd*, "a well constituted individual" may refrain from "blazoning aught calamitous in his history"; he then changed "history" to "family." The mutinous calamity in Melville's family history took place on the USS *Somers*. The two magazine articles revisiting the *Somers* affair prominently featured Lieutenant Guert Gansevoort's role, one in praise, one in condemnation. Perhaps these accounts, and the first publication of Captain Alexander Mackenzie's letter to the naval court of inquiry, were not the reason Melville reworked his tale. Certain it is, however, that *Billy Budd* reimagined the familially based conflicts which the *Somers* mutiny had first brought to Melville's fiction forty years before.

Critics who have argued whether the *Somers* affair provided a "sufficient source" for *Billy Budd* have missed the point. On both the *Somers* and the *Bellipotent* two crew members spoke of mutiny; one brought the tale to a superior, and he told the captain. Both captains initially discounted the story, but then precipitously determined to hang the alleged mutineers. Each convened a court (composed, with one exception, of the same officers on both ships). The first lieutenants presided formally over those courts, but each was "overrulingly instructed" by his captain. In spite of ambiguous evidence, and in the absence of an actual mutiny, both courts sentenced the accused to death. On each ship a condemned sailor blessed the authority about to hang him. First published reports grossly exaggerated both mutinies, requiring an accurate narrative to correct them.

Melville turned fact into fiction, of course, and it would be foolish to look for perfect fidelity to characters and events on the *Somers*. But

Melville did not make a novel from history. Instead he purified complex, novelistic, historical material, splintering a potential novel into a spare, spectral, dualistic, historical fiction. *Billy Budd* anticipates the Kafkaesque strand of literary modernism. Melville borrowed interior details from the *Somers* affair, as we shall see, even more striking than the external parallels. As he did so, however, he took the *Somers* through the looking glass. Inverting the form of the story, he overturned and fulfilled its meaning. The radically altered perspective from the antebellum *Somers* to *Billy Budd* indicates a shift in consciousness, not toward the recovery of society (as has been said of the evolution of American literature and social thought), but toward its exclusion.

Guert Gansevoort was, at the time of the *Somers* affair, the descendant "in primogeniture" of Colonel Peter Gansevoort, . . . the locus of authority in his and Melville's generation. Melville's father, it will be remembered, outfitted the young midshipman for sea. "He will be an honor to the family and. to the star spangled banner," wrote Allan Melvill, and "fight bravely his way to a pair of epaulettes." Herman Melville followed his cousin to sea, but he did so as a common sailor, not an officer. Melville stood with the executed sailor sons on the *Somers* against his own family. White-Jacket questioned the guilt of the hanged men, called their executions "murder," and imagined himself "at the end of a rope" as one of the *Somers* mutineers.

At the end of his life, in the poem "Bridegroom Dick," Melville again imagined he was under Guert's naval command. He placed himself on "the brig-o-war famed,/when an officer was hung for an arch-mutineer." Melville called the figure modeled on Guert, "Tom," giving him the name of his Melvill grandfather, uncle, and ship's-captain brother. This time he elegized Guert's role on the *Somers*. Guert had publicly supported the executions. But Thurlow Weed, politician friend of the Spencers and the Gansevoorts, reported in the 1880s that Guert privately opposed the hangings, and remained silent from loyalty to his captain. "Bridegroom Dick" celebrated Guert, "true to himself and loyal to his clan," for his silence over the *Somers* affair.

By the 1880s, Guert was dead. The mutiny had taken a large personal toll, and two courts-martial flawed his subsequent career. Guert was given command of the USS *Roanoke* during the Civil War. "I hope he will yet turn out the hero of a brilliant victory," Melville wrote his brother. But Guert lost his ship a few months later in the Caribbean, the scene of the *Somers* hangings. Captain Mackenzie had been accused of executing, not three proven ringleaders of a mutinous conspiracy, but the only three suspects who could navigate the ship. He was formally exonerated, as Guert was twenty years later. Guert lived a recurrent nightmare nonetheless. In the later episode, the secretary of the navy held him "to accountability for the consequences of . . . negligent navigation." He insisted on the responsibility of an officer for the derelictions of his men. This theme, so powerful on the *Somers*, had returned to haunt Guert. To be servant of his captain and the military order did not free an officer from responsibility, but magnified it. Naval officer Guert was a victim, too.

He was victim on the *Somers*, by some accounts, of a deranged captain. "Was he unhinged?" the ship's surgeon wondered about Captain Vere. Mackenzie, too, it was alleged, acted under "a species of insanity." In Melville's words, "No more trying situation is conceivable than that of an officer subordinate under a captain whom he suspects to be not mad, indeed, but yet not quite unaffected in his intellects. To argue his order to him would be insolence. To resist him would be mutiny." Guert's dilemma may have been the surgeon's. but these two officers obeyed an unhinged, human authority. Vere seemed deranged because he submitted to the impersonal, humanly unhinged imperatives of the law.

Mackenzie's religious ceremonies, familial bonds, and intimate personal revelations called his judgment into question. If Vere was insane, it was for denying personal and religious claims. The authority he obeyed fatally separated behavior in the world from human bonds among men below, and from transcendent purpose above. But Vere, like the silent Guert, felt the force of claims on which he could not act. Melville narrated Vere's story from the inside. He retold the *Somers* mutiny to separate the structures of human and state authority which converged on the *Somers*. That separation undercut Mackenzie's defense in order to restore a final harmony the actual captain failed to achieve. It was as if Melville was saying, to Mackenzie, to his own clan, and to himself, the best defense of the murderous authority under which we live must look as I portray it here. We cannot know whether Melville assented to the authority he so depicted, but we can at least look at it straight. Let us first compare Vere's courtroom defense of hanging with Mackenzie's, and then examine the "inside narrative[s]" (as Melville titled *Billy Budd*) that lay within them.

"That floating world, the man-of-war," as Mackenzie's counsel called the *Somers*, purported to integrate the structures of feeling and authority that were distinct on shore. Nature, religion, law, family and the heart sustained a captain's rule. His victims, the heroes of Melville's early romances, denied these claims of integration. On White-Jacket's "world in a man-of-war," the *Neversink*, shipboard authority lacked sanctification.

The legal, familially based military hierarchy shut out nature and the heart. Captain Vere, as if echoing White-Jacket, sharply distinguished legal authority from all humanly responsive structures. The ship was not part of an organic order extending from family to God, as it was for Mackenzie, but a rigidified, lifeless, and self-enclosed structure. This radical break between a sympathetic chain of being and the imperatives handed down from above actually sanctified hierarchy. And it enforced a merger of state and nature, father and son, religion and the law, more thoroughgoing than anything White-Jacket or Mackenzie had imagined.

"A vessel which had been born into our naval family," declared Mackenzie's counsel, faced "Anarchy." "The government of the brig . . . had been despoiled of 'that subordination of the heart' which forms the conservative element in that little floating world, a national ship." How should the captain respond to mutinous conspiracy? "The high seas furnished no learned jurists with whom he might consult. But he had with him a volume of nature's laws, written by the finger of God on the human heart. In that volume he read that necessity ordains its own controlling canons, that they who seek unlawfully to slay may themselves be slain without formal process."

"The high seas" permitted Mackenzie to escape from formal legal processes to nature, God, and the heart. "The ocean . . . is inviolate nature primeval," Vere agreed. "But do these buttons that we wear attest that our allegiance is to Nature? No, to the King." Mackenzie's naval uniform incorporated familial, religious and natural relations; Vere's shut them out. Mackenzie's private conscience sustained his public acts; Vere had relinquished his "private conscience" for an "imperial one." "Subordination of the heart" supported Mackenzie's shipboard authority, and "the human heart" required him to kill. Nature and the heart, tools of order on the Somers, promised chaos on the Bellipotent. "The heart, the feminine in man," asked mercy for Billy; Vere ruled it out.

There were no mutinous acts on the Somers. Mackenzie's trial turned on Spencer's intent and on his own. Did Philip Spencer really mean to kill the captain and other officers, or was his talk a mad joke? Did Mackenzie really fear a mutiny before he reached help? Since Mackenzie had no legal right to kill the sailors, his defender Charles Sumner explained, he must be justified by his intent. "Intent is the essence," the judge advocate agreed. Billy Budd "proposed neither mutiny nor homicide." "In natural justice," Vere explained, a court would consider his intentions. But when a sailor struck and killed an officer, a naval court could not look behind his "deed." "Budd's intent or non-intent is nothing to the purpose."

"The high seas furnished no learned jurists" on the *Somers;* Vere was jurist on the *Bellipotent.* The *Somers* mutineers were slain "without formal process," "according to nature's laws." Vere split apart nature and legality; he invoked the letter of the law. "The finger of God" wrote the judgment against Spencer. "Innocent before God," Billy was guilty under law. Mackenzie observed "as many of the forms as were within my reach," but he lacked legal access to "those forms which would have been perfect." For Vere, "forms, measured forms" were all.

Vere's legal brief against Billy seemed extreme, evidence of his insanity. To give it plausibility, Melville invoked "without comment" the "commander of the *Somers.*" Mackenzie acted, Melville reported, "under the so-called Articles of War, Articles modelled upon the English Mutiny Act." Vere acted under the Mutiny Act; Mackenzie, as Melville charged in *White-Jacket,* did not. Mackenzie knew he had no legal right to execute the sailors. "Does the law justify you?" Philip Spencer asked Mackenzie. "In the necessities of my position I found my law," Mackenzie publicly responded. His counsel invoked "the stern law of necessity." Vere relied on the stern necessities of the law.

Mackenzie's hierarchical forms, seeking to encompass organic forms of life, were emotion-laden and imperfect. The captain's effort to establish an organic, inclusive authority resembled that of other antebellum conservatives, who found the bases for political authority in God, nature, family and the obedient heart. For Vere, form shut out and contradicted feeling. He emptied the formal hierarchy of its integrative comprehensive content. Vere split apart the realms of law and morals, appearance and interior, which antebellum Americans had tried to connect. Melville's Pittsfield neighbor, Oliver Wendell Holmes, Sr. (whose poem had made gentle fun of "the old three-cornered hat, and the breeches, and all that" of Major Melvill), would have found Mackenzie's order congenial; Vere's law resembled his son's.

The jurist Holmes's "bad man theory," like Vere's, "banished" "all words of moral significance" from the law. Legal rules, wrote Holmes, did not rely on conscience. They told the bad man the actions for which he would be punished, and they applied to all men, whether of good character or bad. The law, as Vere insisted, avoided intent; it remained in the realm of appearances. Morals addressed intentions, wrote the younger Holmes; the law had to do with external signs and deeds. Holmes the father had first applied the term "Brahmin" to describe the American aristocracy; his son's generation of patricians no longer ruled as family or Brahmin class; they served an overarching state. Holmes spoke to a generation for whom duty lay in submission to a mechanistic hierarchy, whose distant and mysterious purposes were handed down from above.

Vere's court made a radical attack not only on traditional ideas of the law, but on the traditional form of the novel as well. It may be a strange sort of novel which turns on a judgment in court. But at its inception the novel form was attacked precisely because its detailed accounts of ordinary experience resembled "reading evidence in a court of Justice." Early novel readers, Ian Watt has said, were like members of a jury, interested in the particularities of lives like their own. They did not desire an elevated moral authority to sift out superfluous details and impose a rigid meaning from on high. The details critics frowned on as mere evidence made it possible for readers to join event to motive, to form as idea of character. Vere repudiated such a novelistic theory of the law. "What can be expected from a court," White-Jacket had asked of the judgment on the *Somers*, "when an oligarchy of epaulets sits upon the bench, and a plebian top-man, without a jury, stand judicially naked at the bar?" Billy's "oligarchy of epaulets" was denied the particulars of the case. It judged just the sort of one-dimensional, allegorical figure about whom, says Ian Watt, no real jury would accept evidence. In Vere's court, as in modernist fiction, deeds were not a reliable guide to motives, no more for Billy's attack on Claggart than for Vere's judgment against the sailor. Vere distanced his court from Billy's action, and assigned that action a determinate meaning. He confirmed a pattern beyond that given in the world. He did not allow the court's conclusion to approximate a novel reader's, and grow out of the facts of the case. He excluded the details essential to a full grasp of human life, so that judgment could be handed down from on high. The forms imposed in Vere's court defeated the form of the novel.

The three trials of the *Somers* affair (the trial on the *Somers*, the naval court of inquiry, and Mackenzie's court-martial) had the opposite effect. They revealed the relations among characters and the events on the *Somers* in embarrassing detail. Here trial and novel came together. These trial records give us the *Somers* affair in full, novelistic complexity. They almost create the illusion by which the novelist would have us believe in the reality of his fiction, and speak for themselves.

The full story of *Billy Budd*, on the other hand, required an "inside narrative," which took the reader behind not only the false newspaper report but the judgment in Vere's court as well. Traditional allegory, like Vere's court devalued worldly reality for the sake of a higher meaning; properly deciphered, however, the ordinary world pointed beyond itself to the higher realm. In Vere's court there is no bridge between structures of meaning, but a radical break instead. Splitting inner from outer worlds, Vere's court provokes speculations about Vere's madness.

A merely external account of the action on the *Bellipotent* would be deceptive, the narrator insists, false to its underlying meaning. Vere's separation of public judgment from private motive casts into relief the considerations excluded from the court of law, Billy's innocence and Vere's love. It was the law that blocked Billy, and Vere's love for him, from maturing. The world outside the court, however, even as it made the inside narrative of Vere's relation to Billy available, conspired in that abortive result. The split between heart and law extended outside the court to the tale itself. The inside narrative was necessary to interpret a divided world, which could not speak for itself. Still, it did not restore coherence. Melville performed on the potentially novelistic material of *Billy Budd* the sort of operation which Vere performed in his court.

Melville's earlier sea romances were set outside society; yet they encompassed a wealth of novelistic detail from social and natural worlds. To this mundane material he conjoined another, transcendent order, whose possessed characters and monstrous beings imposed a higher meaning. In *Billy Budd* form has driven out novelistic life. A host of minor characters on the *Somers* complicated that plot; their tangential relationship to the mutiny and executions, present in the trial records, gave those accounts their verisimilitude. *Billy Budd* has few such characters. The protagonists on the *Somers* had histories, brought to bear on and revealed during the action on board, and reported in the trials. The protagonists on the *Bellipotent* are denied the human histories which flesh out novelistic characters. We get the bare outlines of Vere's history, but "nothing was known of [Claggart's] former life," and Billy is a foundling. Lacking history, interiority or complex social location, Billy gains vividness from allegorical association more than human interaction. He is "Adam before the Fall," "a young horse fresh from the pasture"; the associations locate him outside human relations in "unadulterate Nature." Claggart, figure of natural depravity to match Billy's natural innocence, is an allegorical type as well. Both are killed before they can develop characters. Unlike the others, Vere is located in society, but he is uncomfortable there. Unlike the others, he chooses his own fate, but chooses to shatter unified experience, to confirm a world torn between duty and desire. He chooses an action determined by a force from without, taking possession of the self. Motivated from within to be moved from without, Vere becomes an allegorical type of the law.

The characters are given some significant speech; but, since their language cannot bear the full weight of the meaning of the action, conversation plays little role. Mackenzie's trials, and his own reconstructions of shipboard conversation, filled the *Somers* affair with dialogue; Mackenzie recorded his speeches to the crew as well. Billy's stammer underlies the inadequacy of speech to present meaning on the *Bellipotent*. The *Somers* affair ran its course in a time and space more constricted than that typical in a novel. Time and space are further constricted on the *Bellipotent*, depriving characters of a chance to develop and gain consciousness from extended encounters with one another, and with the central moral concerns of the action. Novelistic detail would bridge the gap between the inner meaning and outer force; it would carry the weight of interpretation. Instead, the details of character and plot are subordinated to a central purpose. The deepest reality in *Billy Budd* lies in the text itself, not in a realistic world outside to which the text refers and into which it easily merges. Its very constriction within the text, however, gives the narrative its power. That concentrated, hypnotic impact prohibits fidelity to a sprawling, diffuse social reality. As if overwhelmed by the chaos and ambivalence for which mutiny is Melville's emblem, *Billy Budd* achieves its formal order by withdrawing from society.

Melville's short fiction of the 1850s had already resolved the tension between novelistic material and measured forms in favor of the latter. As in *Billy Budd*, that resolution opened a rift between external authority and the claims of the heart. The divisions insisted on in Vere's court and reproduced outside it should subvert integration. *Billy Budd*, however, rises above that dualism. Unlike the logic in Vere's court, the story which surrounds it suffuses the action with a reconciliatory glow. This harmony depends on the splintering of traditional authority, and it does not reestablish human bonds in the living, complex, object world. The formal harmony of the text records the harmony of merged and sacrificed identities.

In the absence of novelistic verisimilitude, *Billy Budd* resembles a romance. As is true for romance, the mundane world left to itself cannot provide meaning. Romance turns to another world, where the demands of reality are relaxed. *Billy Budd* does escape from society into nature, but Melville's tale, he tells us, is "no romance." The operations that drain it of social complexity imprison rather than liberate its characters. Like Melville's fiction of the 1850s, *Billy Budd* confines us in a denuded, mundane world, from which all possibility of transformation has fled. But unlike the earlier stories, *Billy Budd* gives that world its blessing.

Captain Mackenzie also imposed an interpretation on his man-of-war, in an effort to reconstruct the social order that had broken down on the *Somers*. The trial records reveal the project that lay behind Mackenzie's legal defense. As Vere seized the legal defense and turned it on it head, so Melville took possession of the inside narrative of the *Somers* mutiny. Mackenzie's crew, he told them after the hangings, should "draw two useful lessons" from the mutineers' example, "a lesson of filial piety, and of piety toward God." The lesson of filial piety responded to the central inside drama on the *Somers*, and we shall examine it first.

The executions on the *Somers*, it will be recalled, fatally merged patriarchy and the state. Mackenzie and Guert Gansevoort, in the name of protecting their midshipmen children against Philip Spencer's temptation to rebel, killed the son of the secretary of war. Young Melville and Philip Spencer had followed similar paths. Both came from the revolutionary aristocracy, both rebelled against their families when they went to sea, and both were accused of mutiny. The author of *Billy Budd* was closer to John Spencer's position than he was to Philip's. His own son, Mackie, had died at Philip's age and, like John Spencer, he had lost another itinerant son as well. But John Spencer, acting from a position of power, sought retribution against Mackenzie. *Billy Budd* eliminated familial power and loyalty as competitors with formal naval authority. It purified the family drama of its social complexity. Gone was the ship full of children. Gone were the three hanging sailors, merged into one. Gone was the aristocratic father ashore. There was a single father-captain on the *Bellipotent* who, faced with a threat to his authority, killed a single sailor-son.

Redburn and White-Jacket, personas of the youthful Melville, sought paternal captains at sea. They met disappointment. *Billy Budd* did not so much change sides and choose father over son as change the terms of the story. Family, joined in confused complexity to shipboard hierarchy on the *Somers*, White-Jacket's *Neversink*, and Redburn's *Highlander* as well, was simplified and separated from it on the *Bellipotent*. That separation at once safeguarded the ship and reunited the family.

"The best and only service he could do his father was to die," Mackenzie told Philip Spencer as he killed him. That "lesson of filial piety," enforced on the *Somers*, was consummated on the *Bellipotent*, too. Vere's "fatherly feeling" embarrassed Billy, made his stutter worse, and drove him to strike Claggart; "the disciplinarian" who replaced "the father in Vere" "ordered his son away to execution." Foundling Billy was not, as some critics have surmised, the actual "by-blow" of aristocratic Captain Vere. Nevertheless, lacking a family history (such as Spencer's), he lacked an identity independent of Vere's. To join Billy more closely to Vere, Melville eliminated Spencer's bad father ashore, the war secretary who would intervene to save his reprobate son, and was Mackenzie's superior and competitor. Melville also eliminated the captain's good son at sea, Oliver Hazard Perry, Jr.

Mackenzie . . . originally blamed young Perry for the loss of the *Somers*'s top-gallant mast. He shifted the onus to Elisha Small, arrested Small and Samuel Cromwell, and then hung all three accused mutineers. Perry belonged to the most important family in the American navy, one into which Mackenzie had married. His father was above Mackenzie in the naval hierarchy, and his uncle had befriended the captain when Mackenzie was a merchant seaman. Mackenzie wanted to underline the distinction between Perry's innocence and Spencer's guilt. He called Spencer "the base son of an honored father." He proposed that Perry fill the midshipman's slot "left vacant" by Spencer's execution.

The *Bellipotent* also contains a depraved son. When Claggart informs Vere of Billy's mutinous intentions, he is "the spokesman of the envious children of Jacob deceptively imposing upon the troubled patriarch the blood-dyed coat of young Joseph." Claggart's "mesmeric glance" "transfixed" Billy. As the "infernal expression" in Spencer's "staring eyes" "satisfied [Guert] at once of the man's guilt," so Claggart's "protruding alien eyes" symbolize his guilt. Melville may have borrowed Claggart's eyes from Spencer. Like Spencer, Claggart is an intruder new to his ship and undesired by his captain. But Billy, not Claggart, meets Spencer's fate. The executed son has made no plans to kill his captain; the captain who kills him has no favorite waiting in the wings. Yet the result is the same. Aggression and self-interest contaminated the *Somers* executions; Mackenzie justified them in bad faith. Like Mackenzie, Vere is torn between demands internalized from above, and resistance from below. But no familial bonds contaminate his identification upward; love is reserved for the victim below.

Just as *Billy Budd* removed family as a competing structure of power, so it eliminated aggression as a motive for murder. Melville purified Billy and Vere of bad motives. Mackenzie had contrasted the "advantages" of Philip Spencer's "distinguished social position" to his own "nearly thirty years of faithful servitude" in the navy. There was resentment in that comparison, and it called the captain's motives into question. Vere is "by birth" an aristocrat, like Spencer; like Mackenzie, he has chosen "disinterested" naval servitude. But on the *Bellipotent*, unlike the *Somers*, aristocratic bonds do not come into conflict with loyalty to the state. Vere defends his act as the product of a "pure sense of duty," unaffected by and thus not spoiling his pure "sense of love." Separated from love, duty justifies the public hanging; separated from duty, love allows the private reconciliation.

Mackenzie had wanted Spencer to admit he was guilty of mutiny, and to exonerate his executioner. When the captain informed Spencer of his fate, he tried to extort a confession. The two held a prolonged, private conversation, inaudible to the sailors standing nearby. Transcribing his notes of that interview into an official report, Mackenzie manufactured a reconciliation that had not taken place. It took place on the *Bellipotent.* "Captain Vere himself," wrote Melville, "communicated the finding of the court to the prisoner. . . . [W]hat took place at this interview was never known" for certain either. "There is no telling the sacrament." Melville stripped the scene of the dialogue so obtrusive and unconvincing in Mackenzie's report. The narrator, freed from fidelity to his characters' speech, imagines a frieze of frank disclosure and embrace: "He was old enough to have been Billy's father. The austere devotee of military duty, letting himself melt back into what remains primeval in our formalized humanity, may in the end have caught Billy to his heart, even as Abraham may have caught young Isaac on the brink of resolutely offering him up in obedience to the exacting behest."

If Billy did "know our hearts," Vere had hoped, "he would feel even for us on whom in this military necessity so heavy a compulsion is laid." Billy does feel for Vere. His "God bless Captain Vere!" echoes and personalizes Elisha Small's dying words on the *Somers,* "God bless that flag!" Separating love from duty, family from the state, Melville has reconciled father and son.

"Press closely to your snowy breast our lovely rose buds who reflect their Mother's brightness," Allan Melvill wrote his wife from Paris. Billy Budd is folded into Abraham's bosom. Allan Melvill died and abandoned his son. Mackie Melville died and reproached his father. Stanwix Melville abandoned his father and died. In *Billy Budd* a father confines his son, orders his death, and wins his blessing. Compartmentalizing his love and his duty, Vere preserves both. Since the order to execute comes from outside the self, it does not contaminate the love that comes from within. But the reverse is not so clearly the case, and calls Vere's division into question. Vere's hatred does not condemn Billy (as Mackenzie's may have condemned Spencer), but duty alone does not kill Billy either. He is killed by love.

Shipboard authority was arbitrary and murderous for young Melville. He symbolized that authority with the emblem of chattel slavery, the whip. An officer's sadistic whim exposed sailors to the pain and humiliation of public flogging. The captain who controlled the whip brutalized his men. Melville marked the chapter in *White-Jacket* titled "The Flogging" while writing *Billy Budd,* for the scourge was a portent of Billy's doom.

Billy lives in terror of the whip after he observes his first flogging (of a sailor "absent from his assigned post," the offense which nearly got White-Jacket flogged). The petty troubles Claggart brings on Billy threaten him with whipping. And as master-of-arms, Claggart would hold Billy's shirt and supervise his punishment, the task enjoyed by his prototype, Bland, on the *Neversink.* Joseph's metaphorical "blood-dyed coat," which Claggart presents to Vere, foreshadows the actual "bloody shirt" of a flogged bluejacket. Billy's "significant personal beauty" has unmanned Claggart. When Billy spills "the greasy liquid" soup across Claggart's path, Claggart "playfully tapped him from behind with his rattan." Whipping would consummate the erotic sadism hinted at here.

Floggings allegedly provoked the *Somers*'s sailors to mutiny; flogging enforced discipline on them after the hangings. On "vessels blessed with patriarchal intellectual captains," said White-Jacket, "scourging is unknown." Just as White-Jacket condemned the *Somers* executions, so he defended murder and mutiny as the natural right of a sailor threatened with the whip. But White-Jacket commited neither crime. Billy, "as incapable of mutiny as of willful murder," is judged guilty of both. Terrified that Claggart's accusation of mutiny will get him flogged, he strikes the master-of-arms. Billy escapes the scourge, to succumb to Captain Vere's paternal embrace. Guert gave the hanging order, "Whip!" on the *Somers*, and Billy dies with the "ignominious hemp around his neck."

Joseph's brothers, meeting some Ishmaelites, sold their father's favorite son to slavery. Melville marked the passage in his Bible. *The Selling of Joseph* was a famous antislavery tract, and Theodore Parker used Joseph's story to interpret the fate of the fugitive Thomas Sims. "This is the coat of Thomas Sims," he told his congregation, holding aloft the garment. "See how they rent the sleeve away! . . . Let the kidnappers come up and say, 'Massachusetts! Knowest thou whether this be thy son's coat or not?' Let Massachusetts answer: 'It is my son's coat. An evil beast hath devoured him.' " Parker's biblical invocation recalls *Moby-Dick;* no leviathan, by contrast, swallows Billy Budd. Joseph's envious brother, Claggart, fails to sell him into slavery among the Ishmaelites; he offers him up to the "troubled patriarch" instead.

"Patriarchal intellectual" Captain Vere, drained of sadistic pleasure in discipline, gains fatal power over Billy in return. In the fiction of Melville's middle period, *Israel Potter, Benito Cereno* and *The Confidence-Man,* trust placed one at the mercy of others; trusting in Vere, Billy has no defense against him.

Descended from Melville's Ishmaels, Billy is a child of nature. He had independence on the merchant ship, *Rights-of-Man,* from which he was impressed. But Billy's desire to please Captain Vere deprives him of autonomy. The "fatherly" words from Vere bring a "crucifixion" to Billy's face; he stutters in anxiety to speak his innocence to the Captain. Billy is consciously submissive, but critics have heard in his stutter an unconscious hostility to authority. Billy stutters only when his loyalty is questioned, as if his tongue withholds assent and prevents him from dissembling. Does the stutter block anger he is not allowed to express? In American folk tales (long before Freud) obstructed speech leads to frontier violence. Like the proverbial backwoodsman, Billy chokes with rage and strikes his accuser.

Both Billy's stutter and the blow from his fist are involuntary, for Billy never even contemplates rebellion. Claggart, thinking he can tempt an impressed sailor to mutiny, offers him two guineas. Innocent Billy, bewildered by the bribe and its purpose, confuses them with buttons. Had he been conscious enough to own his aggression, he could have established independence from authority; he could have known enough to protect himself from its seductions. Instead Billy's overidentification with Vere progressively infantilizes him. He is reduced from establishing order on the *Rights* to a stuttering protest of loyalty to Vere. The fist, which gave him power on the *Rights,* places him under Vere's power on the *Bellipotent.* At his trial he offers Vere the trust which Babo dissembles toward Benito Cereno, the trust of a "dog" for his "master." Caught up by his father in sacramental sacrifice, the boy is saved from his "virgin experience of the diabolical." In his "white jumper and white duck trousers" the night before he is to die, Billy is like a "patch of discolored snow . . . lingering at some upland cave's black mouth." Lying ironed between two guns, he has "the look of a slumbering child in his cradle." His benediction to Captain Vere is "wholly unobstructed"; the stutter is gone. The "nightingale" that snake-like Claggart fails to devour is finally "licked up by the sun."

Indians, it was said, melted away before civilization, like snow in the sun. Billy meets their fate. The ultimate indignity to White-Jacket's manhood is flogging. Vere's love overwhelm's Billy's resistance far more effectively. Love, supposedly separated from duty, works in conspiracy with the law. The Ishmaelite child of nature brought back into the naval family becomes an Isaac. He willingly does "his father" the service Captain Mackenzie had enforced on young Spencer, "the service . . . to die."

Vere is the only figure in the story whose interior we are given, the only one who can be said to make a choice . . . like Guert on the *Somers,* Vere chooses to act under orders. He chooses to force himself and his sailors into a structure predetermined from without. Deciding immediately that Billy must hang, Vere prevents his fellow characters from developing, in free social action, lives of their own. Duty from without connected organically to desire from within would endanger both. Did Vere need to split them apart to allow each a separate and finally reenforcing existence? Did he have a stake, from within, in Billy's death? Consider first, the nature of Vere's authority; second, his need to keep love safely out of his living personal and social worlds, and finally the resultant bond of victimhood he shares with Billy.

Billy, like Admiral Nelson, has natural authority; Vere has none. With his "queer streak of the pedantic," he lacks the personal presence to inspire loyalty among his crew. Claggart's allusion to a mutiny that threatens the captain's life makes public the unthinkable; Vere impatiently refuses to hear of it. Perhaps the insecurity of his authority and Mackenzie's helped both captains determine, at their first interviews with the accused, to hang them. ("Struck dead by an angel of God! Yet the angel must hang!" said Vere. Talk of mutiny was "only a joke," pleaded Spencer. "That joke may cost you your life," responded Mackenzie. Though both captains were only short sails from other American ships, neither chose to admit weakness and seek help there.) Vere is first merely a "Jacob" to Billy's "Joseph," and Jacob was Melville's avatar of legal, bookish, manipulative authority; he had stolen Esau's birthright. Vere is Jacob in the scene in which Claggart informs against Billy, and his authority is insecure. As Jacob, "the troubled patriarch," he does not control the action. As Abraham sacrificing Isaac, he does. Mackenzie after the hangings "once more was completely commander of the vessel that was entrusted to me"; so Vere gains authority as he demonstrates his power to take Billy's life.

Vere admires Billy as a "specimen . . . who in the nude might have posed for a statue of a young Adam before the Fall." He wants to promote Billy "to a place that would more frequently bring him under his own observation." Vere wants Billy close to him, as the Wall Street lawyer wants Bartleby. But intimacy endangers these legalists. When Vere rejects the "feminine" mercy that would have spared Billy, is he speaking for himself as well as for the law? Perhaps the "all but feminine" Billy is a "mantrap under the daisies" for the "undemonstrative" Vere as well as for Claggart.

Love may not have posed an erotic danger to Vere. But certain it is that his love for Billy could not flourish in the world. Love took the protagonist of the European novel into society; it brought pleasure into conflict with order. The barren world of the *Bellipotent*, with its fragile order, provided no nourishment for love. Just as family provided no structural mediation between society and the heart, so there were no legitimate social objects of aggression or love. Splitting intimate love from public duty,

Vere eliminated a social ground. Where libido and deepest meaning remain private, explosive emotions are forced back into dangerous intimacy. Vere's desire for Billy is forbidden, not simply because it is homoerotic, but because it is incestuous as well. As in the withdrawn, sentimental family on which Vere's feeling for Billy is a kind of comment, the only love possible in so constricted a space is a *Liebestod*.

Vere experienced love only when it did not threaten duty. His helplessness was a condition for his compassion. Had he the power to alter Billy's fate, their love would open dangerous social possibilities; it might undercut Vere's commitment to the state, and perhaps his masculine identity as well. The living Billy was a threat to Vere's authority. He embraced the doomed sailor. Like the philanthropists who pitied Indians they could not save, Vere found it safer to embrace the dying child of nature than to sustain the living one. But since it was Vere who decided Billy's fate, he chose a duty which consummated his love.

Shared impotence connected Vere to Billy; their bond went beyond love to identification. The private Vere took on himself the burden of the suffering for which the public Vere was responsible. Mackenzie killed one sailor-boy to preserve the innocence of another. Vere preserved the innocence of the one he killed. Billy's benediction revealed that Billy was at peace and that Vere was not, "that the condemned one suffered less than he who mainly had effected the condemnation." This was not disinterested compassion; Vere recognized the fate of his own private self.

Mackenzie sacrificed the child of the secretary of war. The Mutiny Act, "War's child," forced Vere to sacrifice Billy. But it also kept Vere a child of the law. God saved Isaac from the altar and made Abraham, in Melville's words, "the father of a great multitude of men." The Abraham who must kill Isaac is sacrificed, too. Joseph Brant named his son Isaac, and Isaac "raised his parricidal hand against" his father. He came at Brant with a knife, in the account Melville read, and Brant was forced to kill him. Captain Vere, like "the great Captain of the six nations," killed an Isaac. Both killings, far from establishing paternal authority, brought it to an end. Hanging Billy, Vere offered up his own generative powers to the military state. That sacrifice completed the *Liebestod*; Vere and Billy shared the masochistic bond of victims.

When he hears Billy bless him, "Captain Vere, either through stoic self-control or a sort of momentary paralysis induced by emotional shock, stood erectly rigid as a musket in the ship-armourer's rack." While Vere is stiff, Billy remains limp. Vere's rigidity is at once that of the guns between which Billy has lain ironed, and the "euthanasia" which saves Billy from the normal posthanging ejaculation. Vere's erect posture is no symbol of personal power, however. It recalls the motion of Claggart's body, felled "like a heavy plank tilted from erectness." Like the "scabbard artificially stiffened," of Benito Cereno, musket-rigid Vere is "empty." He has been possessed from without, by the daemon of military form.

Mackenzie "put on my full uniform, and then proceeded to execute the most painful duty that has ever devolved upon an American commander—*that of announcing to the criminals their fate.*" Mackenzie's "imposing costume—feathers and chapeau, gold lace and embroidery, sword and epaulettes" made a striking contrast to the bagged, ironed, helpless sailors. To Jacksonian Democrat Thomas Hart Benton, the contrast exposed Mackenzie's arrogance. To White-Jacket, choosing the "judicially naked topman" over the "oligarchy of epaulets," it would have as well. To Vere, however, "these buttons that we wear" on naval uniforms did not free officers for self-aggrandizement; they constrained them to "self-abnegation." Dressed in his military uniform at Billy's hanging, Vere is also an offering to the state.

Admiral Nelson had put on his full naval uniform, Melville imagined, to meet a glorious death at Trafalgar. "Dress[ing] his person in the jeweled vouchers of his own shining deeds," he "adorned himself for the altar." The "military button" on which Richard Henry Dana commented during Mackenzie's trial, was a badge of personal glory for Nelson. It had once been so for Melville as well. Writing his cousin, Henry Gansevoort, wounded in the Civil War, Melville imagined himself "some paces from you, in an erect attitude, and with manly bearing, giving you the military salute . . . May two small but choice constellations of stars alight on your shoulders. . . . And after death (which God long avert, and bring about after many great battles, quietly, in a comfortable bed, with wife and children around) may that same name be transferred to heaven—bestowed upon some new planet or cluster of stars of the first magnitude."

Melville's "erect" bearing, however, predicted no fame for his cousin. Henry died a bachelor, like Vere, with neither children to keep alive his memory, nor "constellations of stars" on his uniform. Vere died before Trafalgar, unknown and forgotten, Billy's name on his lips. His "heart" "in duty's course half-broken," like Mackenzie's in the ballad memorializing the *Somers* affair, may have been "calm as the stars." But instead of his name bestowed on a cluster of stars, he was absorbed back into "the Starry Vere." Decades earlier Allan Melvill had discovered his ancestral coat of arms in Scotland. He wrote his wife, "My father's arms are crescents, my mother's stars, which seem to betoken the loftiness of their origin." The aristocrat Vere also had a lofty origin. He was "in a domestic heaven nursed. . . . Of Fairfax and the Starry Vere." Starry Vere would die (if we imagine him an American) the anonymous servant of Elisha Small's flag.

Henry Gansevoort had admired Melville's "description of the wavy folds of the star spangled banner," in the "America" of *Battle-Pieces*. He liked the comparison of the flag to the ocean. As epauletted officers defended "the star spangled banner," to return to Allan Melvill's prophecy for Guert, they disappeared into it. The "eagle" "aloft" would "guard . . . the starry folds" of the American flag, in Melville's "Eagle of the Blue," when the Melvills and Gansevoorts who raised it were forgotten. The bronze eagle, stars and stripes of the custom-house badge would replace the "eagle wings in gold" of Cincinnati.

Welcome the "Great Khan of Tartary" to Albany, Melville told Abraham Lansing, "but not a Custom House Inspector." "The nothingness of things glorious, redounds to the glory of Omnipotence," he wrote at the end of his life.

> Two or three hundred years ago, to the amazement of the telescopes, a strange star appeared in the constellation of Cassiopeia, and shining there like a planet for a brief term, abruptly disappeared. . . . [E]xtinction is signalized in the instance of stars of magnitude; and in corresponding degree the glory of God is magnified . . . to whom the planets are of even less consideration than to the Grand Mogul his golden buttons.

Redburn was baptized "Buttons" on his first sea voyage, in mockery of the family smoking jacket he wore to sea. This jacket of inherited authority isolated Redburn from the common-sailor crew. Uniformed authority also separated family members from one another on the *Neversink*. "A Man-of-War Button Divides Two Brothers," it will be remembered, and common-sailor Melville and his midshipman cousin, Stanwix Gansevoort, were the actual kinsmen behind the "sailor frock" and the "anchor button." Stanwix was Guert's brother, while White-Jacket, in the aftermath of the *Somers* affair, was imagining himself as Guert's victim.

Redburn's buttons were "evanescent"; they symbolized a declining family; Guert and Stanwix, like Vere, replaced them with the buttons of the state. Now, however, the naval uniform was no longer a way for revolutionary aristocrats to sustain their familial power. On the *Neversink* the "large brass buttons" divided inheritors of clan authority from family outcasts. "These buttons that we wear" still separated Vere from Billy to be sure. But the naval button on Captain Vere's uniform was evanescent, too. Choosing the form of "the military button" over Billy's life, Vere shared his sacrifice.

The name Buttons signified not only Redburn's failed inherited authority, but his sexual innocence as well. Redburn's melancholy cut him off from life. "Upon his young soul the mildew has fallen; the frost which with others is only blighted after ripeness, with him is nipped in the first blossom and bud." Redburn, the promise of maturity before him, lost the name of Buttons. Billy remained a bud. And Vere died a bachelor, too. In "The Paradise of Bachelors and the Tartarus of Maids," Melville had played with the double meaning of bachelor's buttons, as buttons on bachelors' shirts, and as tiny flowers, to invoke sexual sterility. *Billy Budd*, to a similar effect, invoked the conjoined meanings of button and bud. Among the uses of "button" given in the *Oxford English Dictionary* are these two: "The simple flowerets . . . open their infant buttons" and "a custom-house officer in his brass-buttoned jacket," Billy Budd is the bachelor Vere's button; the uniformed captain has merged with the sacrificed son.

Billy Budd fulfilled the "lesson of filial piety" Captain Mackenzie had taught on the *Somers*. It also consummated his lesson of "piety toward God." Worldliness, said the Puritan minister Richard Baxter, should lie on the shoulders of the "saint like a light cloak which can be thrown off at any moment." The saint went into the world, in Max Weber's formulation, but was not of it. But "fate decreed that the cloak should become a housing hard as steel." Vere was a worldly ascetic, like Weber's Protestant monk, but the disappearance of otherworldly conviction left him encased in an iron cage. The Calvinism to which Melville returned with Vere was radically split between legalism and piety. Piety in Vere's monkish world had nothing to do with regeneration; it meant only the sacrifice to legalism. Melville's religious images decomposed Christianity into the parallel structures of military hierarchy on the one hand, nature on the other. As with the state and the family, the fracture of integrated, religious authority finally merged the divided, frozen structures together.

The *Bellipotent* is a negative church, to which Vere owes "monastic obedience." The "self-abnegation" of a "true military officer" is like that of a "true monk." The chaplain, "minister of the Prince of Peace serving in the host of the God of War," also "subserves the . . . cannon." Such images, instead of locating military obedience in a hierarchy of obligations under God, juxtaposed military to religious commands. Billy, echoing and undercutting the sacrament, has "eaten the King's bread and [is] true to the King." The gun bays are "like small confessionals . . . in a cathedral"; Billy lies ironed in one. The sailors hear Billy's sentence "in a dumbness like that of a seated congregation of believers in hell listening to the clergyman's announcement of his Calvinist text."

These images break apart the easy transition from obeying human authority to "piety toward God" invoked in Allan Melvill's liberal Christianity and on the *Somers*. The *Bellipotent's* "Minister of the Prince of Peace" serves "the God of War." Mackenzie sacrificed the son of the minister of war to God. He had brought a divinity student on board to hold church services and give moral and religious instruction to the crew. But their moral "depravity" made the sailors ripe for mutiny; Mackenzie turned revivalist and restored their piety with hangings. He conducted a religious service, thanking God for deliverance from danger. "I urged the youthful sailors to cherish their Bibles," he reported. "I endeavored to call to their recollection the terrors with which the three malefactors had found themselves suddenly called to enter the presence of an offended God." Mackenzie hoisted a cross above the Stars and Stripes. At the end of his sermon, he read the Psalm 100 to his crew: "I could not but humbly hope that divine sanction would not be wanting to the deed of that day."

Identifying political with religious confession, Mackenzie urged Spencer, for the sake of his soul, to admit he had planned a mutiny. He "repeated to [Spencer] his catechism, and begged him to offer sincere prayers for divine forgiveness." Mackenzie heard Spencer's deathbed confession of "sins"; translating his notes of that interview into an official report, he changed "sins" to "crimes." Christ saved the soul of "the penitent thief on the cross," the Captain reminded Spencer. The image of "three condemned men . . . dangling from the yard-arm" led Gail Hamilton to think of Spencer not as the thief but as Christ. Gail Hamilton had encouraged the sacrifice of sons during the Civil War; later she wrote "The Murder of Philip Spencer" in protest against his hanging. The image of the resurrection came to her mind in both instances. In a magazine article that Melville used as a source for *Billy Budd*, she saw Spencer "glorified . . . by the light shining upon him through the opening gates of death." As Billy "ascended," "the vapory fleece hanging low in the East was shot through with a soft glory as of the fleece of the Lamb of God seen in mystical vision." The body of the executed sailor, Samuel Cromwell, as described in Mackenzie's report, "rose dipping to yard-arm" in the sea. Billy "ascending, took the full rose of the dawn." The sacrificed Isaac, not replaced by a ram on the altar, is Christ.

The "God of war" who demanded Billy's life took Melville back beyond the sentimental Protestantism of the nineteenth century to Calvinist orthodoxy. The breakdown of the links between family, religion, state and society released an angry God. *Billy Budd* reimagined the vengeful, omnipotent Puritan deity who, behind a legalist façade, saved and damned arbitrarily. From this orthodox perspective, to quote Weber again, "the death of the savior may be viewed as a means of mollifying the wrath of God, before whom the savior appears as an intercessor for men." Such a God, punishing assertions of human autonomy, denied that the mind or will of man could make sense of the world. "Extinction," in Melville's words, "magnified the glory of God."

Decades earlier Judge Shaw had ruled that a church belonged to its living congregation. The decision allowed the religiously liberal, worldly elite of Massachusetts to expropriate historically Calvinist churches. Shaw's decision, complained Harriet Beecher Stowe, "nullified . . . the peculiar features of church organization so carefully ordained by the Pilgrim fathers." It was a judgment against traditional orthodoxy and for living power. *Billy Budd* reversed it.

But in an other sense, Shaw's judgment anticipated Melville's. It shattered the alliance between the State Street merchants and the religious establishment. It pointed toward a self-sufficient world, deprived of transcendental sanctification. *Billy Budd* carried that tendency to its not so benevolent conclusion, for it imposed a Calvinist structure on the world Shaw was freeing from God. The *Bellipotent* hierarchy was beyond human appeal, yet it was not transcendent either. Failing to point above itself, it offered no redemption. Vere's "monastic devotion" was to "martial duty." The "angel of God" was "the King's bread." "The Omnipotence" demanding Billy's "extinction" was the state.

Billy's sacrifice had another meaning for the sailors, to be sure. For years afterward they searched, "as a piece of the Cross," for chips of the spar on which Billy was suspended. But there is hint here neither of Christian condemnation of the hanging, nor of a regenerate community reborn from Billy's death. Billy's crucifixion is closer to pagan nature ritual than to Christian rebirth. Billy himself could make nothing of the ship chaplain's "ideas of death." "The young barbarian" received his "primer of Christianity, full of transcendent miracles," like some "Tahitian" of long ago. Melville's journey to Polynesia had begun his own creative life. Fearful of cannibalistic absorption into primitive existence, Melville left the South Pacific. Now, at the end of his life, he imagined a cannibalistic death for Billy. Unlike the sacrament of Communion, it left nothing "transcendent" behind. Like the "grand sculptured Bull" of the "Assyrian priests," the handsome sailor was worshiped as a nature god and then sacrificed to nature. "Screaming seafowl," filled with "animal greed for prey," circled his body as it sank into the sea. His spirit, too, "vanished." Cloudy "fleece" of the Lamb of God, it was "licked up by the sun that had late so glorified it." John Winthrop had announced on board the *Arbella* that the Puritans were the mystic body of Christ, regenerated from the blood of the lamb.

Winthrop's community, reborn out of nature in God's love, here comes to an end. "Like smooth white marble in the polished block not yet removed from the marble-dealer's yard," the sculptured Sun-God, "Apollo," is absorbed back into nature.

As White-Jacket imagined himself "at the end of a rope . . . put to bed forever," so "Billy in the Darbies" will "dream fast asleep" in the sea. But White-Jacket, fallen from the yard-arm, had refused a watery grave. He accused Charles Didbin, in his sea-ballards, of promoting an acquiescent, sensual fatalism in the face of death. Like a Didbin sailor, Billy could sing, "as for my life, 'tis the King's." Didbin's ballads were public and patriotic; "Billy in the Darbies," the sailor's ballad that ends *Billy Budd,* is private. But Billy's canine devotion to Vere recalls the "unquestioning dog-like devotion to whoever may be lord and master" celebrated, to White-Jacket's anger, by Didbin. That devotion anticipates the ballad's sensual acceptance of death in its last lines: "Roll me over fair! I am sleepy and the oozy weeds about me twist."

"[A]nd her long hair ran over him, and arbored him in ebon vines." The last line of Billy's ballad echoes the last line of *Pierre.* Isabel's hair and the weeds of the mother-sea dress the young men for death. Hercules, swallowed by a sea-monster, killed the monster and escaped. But his wife stained his white robe with the blood of another beast from the sea. That shirt of Nessus stuck to Hercules' flesh, and devoured him. White-Jacket's garment also "struck to [him] like the fatal shirt of Nessus," but White-Jacket threw it off. The *Neversink* sailors harpooned the jacket, mistaking it for a "white shark," and White-Jacket escaped his watery grave. Billy Budd is returned there.

The oozy weeds beneath the sea that twist around Billy parallel the jacket on board deck that encases Captain Vere. Billy's form dissolved into nature; Vere placed himself within the "measured forms" of the law. But nature is juxtaposed to form, as family to state and religion to war, only to naturalize the forms of human authority. Mackenzie filled military forms with his flawed human content as he explained the executions to his crew. Then he employed an innovative ritual (evidence, to some, of his insanity) and piped the sailors down to quarters. Vere, unwilling to reveal himself in public, said nothing to the crew; he only piped them down. A captain could not, he had earlier explained, justify his course of action to his men. " 'The people' (meaning the ship's company)" lacked the discriminating power required by speech. Subjected to "true martial discipline," on the other hand, they acted under the "promptitude of an instinct." As Vere piped down the starboard watch, so he sounded the "drumbeat to quarters" to calm the troubled crew. Colonel Peter Gansevoort's brass drum, captured from the British and Indians in the Revolution, did not pass into the hands of Billy, the seaman impressed from the *Rights-of-Man*. The British captain appropriated it instead. Rebellious stirrings must be met with the "measured forms" of military ritual, Vere explained, "and this is the import couched in the story of Orpheus and his lyre spellbinding the wild denizens of the wood."

Thoreau's "Civil Disobedience" distinguished resistance to nature from resistance to the law. Since the law was partly a human force, Thoreau appealed beyond the law to speech among men. But he would not resist "a purely brute or natural force," he explained. "I cannot expect, like Orpheus, to change the nature of the rocks and trees and beasts." "Civil Disobedience" separated men from nature to underline human autonomy. Melville, registering nature's power over humankind, dissolved the boundary Thoreau tried to establish. Melville had originally given Orpheus's musical power to youth, to Harry Bolton and Isabel. Vere expropriated it. The sailors responded to his drumbeat, as Pierre had responded to Isabel's guitar, "under the promptitude of an instinct."

Authority repossessed instinct on the *Bellipotent*. Uniforms and rituals naturalized man-made institutions, placing them beyond human reach. Men regained their location in nature. But this was not the rights-granting nature of the Declaration of Independence, but a nature in which they were assimilated to beasts. Frozen into forms to protect against chaos, society conspired with nature in *Billy Budd* against a human ground.

The officer in Franz Kafka's penal colony, faithful to the memory of the former commandant, places first a disobedient soldier and then himself on the punishing machine. The machine breaks down, however. It fails to write his punishment on the officer's body so that, "decipher[ing] it with his wounds," he will die redeemed. It merely tortures him meaninglessly to death. Kafka's machine goes beyond Melville's uniform, and Kafka's officer, releasing the soldier, establishes no sacrificial bond with him. Nevertheless, Vere shares the officer's fate. The buttons that he wears place him under the law. "However pitilessly that law may operate," Captain Vere tells his officers, it is "operating through us."

But Vere was more than an offering to a forgotten "old ancestor" commandant and his disintegrating machine. He was a sacrifice both to the Cincinnati badge of Revolution, and with it. Families like the Melvills and Gansevoorts, fighting for natural rights, made the American Revolution. Captain Vere, impressing Billy Budd from the *Rights-of-Man*, served the British crown. He chose a peculiarly modern form of servitude. "We live and have our being" in God, preached St. Paul. "For we are also his offspring." "We move and have our being" in nature, said Vere, but we are officers of the king. Religion no longer joined nature to culture. Drained of religious meaning, state authority offered no redemption, but religion blessed it nonetheless. Echoed by the crew, Billy's last words quieted the threat of mutiny the execution had raised. Billy's benediction, "God bless Captain Vere!" sanctified the state.

P. ADAMS SITNEY

Ahab's Name: A Reading of "The Symphony"

IS AHAB, AHAB?

In "The Symphony," the one hundred and thirty-second chapter of *Moby Dick*, the captain's dialogue with his first mate, Starbuck, drifts into a soliloquy in which he questions his control over his acts:

> What is it, what nameless, inscrutable, unearthly thing is it; what cozening, hidden lord and master, and cruel remorseless emperor commands me; that against all natural lovings and longings, I so keep pushing, and crowding and jamming myself on all the time; recklessly making me ready to do what in my own proper, natural heart, I durst not so much as dare? Is Ahab, Ahab? Is it I, God or who, that lifts this arm? But if the great sun move not of himself; but is as an errant-boy in heaven; nor one single star can revolve, but by some invisible power; how can this one small heart beat; this one small brain think thoughts; unless God does that beating, does that thinking, does that living, and not I.

In this context the tiny sentence "Is Ahab, Ahab?" appears innocent enough. The force of fate makes the captain doubt his identity. For years I read this question ignoring the comma, supporting myself with the commonplace of editors that Melville was an ungrammatical punctuator, as if the sentence were the interrogative form of the tautology: Ahab is Ahab. But what might the question "Is Ahab Ahab?" or "Is X X?" when X stands for a proper noun, mean? In the form of a question doubt is raised about

---

the *language* of the tautology. It asks if there is not something wrong with the naming of X that represents X as ontologically unstable. Then again, it could be a question about two different meanings of the proper noun. Does the first X correspond fully to the stable meaning of X represented by the second instance of the name? All three readings of the question are relevant to our interpretation of *Moby Dick* as a whole: they correspond to ontological, epistemological, and typological investigations.

I would like to consider the alternatives posed by the problematic comma. If we read the second naming of Ahab as vocative, two interpretations of the sentence are possible. Either "Is Ahab . . .?" questions his existence, or the sentence is incomplete, requiring reference to the previous one. In that case it asks if "Ahab" is the answer to the previous question; is "Ahab" the "nameless . . . thing" that "commands me." In fact, the first English edition of *The Whale*, printed months earlier than the American, explicitly determines this reading. "Is it Ahab, Ahab?" in the English text makes very good sense; for it fits all three opening sentences in this speech into a single form: "What is it . . . Is it Ahab . . . Is it I, God, or who. . . ."

We cannot conclude whether this is one of the many editorial intrusions to be found in *The Whale* or a genuine alternative from Melville's hand. Let's consider the consequences of accepting it as the superior reading. The ontological question posed by both "Is Ahab Ahab?" and "Is Ahab . . .?" disappears. Nevertheless, the repetition of the name in the vocative continues to underscore the potential ambiguity of the name which has both epistemological and typological consequences. It is this doubling of the *name*, consistent in both texts, which I take to be crucial; for it points up the relationship of the name to the dilemmas of identity and responsibility. Therefore, even though I prefer the richer ambiguities of the American version, what follows will not depend upon the choice of texts.

My conviction that "Is Ahab, Ahab?" should be read as the questioning of a tautology rests on the echoing passage two chapters later in "The Chase—Second Day" when the captain refers back to his earlier encounter with the first mate:

> Starbuck, of late I've felt strangely moved to thee; ever since that hour we both saw—thou know'st what, in one another's eyes. But in this matter of the whale, be thy face to me as the palm of this hand—a lipless, unfeatured blank. Ahab is for ever Ahab, man. This whole act's immutably decreed. 'Twas rehearsed by thee and me a billion years before this ocean rolled. Fool! I am the Fates' lieutenant; I act under orders.

"Ahab is for ever Ahab, man" reasserts the ontological question of the earlier chapter in the rhetoric of bravado, taking the tautology out of the realm of time which had oppressed the captain, who feared that Moby Dick would be taken by a rival whaler or that he would not live to do the job. Now that he is in the midst of the "fiery hunt," he speaks as though he were reconciled to his relationship to Fate. But readers soon discover that he is haunted during this speech by hints of the fulfillment of Fedallah's prophecy of his death.

The paired lines "Is Ahab, Ahab!" and "Ahab is for ever Ahab" do not dispell the ambiguities we found in the name, Ahab. The later speech proclaims that Ahab is an ontological entity, that his name is appropriate, and that he conforms to the model of the ancient, Biblical Ahab.

The tone of these speeches is familiar enough. Melville wrote fresh from a reading of Shakespeare. The use of the name, instead of "I," in the mouth of the hero recalls a number of precedents in the plays:

> . . . O Lear, Lear, Lear!
> Beat at this gate, that let thy folly in
> And thy dear judgment out!
> (*King Lear*, Act I, sc. iv.)

> Was't Hamlet wronged Laertes? Never Hamlet.
> If Hamlet from himself be ta'en away,
> And when he's not himself does wrong Laertes,
> Then Hamlet does it not, Hamlet denies it.
> Who does it then? His madness. If it'd be so,
> Hamlet is of the faction that is wronged,
> His madness is poor Hamlet's enemy.
> (*Hamlet*, Act V, sc. ii.)

Shakespeare uses this substitution of the third for the first person, of the name for I, here in parallel speeches by Othello, Brutus, and Timon, to emphasize the machinations of fate or to dramatize the dislocation of selfhood in madness. Its illusion of objectivity indicates that the speaker has submitted to the language and the judgment of the world by renouncing his power to speak for himself. To make such a renunciation is to invoke the discourse of the victim.

Melville became excessively fond of this mode of self-address. It is a mark of Ahab's grandiosity. Interpreting the Ecuadorian doubloon he nailed to the mast as a reward for the first sighting of Moby Dick, he repeats his name four times: "The firm tower, that is Ahab; the volcano, that is Ahab; the courageous, undaunted, and victorious fowl, that, too, is Ahab; all are Ahab; and this round gold is but the image of the rounder globe, which, like a magician's glass, to each and every man in turn but mirrors back its own mysterious self." As much echo as mirror, the coin reflects his name again and again.

In *Moby Dick* calling oneself by name is not Ahab's exclusive privilege. Stubb does it with comic effect when he finds himself unfairly treated by the captain. The narrator calls himself by his pseudonym three times in "A Bower in the Arsacides," as if, taking the side of his readers, he felt the need to demand evidence of his authority for the whale lore he was about to expound. These whimsical versions of the discourse of victimization are not of the same order of frequency or dramatic intensity as Ahab's use of his own name. He embraces and sublimates his victimization, naming himself as if being called Ahab were an honor and a responsibility of which he was proud.

IS AHAB, AHAB WHO PROVOKED THE LORD GOD OF ISRAEL?

When we ask the question, "is Ahab (of Nantucket) Ahab (king of Israel)," we are actually asking in what way the captain of the *Pequod* resembles the wicked king of the First Book of Kings. In the sixteenth chapter, "The Ship," Ishmael told of the peculiarity of Biblical names among Nantucket Quakers. He also speculated that such a name, coupled with the "bold and nervous language" a man learns from solitude with nature, could fashion a being "formed for noble tragedies." Thus, as soon as we learn Captain Ahab's name in the novel, we are instructed to anticipate a tragic appropriateness to it.

The narrator had marshalled typology to give weight to his story in the very first sentence, "Call me Ishmael." He implies that the ad-hoc name is more relevant than the one given him at birth. No one in the novel ever addresses him as Ishmael, or by any other name. By stopping the flow of his narrative, as soon as Captains Peleg and Bildad are introduced and Ahab mentioned by name, in order to warn us of the importance of these names, he invites the reader to investigate Scriptural etymology and narrative.

In a useful note Willard Thorp pointed out that Peleg means "division"; Captain Peleg divides the lays of the ship's income. Bildad was one of Job's comforters; like him the co-owner of the *Pequod* spouts warnings against wickedness. Neither of these men is "formed for noble tragedies." The manner in which Ahab will correspond to his Biblical type is not immediately apparent; only a reading of the whole novel will answer that question. "The Ship" whets our interest in Ahab, who will not appear for another twelve chapters.

More is made of his name in this seductive chapter of initimations than of the other Biblical names. Captain Peleg's attempt to minimalize the implications of Ahab's name only makes it more ominous:

> Captain Ahab did not name himself. 'Twas a foolish, ignorant whim of his crazy, widowed mother, who died when he was only a twelvemonth old. And yet the old squaw Tistig, at Gayhead, said that the name would somehow prove prophetic. And, perhaps, other fools like her may tell thee the same. I wish to warn thee. It's a lie.

As an argument for Ahab's humanity, Peleg adds that he has a young wife and a son. These facts will play no role in the novel until "The Symphony."

The sudden appearance in chapter nineteen of a prophet, named Elijah, who curses Ahab, almost immediately confirms Peleg's warning. Yet the coincidence of two names from the First Book of Kings erodes the authority of his dismissal of the typological significance. Elijah cryptically refers to blasphemies the captain commited and to a prophecy that had been confirmed by his losing a leg. As soon as Ishmael learns Elijah's name, he repeats it with an exclamation mark.

Encouraged by the correspondence of names from the Scriptural narrative of Ahab's wickedness, the reader will look in vain for a Jezebel. Is Ahab Ahab without Jezebel? Certainly, in this novel virtually devoid of women, a moody leader, with a diabolical cosmology, bringing himself and his crew to destruction would justify the name and fulfill the "somehow" of Tistig's prophecy. Nevertheless, if we read "The Symphony" carefully we may find Jezebel haunting the chapter even though we never hear her name. I do not mean to suggest that the "sweet, resigned girl" Ahab married is a figure for the Sidonian princess. On the contrary, her non-correspondence to the Biblical narrative seems to guarantee her ineffectiveness in *Moby Dick*. "The Symphony" dramatizes the impossibility of Ahab's acting on her behalf.

In the chapter's opening paragraph Melville conflates two themes typical of *Moby Dick*, the reduction of space to an undifferentiated plane and the domination of a single color, and introduces a third, the feminization of a part of the natural world:

> It was a clear steel-blue day. The firmaments of air and sea were hardly separable in that all-pervading azure; only, the pensive air was transparently pure and soft, with a woman's look, and the robust and man-like sea heaved with long, strong, lingering swells as Samson's chest in his sleep.

The reduction of the visible world to an undifferentiated monochromatic plane is the final version of a disorientation of spatiality that began in the dark of New Bedford with Ishmael's stumbling into a Negro church where he caught enough of the sermon to know it was about "the blackness of darkness." The Spouter-Inn's befogged oil painting, which poses the first puzzle for interpretation the narrator faces, and the crucial meditation on blankness in "The Whiteness of the Whale" would be the other moments in this series. "The Symphonys'" pervading blueness, then, completes the long-interrupted triad.

This is also the final instance of a more continuous play on color which progressed from the early passages on blackness and whiteness to the chromatic richness of silver ("The spirit spout"), yellow ("Brit"), and crimson ("Stubb Kills a Whale") before reaching the lush blindness of blue on blue, a visual equivalent of the riddle of differentiation posed by the question, "Is Ahab, Ahab?"

Against the backdrop of blueness Melville inscribes a parody of Genesis 1. In the opening paragraph the narrator mimes the work of God on the second day: he divides the firmaments. In the subsequent four paragraphs the work of the fifth, fourth, and sixth days, in that order, finds counterparts in the chapter as the creatures of air and sea, the stars, and, lastly, man are represented in the hitherto pervading blueness.

The world is remade in the first paragraphs of "The Symphony" in order to revise the place of woman in the scheme of Genesis. In the alternative cosmology nature itself is sexualized, and copulates. The feminine dimension appears benign and passive in the language of the chapter, but the metaphorical undercurrents suggest an active and destructive femininity. The simile of Samson's chest describes the latent power of the rolling ocean. However, crowding upon this image, comes the unstated allusion to his betrayal by Delilah. The only mention of Samson's sleep in the Old Testament is part of the narrative of her treachery: "And she made him sleep upon her knees; and she called for a man, and she caused him to shave off the seven locks of his head; and she began to afflict him, and his strength went from him" (Judges, xvi, 19).

The subterranean logic of this passage contradicts the literal meaning. One day in the voyage of the *Pequod* brings to mind the first six days of Creation. The explicitly developed image of masculine sexual conquest of an innocent, gentle woman suggests erotic violence by the "murderous" male; but the simile of Samson brings into play the erotic manipulations of a castrating female. Furthermore, I believe there is a silent symbolical equation of the unnamed Delilah with the unnamed Jezebel.

Melville renders Ahab's ambiguous position in this amorous spectacle with a verbal deviousness that deserves our attention. The fourth and fifth paragraphs postpone their grammatical subjects for seven and twenty-seven words respectively. In both cases it is possible to anticipate a different subject. First, we might read "Aloft, like a royal czar and king," as if Ahab himself were to be the subject. Instead it is the sun. The previous paragraph, describing the identity of the air and the sea—"it was only the sex, as it were, that distinguished them"—would lead the reader to expect a human agent to be introduced as the figure reading this sexual discrimination into the field of vision. Conversely, the fifth paragraph unreels a long series of past participles which can be read as a continuation of the description of the elemental love-making of the previous paragraph. The words "Tied up and twisted; gnarled and knotted with wrinkles; haggardly firm and un-yielding. . . ." ambiguously fuse the delayed subject to the previous picture of copulation. The first four words could continue that primal scene un-problematically. Only after a fourteen word description of his eyes, does the phrase "untottering Ahab" specify the grammatical subject. We do not learn what he is observing, only that he faces "the fair girl's forehead of heaven." The paratactic construction permits us to read Ahab as alternate-ly a participant and an observer in the primal scene of nature, until the grammatical meaning asserts itself, terminating the images of sexual intercourse.

The ambiguity of watching or participating in intercourse frequently characterizes the primal scene in psychoanalytical literature. It is important that Melville not only suggests this oscillation in his text, but he forces the reader into repeating this ambiguous situation in the process of dis-cerning what is happening in the chapter. This strategy volatilizes the undersong of the text. As we focus upon the erotic representation, inti-mations of more than we can discern through the denotations of the de-scriptive language direct our attention to the repressed figuration of the narrative. Ahab even comes to represent the reader's problem here.

After a puzzling paragraph which I shall address shortly, Ahab finally directs his gaze to the sea. Therefore, he has looked at both participants in the sexual scene. But in looking at the sea, "he strove to pierce the profundity." The path to this "profundity" is through his own reflected image. His narcissistic identification with the male half of the elemental coupling brings him into contact with the contradictory, but unreconciled, images of female as innocent bride and castrating traitor. Although he cannot pierce this profundity, he is shaken by a feeling of the emptiness of his life, which is expressed first by a tear.

IS AHAB ISHMAEL?

In the preceding discussion I have been reading "The Symphony" as if the narrator, Ishmael, were identical with the author, Melville. The paragraph I mentioned, which comes between the introduction of Ahab and the scene of his gazing at the sea, makes that difficult.

In an apostrophe to the innocence of the air and sky, the narrator asserts his authority within the chapter by inscribing the pronouns "us" and "I." However, the image he uses to personify the "invisible winged creatures" of the air has eluded convincing interpretation:

> But so have I seen little Miriam and Martha, laughing-eyed elves, heed-lessly gambol around their old sire; sporting with the circle of singed locks which grew on the marge of that burnt-out crater of his brain.

Charles Feidelson, the most discreet of the commentators, has noted that the reference to Miriam and Martha and their sire is not known. Mansfield and Vincent, at the other end of the editorial spectrum, fantasize that Melville has invented names for Lot's incestuous daughters here. Murray points to the description of Teufelsdröch in Carlyle's *Sartor Resartus*: "as of some silent, high-encircled mountain-pool, perhaps the crater of an extinct volcano, into whose black depths you fear to gaze. . . ." (Bk. 1, ch. 4), and identifies the innocent figures as Hawthorne's children under pseudonyms. In his fascinating and provocative annotations, Harold Beaver acknowledges some point to the private joke about Hawthorne, adding that Ishmael speaks as if he were Lazarus, recalling a scene of his two sisters. The variety and ingenuity of these glosses underscore the problem.

Not only is the allusion obscure, but the testimony of Ishmael seems unnecessary. None of the editors addresses the *strangeness* of Ishmael's intrusion here. Until "The Symphony," the narrator had not made his presence known by speaking in the first person since "The Candles," thir-teen chapters earlier. He will not utter "I" again in the three concluding chapters of the chase of Moby Dick. The first person reemerges, in the "Epilogue," with Ishmael himself as he accounts for his surprising survival after the whale wrecked the *Pequod*.

Only Beaver notices the presence of the narrator when he annotates this paragraph. If we understand Lot or Hawthorne to be the old sire, then, the declaration, "But so have I seen. . . ." only confuses the analogy to Ahab. Referring back to the third chapter, "The Spouter-Inn," Beaver suggests that Ishmael, who already knows the conclusion of the novel as he writes it, identified with Lazarus. But if that is true, who is the old sire? Why does he write "their" not "our" old sire? The New Testament tells us nothing of Lazarus' father. Perhaps the British editors saw the oddity of this passage; they omitted it from *The Whale*.

Although I have no superior reading for the "laughing-eyed elves," I dwell on this passage just because the narrator asserts himself here. What he has seen and what he sees is crucial for a reading of *Moby Dick*. We should recall that the narrative style shifts decisively after the *Pequod* leaves Nantucket harbor. The intense subjectivity of the first twenty chapters quickly dissolves. Ishmael suddenly begins to ventriloquize conversations and monologues to which the circumscribed narrator of the book's initial chapters would have had no access. The theatrical title of the first chapter in which this is evident, "Enter Ahab; to Him, Stubb," lends support to Charles Olson's contention that there were two versions of the novel; one centering on the Ishmael-Queequeg relationship; the other, an Ahabiad, written after Melville had immersed himself in Shakespeare. Certainly, the narrator becomes a self-conscious Shakespearean only after boarding the *Pequod*. Even his taxonomy of whales takes the form of Octavos and Folios. Yet, this bookish whalelore emerges with an authority we would not have expected from the landed Ishmael. Moreover, his excursions into fictional omniscience correspond to an abandonment of the timid and often puzzled persona he had so meticulously created in the early pages of the novel. In the middle chapters, vestiges of the initial Ishmael show through those passages where he is in contact with Queequeg.

As the narrative progresses there is a further loss of Ishmael's voice. The final thirty chapters have little or nothing of the scholarly whale lore that dominated the sixty before them. The most obvious consequence of this negligence of self-portraiture is the collapse of the vivid distinction between Ishmael's mind and Ahab's. Of course, that had been the point of the brilliant essay in intellectual temperament, "The Whiteness of the Whale," where, shortly after seeing Ahab for the first time and hearing of the quest for the white whale, Ishmael talked himself into a terror over the Emersonian theme of "the blank we see when we look on nature."

The last, pale glimpse we get of Ishmael's mind in action occurs in "The Pacific." The long-awaited balm of the Pacific Ocean almost restores his spirits as he tries to shake off the implications of the previous chapter, "Queequeg in His Coffin." The sea itself, "my dear Pacific," becomes for him a tomb and bed of the dreaming dead. Its rhythms quickly seduce him into worship of Pan, at one and the same time a deity of eros and the cause of unexplained panic to the travellers who encounter him. In that final measuring of the intellectual distance between himself and Ahab, Ishmael records how the captain was untouched by the enthusiasm he felt. In fact, "The Pacific" is the precursor of "The Symphony." But in the latter the narrator's consciousness fuses with that of Ahab.

The intrusion of the first person singular into "The Symphony" reminds us that the description of the azure world in the opening paragraphs had been through his eyes. Whenever the narrator writes "I" or "Ahab" in *Moby Dick* he performs a straight-forward act of representation; a sailor or the captain comes into the reader's "view." Those same two words, in Ahab's mouth, are extremely problematic. Ahab's grandiose sense of his own name forecloses the possibility of his telling his own story. When Ishmael describes the world as he encounters it in his fictional persona, there is always a possibility that his neurotic obsessions, which he himself called his "hypos" (slang for hypocondriac delusions) in the opening chapter, inflect or even distort his perceptions. The most massive of his "hypos" in his reaction to whiteness. Perhaps we can read the chapters in theatrical form as marked off from the blinders of his "hypos." They begin to appear shortly before the meditation on whiteness.

Ishmael is almost as obsessed with blueness as he is with whiteness. In chapter thirty-five, "The Mast-Head," he attributes that color to the soul. He describes how the meditative sailor on watch in the mast-head endangers his life by losing himself in thought: he "takes the mystic ocean at his feet for the visible image of the deep, blue, bottomless soul, pervading mankind and nature; and every strange halfseen, gliding, beautiful thing that eludes him; every dimly-discovered, uprising fin of some undiscernible form, seems to him the embodiment of those elusive thoughts that only people the soul by continually flitting through it." Furthermore, in "Queequeg in His Coffin," he portrays the pagan's idea of heaven in terms of blue and white: "for not only do they believe that the stars are isles, but that far beyond all visible horizons, their own mild, uncontinented seas, interflow with blue heavens; and so form the white breakers of the milky way."

The opening of "The Symphony" is not only a description of a day in the Pacific. It is implicity a representation of how Ishmael reacted to the "hardly separable" layers of blue and how he read Creation into it, along with the troubled undersong of female violence. As early as "Loomings" he had confessed an identification with Narcissus. In "The Mast-Head" he comically acknowledged the threatening power of that identification. Ruminating "Pantheists" aloft in the mast feel how the "identity comes back in horror" when they let a foot slip and plunge to death. In fact, much later, in "The Life-Buoy," an anonymous crew member falls from his watch post, his body unrecovered. The description of this "falling phantom" echos "the ungraspable phantom of life" that all Narcissuses seek according to the philosopher of "Loomings." Finally, the only vestiges of the fallen watchman were "white bubbles in the blue of the sea."

Restoring Ishmael to his role as Narcissistic gazer at the beginning of "The Symphony" does not necessitate displacing Ahab. Ishmael reminds us he is there only *after* the scene has been painted. This is a ploy in paragraph arrangement that repeats the strategy of withholding the grammatical subject in two successive, paragraph-long sentences. Ishmael had been forgotten at the beginning of the chapter. Contextual clues point us to read the opening description as if it mimed Ahab's perceptions. Only retrospectively do we learn they were Ishmael's. The effect is a fusion of the two figures. Here the narrator disposes of the accustomed antithesis of I and Ahab.

Not only does he transfer the Narcissus type from himself to the captain by portraying him as he "watched how his shadow in the water sank and sank to his gaze," he adds two other images as well, which had been used to define Ishmael's mentality. They are orphanhood and live burial. The very first mention of sleep in the novel and the earliest menacing woman were evoked when the narrator found himself in Queequeg's embrace. He recalled a punishment inflicted by his stepmother on the summer solstice. In an intermediate state between dreaming and waking, cruelly confined to his bed, he had the uncanny sense of a "supernatural hand" in his. When Ahab drops a tear into the ocean, experiencing the Panic epiphany that Ishmael knew twenty-one chapters before, he is embraced by "the step-mother world," another female image for the mild air. The word "stepmother" reminds us that the mad mother who named Ahab died in his infancy. Yet, the only stepmother in the book is Ishmael's. This term smuggles a sinister note into the superficially benign moment and brings Ahab another step closer to Ishmael.

The third image transferred from Ishmael's psychic history to Ahab is that of Adam buried under time. In the Whaleman's Chapel, the markers for men lost at sea re-inspired the narrator's reverie of paralysis: ". . . in what eternal, unstirring paralysis, and deadly, hopeless trance, yet lies antique Adam who died sixty round centuries ago. . . ." Ahab, in turn, confesses to Starbuck, who saw him drop his tear into the sea, that he feels "as though I were Adam, staggering beneath the piled centuries since Paradise." Then he breaks into a Lear-like cry to be annihilated.

The transference of Ishmael's "hypos" to Ahab prepares the way for the complete divestment of the narrating persona in the book. The final three chapters, the only ones in which Moby Dick appears, have no traces of Ishmael. In fact, when he resurfaces on Queequeg's coffin in the "Epilogue," Ishmael provides the astonishing news that "I was he . . . who, when on the last day three men were tossed from out of the rocking boat, was dropped astern." This is astonishing simply because he had written, in the neutral third person, of an unnamed "third man" falling overboard. This is the most blatant of the retrospective admissions of the narrator.

When he does, at last, plunge to his predicted fate as a modern Narcissus, we do not see him, nor does he really drown.

We know that Melville wrote the end of the novel in a feverish rush; the epilogue and two paragraphs of "The Symphony" were among the passages that do not appear in the British edition, which preceded the American. However, haste and sloppiness do not account for the disguise of Ishmael in the finale. Something more is at stake. There is a deliberate gesture of calling our attention to the loss of the first person voice by the end of the book. Even the phrase "I was he. . . ." reflects, on the level of grammar, the fated substitution of Ishmael from the otherwise unknown bowsman, who, replacing the dead Fedallah, left a position to be filled. In a sense Ishmael does die: "I" becomes "he." He does not, like Pip, lose the capability of saying both "I" and his own name, after falling into the sea. He has already lost his name and his autonarrating authority in the final chapters. The epilogue restores both to him. But before that he was buried as the "third" person—Melville wrote "third man"—when he was lost.

IS AHAB FEDALLAH?

The two blue fields, air and water, are projections of sexual difference on what Ahab called "the pasteboard mask" of the visible world. Its imminent blankness generated Ishmael's horror and Ahab's violent, Oedipal quest. Starbuck, who lacks the Emersonian absolutism of either Ishmael or Ahab, attempts to divert the tragic conclusion by promoting the differences emerging in the seascape. He humanizes and idealizes the female figures, otherwise virtually expelled from the novel.

Earlier he had failed as an imitator of Ahab. His monologue in the chapter called "The Musket" brings his own wife's name—Mary—into the text for the first time. But even the thought of her and of his son cannot bring him to murder the captain. Thinking back to the oath on the Quarter Deck, he realizes that his mutiny would earn him the name of Ahab. He rejects that option: "Aye, and say'st the men have vowed thy vow; say'st all of us are Ahabs. Great God forbid!"

When "the step-mother world" coaxed a tear from Ahab, breaking his Narcissus-like trance, Starbuck approached him. In the ensuing dialogue, he vainly attempted to convince the captain to abort his quest and sail for Nantucket. For a moment, the mate seemed to penetrate Ahab's solipsism. The captain was attracted by the mirroring of his first mate's eyes: "Let me look into a human eye; it is better than to gaze into sea or

sky; better than to gaze upon God." Sea and sky stand for sexualized nature
here; coming face to face with God has the Mosaic consequence of death,
as a careful reader of chapter eighty-six would know. In facing Starbuck,
Ahab turns from the primal scene of nature and from his Oedipal rage
at the apotheosized whale toward a domestic humanism that cannot
satisfy him.

In Starbuck's eyes Ahab sees his own shunned family. Rather than
divert his course, he urges the mate to remain on board when the boats
are lowered to chase Moby Dick. The dialogue they share does not effect
the drama. The narrator compares it to an apple of Sodom, drawing his
allusion from *Paradise Lost,* according to all the annotators. This vegetative
image of delusive nourishment actually completes the very first portrait of
Ahab the narrator drew at the end of the twenty-eighth chapter. There
an allegorical figure pictures April and May as tripping "dancing girls" (like
elfin Martha and Miriam later) returning to "the wintry, misanthropic
woods," where even strongest "thunder-cloven oak" would respond to them
by sending "forth some few green sprouts, to welcome such glad-hearted
visitants; so Ahab did, in the end, a little respond to the playful alluring
of the girlish air."

In *Moby Dick* dialogue itself leaves cinders in the mouth of advocates
of reason. No characters are more fit for verbal exchange than Starbuck
and Ahab, yet this is the only moment in which meaningful discussion
even seems possible. Nor can Ahab speak fruitfully to the captain of the
Samuel Enderby, who lost his arm to the white whale. The intimate companions Ishmael and Queequeg are constrained by the latter's "broken
phaseology" and many incomprehensible words. Fedallah speaks oracularly
to Ahab; he, in turn, misconstrues the sense of Fedallah's words as fatally
as Macbeth the rhymes of the witches. Stubb sadistically forces the old
black cook, Fleece, to preach to sharks or "diddles" the French-speaking
captain of the *Rosebud* (itself a ribald joke about female sexual anatomy)
out of ambergris through an interpreter. Neither the carpenter nor the
blacksmith truly converses with Ahab; they respond to his monologues. Of
course, Ahab prefers monologue. He keeps Pip by his side after the cabinboy
had seen "God's foot upon the treadle of the loom, and spoke it" in a
schizophrenic idiolect without control over his name or the first person
pronoun. Pip's eyes, as well, suit Ahab because he does not see his "reflection in the vacant pupils."

The voices of *Moby Dick* are heard in sermons, formal tales of the
adventures of ships encountered at sea, pandemonian rallies in the cult of
white-whale hatred, and, above all, in monologues, which increase in

frequency in the final section of the book, once Ishmael has completed his inventory of the ship and his whale lore.

At the end of "The Symphony" the reader feels the predominance of monologue over dialogue when he learns, again after the fact, that Starbuck had "stolen away" during Ahab's climactic rumination on fate. This delayed revelation necessarily identifies us with the monomaniacal Ahab; we are bound by his speech even when no one else is listening; like Ahab, we do not realize we are alone. In this manner, the shift of emphasis from a language controlled by Ishmael to one articulated by Ahab finds a dramatic form.

The speech itself contains a drift of tone. From the high rhetoric of the opening questions which try to displace responsibility for the deadly quest from Ahab to a god of fate, the monologue comes to speak of the naturalization of predatory instincts. God and man become consubstantial through murder. Finally, it beautifully tails off with a pastoral image that reinterprets the softening force of the weather. Eliminating the sexuality of the opening paragraphs, unless a faint trace of Samson can be detected in the picture of the mowers sleeping in hay, Ahab tortures himself with a parable about the destructive power of time. The sleeping mowers have not been given enough time to complete their appointed task. In their deathly sleep there is also an echo of his own castrative scar: "Sleep, Aye, and rust amid greenness; as last year's scythes flung down, and left in half-cut swaths."

Ultimately the erotic softening engendered by the imagined intercourse of sea and air brings home to Ahab his fateful crippling. He fancies the reapers are asleep "somewhere under the slopes of the Andes." The mild wind, then, blows from the symbolic world of the doubloon, nailed to the mast for the man who first sights Moby Dick. Of course, that will be Ahab himself. The coin, as he interpreted it, showed "Ahab . . . Ahab . . . Ahab . . . Ahab." His interrupted attempt to penetrate the profundity brings him to a depth somewhere under Ahab.

Throughout the novel, the depths of Ahab's mind are associated with the ghostly Fedallah. Before Fedallah made his first appearance, Ishmael had compared "the larger, darker, deeper part" of Ahab's mind to the Roman baths under the Hotel de Cluny where a "captive king" upholds "on his frozen brow the piled entablatures of ages." Fedallah gives him what he most needs, the assurance that he will not be undone by time. Rather, Ahab takes that assurance by reading Fedallah's prophecy to his own advantage. When he completes his speech and notices that Starbuck has departed, he goes back to studying his image in the sea-mirror:

Ahab crossed the deck to gaze over on the other side; but he started at two reflected, fixed eyes in the water there. Fedallah was motionlessly leaning over the same rail.

In the end of the chapter, as again and again within it, we have to read backwards. The eyes of Ahab sees reflected are his shadowy harpooner's. But here the final sentence is poised ambiguously. We can read the conclusion as Ahab startled by his own fixed eyes with Fedallah monitoring him. Then again, if both sets of eyes are superimposed on the same reflecting surface, we find ourselves in the now familiar but still disturbing realm of what is "hardly separable." They are eyes without a name.

Chronology

1819	Herman Melville (or Melvill) born on August 1 in New York City, the third child of Allan Melville, an importer, and Maria Gansevoort Melville.
1826	Melville attends the New York Male High School.
1830–32	Allan Melville's importing business fails, and he moves the family to Albany. Herman becomes a student at the Albany Academy until his father's death in 1832. Then he works at various jobs: a bank clerk, a helper on his brother's farm and an assistant in his brother's fur factory and store.
1835–38	Continues his education at various high schools; supplements the family income by teaching.
1839	"Fragments from a Writing Desk" published May 4 and May 18 in the *Democratic Press and Lansingburgh Advertiser*. Melville works his way to Liverpool and back on the *Saint Lawrence*, a merchant ship.
1841–44	Melville leaves Fairhaven, Massachusetts as a sailor on the whaler *Acushnet*, bound for the South Seas. Jumps ship in the Marquesas Islands, where he lives among the natives for about a month. After a series of adventures, travels home as a passenger on the frigate *United States*.
1846	Publishes *Typee*. Brother Gansevoort dies.
1847	Publishes *Omoo*. Marries Elizabeth Shaw, daughter of Chief Justice Lemuel Shaw of Boston.
1847–50	Melville tries to earn a living as a writer, producing occasional articles and reviews. Makes acquaintance of George and Evert Duyckinck, and other New York literary figures.
1849	Publishes *Mardi* and *Redburn*. Travels to Europe. Son Malcolm born.
1850	Publishes *White-Jacket*. Purchases Arrowhead, a farm near Pittsfield, Massachusetts. Begins his friendship with Nathaniel Hawthorne, who lives in nearby Lenox.
1851	Publishes *Moby-Dick*. Son Stanwix born.
1852	Publishes *Pierre*.

1853–56	Daughter Elizabeth born. Writes stories and sketches for *Putnam's Monthly Magazine* and *Harper's New Monthly Magazine*.
1855	Publishes *Israel Potter* as a book, after serialization in *Putnam's*. Daughter Frances born.
1856	*The Piazza Tales* published. Melville travels to Europe and the Near East for his health.
1857	*The Confidence Man*, which Melville has left with his publisher before he began travelling, is finally published. Melville returns to the United States.
1857–60	Melville supports family by lectures on such topics as "Statuary in Rome," "The South Seas" and "Travelling."
1863	Melville sells Arrowhead, and moves his family to New York City.
1866	Publishes a collection of poems, *Battle-Pieces and Aspects of the War*. Son Malcolm shoots himself; son Stanwix runs away to sea.
1876	Publishes *Clarel*.
1886	Son Stanwix dies.
1888	*John Marr and Other Sailors* privately printed.
1891	*Timoleon* privately printed. Melville dies on September 28.
1924	First publication of *Billy Budd*.

Contributors

HAROLD BLOOM, Sterling Professor of the Humanities at Yale University, is the author of *The Anxiety of Influence, Poetry and Repression* and many other volumes of literary criticism. His forthcoming study, *Freud: Transference and Authority*, attempts a full-scale reading of all of Freud's major writings. A MacArthur Prize Fellow, he is the general editor of *The Chelsea House Library of Literary Criticism*.

CHARLES OLSON, considered by many to have been the major poet of his American generation, is remembered most for his *Maximus Poems*.

NEWTON ARVIN was Professor of English at Smith College. His seminal books upon American literature, besides his work on Melville, include studies of Whitman and Longfellow.

HERSHEL PARKER is Professor of English at the University of Delaware, and has edited Melville extensively.

GUY CARDWELL is Professor Emeritus of English at Washington University. His scholarly work includes essays on Faulkner and Timrod.

R. W. B. LEWIS is Neil Gray Professor of Rhetoric at Yale University. His books include studies of Hart Crane and Edith Wharton, and the celebrated study of 19th century American literature, *The American Adam*.

PAUL BRODTKORB, JR. is Associate Professor of English at Hunter College. Besides *Ishmael's White World*, he has written essays on *The Confidence Man, Billy Budd* and Hawthorne's *The Marble Faun*.

ROBERT PENN WARREN, our major living poet, is also famous as novelist, critic, and social historian. His central books include *All The King's Men* and the five versions of his *Selected Poems*.

ELAINE BARRY is Associate Professor of English at Monash University, Victoria. Her publications include *Robert Frost on Writing* and *Robert Frost*.

RICHARD H. BRODHEAD is Professor of English at Yale University, and is the author of *Hawthorne, Melville and the Novel*.

EDGAR DRYDEN is Professor of English at the University of Arizona. He is the author of critical studies of Hawthorne and of Melville.

BRYAN C. SHORT is Chairman of the English Department of North Arizona University at Flagstaff. He is at work on a study of Melville's sources.

MICHAEL PAUL ROGIN teaches English literature at the University of California at Berkeley. He is the author of *Subversive Genealogy: The Politics and Art of Herman Melville.*

P. ADAMS SITNEY teaches film and literature at Princeton University and is the author of *Visionary Film.*

Bibliography

Arvin, Newton. *Herman Melville*. New York: William Sloane Associates, 1950.

Beaver, Harold. "Melville and Modernism." *Dutch Quarterly Review of Anglo-American Letters* 1, vol. 13 (1983): 1–15.

Bender, Bert. "*Moby Dick*, An American Lyrical Novel." *Studies in the Novel* 10 (1978): 346–56.

Blau, Richard Manly. "*Pierre*: Let Them Look Out For Me Now!" and "*White Jacket*: To Scourge a Man that is a Roman." *The Body Impolitic, Costerus* 22 (1979): 113–200.

Bowen, Merlin. *The Long Encounter*. Chicago: The University of Chicago Press, 1963.

Brodhed, R. H. *Hawthorne, Melville and the Novel*. Chicago: The University of Chicago Press, 1976.

Cook, Charles H. Jr. "Ahab's 'Intolerable Allegory'." *Boston University Studies in English* 1 (1955–56): 45–52.

Dryden, Edgar A. *Melville's Thematics of Form*. Baltimore: The Johns Hopkins University Press, 1968.

Edinger, Edward A. *Melville's Moby Dick: A Jungian Commentary*. New York: A New Directions Book, 1978.

Fischer, Marvin. *Going Under*. Baton Rouge: Louisiana State University Press, 1977.

Fogle, Richard Harter. "The Themes of Melville's Later Poetry." *Tulane Studies in English* 11 (1961): 65–86.

Glick, Wendell. "Expediency and Absolute Morality in *Billy Budd*." *Publications of the Modern Language Association* 68 (1953): 103–10.

Johnson, Barbara. "Melville's Fist: The Execution of *Billy Budd*." *Studies in Romanticism* 18 (Winter 1979): 567–99.

Justman, Stewart. "Repression and Self in *Benito Cereno*." *Studies in Short Fiction* 15 (1978): 301–06.

Kazin, Alfred. "An Introduction to *Moby Dick*." In *Moby Dick*. Boston: Houghton Miflin Company, 1956.

Kemper, Steven. "*Omoo*: Germinal Melville." *Studies in the Novel* 10 (1978): 420–30.

Lawrence, D. H. "Herman Melville's *Typee* and *Omoo*." *Studies in Classic American Literature*. New York: Thomas Seltzer, Inc., 1923.

———. "Moby Dick, or the White Whale." *Studies in Classic American Literature*. New York: Thomas Seltzer, Inc., 1923.

Lee, A. Robert. "*Moby Dick*: The Tale and the Telling." In *New Perspectives on Melville*. Edited by Faith Pullin. Kent, Ohio: Kent State University Press, 1978.

Lewis, James W. "The Logic of Broken Promises: Religion and Sex in Melville's Shorter Fiction." *North Dakota Quarterly Review* 47 (1979): 19–33.

Manlove, C. N. "An Organic Hesitancy: Theme and Style in *Billy Budd.*" In *New Perspectives on Melville.* Edited by Faith Pullin. Kent, Ohio: Kent State University Press, 1978.

Mason, Ronald. *The Spirit Above the Dust.* Mamaroneck, N.Y.: Paul P. Appel, 1972.

Matthiessen, F. O. *American Renaissance.* New York: Oxford University Press, 1941.

Melville, Herman. *Clarel.* Edited by Walter Bezanson. New York: Hendricks House, 1960.

———. *Selected Poems of Herman Melville.* Edited and with an introduction by Robert Penn Warren. New York: Random House, 1969.

———. *Poems of Herman Melville.* Edited by Douglas Robillard. New Haven: College and University Press, 1976.

Mumford, Lewis. *Herman Melville.* New York: Harcourt Brace and Company, 1929.

Murray, Henry A. "In Nomine Diaboli." *New England Quarterly* 23 (1951): 435–52.

Novak, Frank G. "Warmest Climes but Nurse the Cruellest Fangs." *Studies in the Novel* 15 (1983): 332–43.

Obuchowski, Peter A. "*Billy Budd* and the Failure of Art." *Studies in Short Fiction* 15 (1978): 445–52.

Pullin, Faith. "Melville's *Typee:* The Failure of Eden." In *New Perspectives on Melville.* Edited by Faith Pullin. Kent, Ohio: Kent State University Press, 1978.

Rosenberry, Edward H. *Melville.* Boston: Routledge and Kegan Paul, 1979.

Sewall, Richard B. *The Vision of Tragedy.* New Haven: Yale University Press, 1959.

Sherrill, Rowland A. *The Prophetic Melville: Experience, Transcendence and Tragedy.* Athens, Ga.: University of Georgia Press, 1979.

Short, Bryan. " 'The Redness of the Rose': The *Mardi* Poems and Melville's Artistic Compromise." *Essays in Arts and Sciences* 5 (1976): 100–12.

Stein, William Bysshe. *The Poetry of Melville's Late Years.* Albany: State University of New York Press, 1970.

———. "Melville's Poetry: Two Rising Notes." *Emerson Society Quarterly* 27 (1962): 10–13.

Stern, Milton R. *The Fine Hammered Steel of Herman Melville.* Urbana, Ill.: University of Illinois Press, 1968.

Watters, R. E. "The Meanings of the White Whale." *University of Toronto Quarterly* 20 (1951): 155–68.

Withim, Phil. "*Billy Budd:* Testament of Resistance." *Modern Language Quarterly* 20 (1959): 115–27.

Zoellner, Robert. *The Salt Sea Mastodon.* Berkeley: University of California Press, 1973.

Acknowledgments

"Call Me Ishmael" by Charles Olson from *Call Me Ishmael* by Charles Olson, copyright © 1947 by Charles Olson. Reprinted by permission.

"The Early Novels: *Typee, Omoo, Redburn, White-Jacket*" by Newton Arvin from *Herman Melville* by Newton Arvin, copyright © 1950 by William Sloane Associates, Inc. Reprinted by permission.

"The Metaphysics of Indian-Hating" by Hershel Parker from *Nineteenth-Century Fiction* 18 (September 1963), copyright © 1963 by The Regents of the University of California. Reprinted by permission.

"Melville's Gray Story: Symbols and Meaning in 'Benito Cereno' " by Guy Cardwell from *Bucknell Review* 8 (May 1959), copyright © 1965 by D. C. Heath & Co. Reprinted by permission.

"Melville After *Moby-Dick:* The Tales" by R. W. B. Lewis from *Trials of the Word: Essays in American Literature and the Humanistic Tradition* by R. W. B. Lewis, copyright © 1965 by R. W. B. Lewis. Reprinted by permission.

"Ishmael: The Nature and Forms of Despair" by Paul Brodtkorb, Jr. from *Ishmael's White World* by Paul Brodtkorb, Jr., copyright © 1965 by Yale University Press. Reprinted by permission.

"Melville the Poet" by Robert Penn Warren from *Selected Essays of Robert Penn Warren* by Robert Penn Warren, copyright © 1966 by Vintage Books. Reprinted by permission.

"The Changing Face of Comedy" by Elaine Barry from *American Studies International* 4, vol. 16 (1978), copyright © 1978 by *American Studies International*. Reprinted by permission.

"*Mardi:* Creating the Creative" by Richard H. Brodhead from *New Perspectives on Melville* edited by Faith Pullin, copyright © 1978 by Edinburgh University Press. Reprinted by permission.

Index